PUBLICATIONS

OF THE

ILO

The International Labor Organization (ILO) was created under the Treaty of Versailles in 1919, and became in 1946 the first specialized agency associated with the United Nations. The ILO is unique among world organizations in that workers' and employers' representatives have an equal voice with those of governments of its 132 member countries.

The publications of the I.L.O. provide a unique source of information in a variety of fields as well as labor and social affairs.

The Impact of International Labor Conventions and Recommendations

In pursuance of one of its main constitutional functions, the ILO has, since 1919, laid down standards on a wide variety of questions of social policy, chiefly through Conventions and Recommendations formally adopted by its general conference. The present volume is a timely assessment of the influence which international labor standards have exerted on the law and practice of individual countries, as well as on international action outside the ILO itself. This book includes a comprehensive review of the question of the ratification of ILO Conventions and its effects, and of the results achieved through the procedures for supervising the application of ILO standards.

104 pp. cloth **$11.95** paper **$7.95**

Freedom of Association and Economic Development

Is freedom of association compatible with economic development; or is the one bound to be a brake on the other? This is a very typical issue in numerous countries where economic development is acquiring momentum. In this book, the author, a well-known specialist on questions of development and trade unionism, argues that the two are by no means incompatible. 170 pp. cloth **$11.95** paper **$7.95**

1976 Yearbook of Labor Statistics

The Yearbook presents a summary of the principal labor statistics in some 190 countries or territories in such areas as:—total and economically active population—employment—unemployment—hours of work—labor productivity—wages—industrial accidents—industrial disputes—consumer prices (including general indices for food, fuel, light, clothing and rent). *Standing orders are available for this publication.*

$37.95

Bulletin of Labor Statistics

Complements the annual data given in the YEARBOOK OF LABOR STATISTICS. The Bulletin is published Quarterly, with eight supplements.

Single: **$5.95** Yearly: **$17.95**

Combination Yearbook and Bulletin: **$44.75**

Send orders and requests for Free Catalog to:
INTERNATIONAL LABOR OFFICE
Suite 330 A, 1750 New York Avenue, N.W.
Washington, D.C. 20006 • (202) 634-6335

VOLUME 431   MAY 1977

THE ANNALS

of The American Academy *of* Political
and Social Science

RICHARD D. LAMBERT, *Editor*

ALAN W. HESTON, *Assistant Editor*

INDUSTRIAL DEMOCRACY IN INTERNATIONAL PERSPECTIVE

Special Editor of This Volume

JOHN P. WINDMULLER
Professor
New York State School of
Industrial and Labor Relations
Cornell University
Ithaca, New York

PHILADELPHIA

The articles appearing in THE ANNALS are indexed in the *Reader's Guide to Periodical Literature*, the *Book Review Index*, the *Public Affairs Information Service Bulletin*, *Social Sciences Index*, and *Current Contents: Behavioral, Social, Management Sciences* and *Combined Retrospective Index Sets*. They are also abstracted and indexed in *ABC Pol Sci, Historical Abstracts, United States Political Science Documents, Abstracts for Social Workers, International Political Science Abstracts* and/or *America: History and Life*.

International Standard Book Numbers (ISBN)

ISBN 0-87761-215-3, vol. 431, 1977; paper—$4.00
ISBN 0-87761-214-5, vol. 431, 1977; cloth—$5.00

Issued bimonthly by The American Academy of Political and Social Science at 3937 Chestnut St., Philadelphia, Pennsylvania 19104. Cost per year: $15.00 paperbound; $20.00 clothbound. Add $1.50 to above rates for membership outside U.S.A. Second-class postage paid at Philadelphia and at additional mailing offices.

Claims for undelivered copies must be made within the month following the regular month of publication. The publisher will supply missing copies when losses have been sustained in transit and when the reserve stock will permit.

Editorial and Business Offices, 3937 Chestnut Street, Philadelphia, Pennsylvania 19104.

CONTENTS

iii

CONTENTS

CONTENTS

UNITED STATES HISTORY AND POLITICS

SOCIOLOGY

ECONOMICS

PREFACE

In the United States, the concept of industrial democracy is largely associated with the institution of collective bargaining. Industrial democracy is regarded as achieved whenever strong and independent unions gain the right to share effectively with management in making the basic substantive and procedural rules that determine the employment relationship. Participation occurs not only through the negotiations leading to the conclusion of a collective agreement but also through the continuing role of the union in administering the agreement during its lifetime. Until recently this interpretation was also current in Great Britain, and it would be fair to say that even now both the American and the British systems of industrial relations, with their emphasis on adversary collective bargaining, are close reflections of this view of industrial democracy.

In most of Western Europe, however, and in a number of other countries industrial democracy and its companion terms, such as worker participation in management, have acquired quite different meanings. Industrial democracy there refers often, though not always, to various schemes designed to associate employees or institutions representative of employee interests more closely with the internal decision-making process in the units constituting the private or public sectors of the economy. Without abandoning collective bargaining or even demoting it to a subordinate position, industrial democracy in these countries is conceived of as a means of direct employee access to the policy-making and operating levels of individual enterprises, especially the larger ones. The aim is to transform, or to reform, long established patterns of authority and power in industry by granting to employees a degree of influence over all vital affairs of the enterprise which more nearly approximates that of employers, shareholders, and their representatives in management. It is revealing of this meaning that in France the term in current usage is not industrial democracy but "the reform of the enterprise," while in Germany a principal component of industrial democracy is known as codetermination (Mitbestimmung), that is, employee codetermination in the management of the enterprise.

The prevailing meaning of industrial democracy, however, is by no means exhaustive of the conceptual and terminological varieties. In an increasing number of countries, the emphasis on employee participation in decision making is being extended by schemes intended to achieve employee participation in the ownership of industrial capital. As in the case of shared decision making, there are substantial differences between the several plans to achieve employee participation in ownership, with some plans envisaging a far-reaching redistribution of wealth and, thus, also of power. It is entirely conceivable that the long-term consequences of capital-sharing plans, or at least of the more sweeping ones, will be even greater in terms of ultimate employee and union control over economic policy making than the introduction of new forms of shared decision making in industry.

Still another meaning of industrial democracy refers to rather widespread efforts to restructure the organization of work so as to enhance its attractiveness or quality. The link between industrial democracy and what is sometimes referred to as the humanization of the work environment consists of attempts to confer on the individual worker, or a particular work group, more power over the performance of required tasks in the production process than has been customary. Changes of this kind are usually expected not merely to lead to improvements in morale and output but also to alter in some fashion the hierarchical relationships characteristic of the organization of work in almost all industrial societies.

Industrial democracy cannot be regarded in isolation from ideological and political motivations and objectives. Its leading supporters in most countries—aside from intellectuals of various viewpoints—have been trade unions and allied political parties. Conversely, its leading opponents have been employers and their associations, as well as political parties associated with their views. At least to some degree, both the proponents and the opponents of industrial democracy in one or more of its variants regard it—with satisfaction or apprehension—as a means of changing the existing distribution of power not only in industry but eventually also in society at large. Others hope or fear, as the case may be, that it will in the end lead to a complete transformation of the social order toward some form of participatory collectivism.

To be sure, not all trade unions support industrial democracy, nor do all employers adamantly oppose it. Some unions reject it as an undesirable diversion from their central bargaining tasks, while others regard it as a potential dilution of their commitment to establish a socialist society. On the other hand, there are employers who regard certain forms of industrial democracy as a necessary device for "derevolutionizing" the labor movement, while others welcome its promise of significant improvements in job satisfaction and productivity.

The existence of a politico-ideological dimension to industrial democracy emerges clearly from the case of Yugoslavia, which has proclaimed self-management as the basis of society itself, including of course the industrial segment. Moreover, Yugoslavia has become to some extent a model for certain less developed countries (such as Peru, India, Algeria) that are attracted by the vision of a socialist society but repelled by the reality of its implementation in the Soviet Union and Eastern Europe.

Whatever may be the motivations or the ultimate goals, there is no doubt that the widespread preoccupation with industrial democracy, at least among many industrially advanced countries, requires close attention. It seems inevitable that current trends will bring about, indeed in several instances have already brought about, significant changes in various national systems of industrial relations. The essays in this volume attempt to indicate, with special reference to labor-management relations, what has already occurred in a representative selection of countries and where they seem to be headed.

A note of caution is appropriate. Discussions of a trend extending across a broad range of countries may easily create an impression of a universal and inexorable force at work. That would be misleading here. In spring 1976, for example, the Swiss electorate rejected by wide margins two referendum proposals favoring worker participation in management. Likewise there are no significant indications of interest in industrial democracy schemes among American unions and employers, except perhaps for scattered efforts to improve the quality of work. Among less developed countries, too, there are few indications of sustained interest, and insofar as experience may serve as a reasonable guide to action, the failures of Peru and India presented in this volume hold out scant promise of success elsewhere. As to the Soviet Union and most other Eastern European countries, there is little prospect of early change in the direction of more industrial democracy.

One is thus left with the distinct impression that, at least for the time being, most innovations associated with the term industrial democracy will be confined to the countries of Western Europe, including Great Britain. That is where the impetus now is and where further reinforcement can be expected from current efforts to build some form of institutionalized industrial democracy into the supranational body of rules for European corporations that is gradually emerging from the European Community. Hence, this volume of essays on industrial democracy has allocated more space to Western Europe than to other parts of the world.

JOHN P. WINDMULLER

Toward the Participatory Enterprise:
A European Trend

By KENNETH F. WALKER

ABSTRACT: Workers' participation in management has been extending in various forms in Europe during the third quarter of the twentieth century, and in the last quarter the business enterprise in Europe will evolve into a pattern of organization that may best be designated "the participatory enterprise." This evolution will involve changes in conceptual models of the enterprise and continued effort to resolve certain practical problems that appear to be inherent in participation. Unlike classical models of organization, the participatory enterprise is a coalition of conflicting and cooperative interests. Further progress is required in clarifying the causal relations involved in participation, which the small research effort to date reveals to be more complex than is often assumed. Experience shows that participation does not remove problems of human interaction and relations, but changes their character. It is time to abandon global thinking about participation and move to a more discriminating approach which does not seek final solutions but recognizes that participation is a living, evolving process, the outcome of which cannot be predicted in detail.

Kenneth F. Walker is Professor of Industrial Relations at the European Institute of Business Administration (INSEAD). He received his B.A. in economics and psychology, his M.A. in psychology, and his postgraduate diploma in anthropology from the University of Sydney and his Ph.D. in economics from Harvard University. He has served as a lecturer in economics at the University of Sydney, Professor and Head of the Department of Psychology at the University of Western Australia, visiting Professor of Psychology at the University of Michigan and Birkbeck College, London University, and Director of the International Institute for Labor Studies in Geneva. His publications include Industrial Relations in Australia, Research Needs in Industrial Relations, and Australian Industrial Relations Systems.

WORKERS' participation in management, in one form or another, is now widely practiced in the industrial world, and its extension is continuously debated. Although the problem of in what ways, and to what extent, workers should and can take part in managerial functions has been on the agenda of various social reformers since the nineteenth century, it was only in the third quarter of the twentieth century that large-scale attempts were made to put the idea into practice. While the various forms of workers' participation in management have fallen short of the hopes of their advocates, and various practical problems have been encountered, the trend toward increasing participation is unmistakable.

During the final quarter of the twentieth century, it may be expected that the business enterprise in Europe will evolve into a pattern of organization that may best be designated "the participatory enterprise." This evolution will involve developments at the conceptual level and also at the practical level.

At the conceptual level, changing models of the enterprise are opening the way to a more fruitful formulation of the participation problem in organization theory. Further conceptual progress is being made in clarifying various propositions (usually implicit in the controversial debates over participation and industrial democracy) concerning the cause-and-effect relationships involved and in stating them in testable form.

At the practical level, experience of the last 25 years indicates that certain problems may be inherent to workers' participation in management. Recognition of such problems, and of the limitations which they impose, can open the way to formulation of realistic goals for the operation of the various forms of participation in management.

After a brief review of the trend toward the extension of workers' participation in management, this paper will address the problems of conceptual clarification and summarize the practical problems that have been found in the way of the practice of workers' participation in management.

THE TREND TOWARD PARTICIPATION IN MANAGEMENT

It is convenient to distinguish three principal forms of participation in management. The first may be called representative integrative participation. It consists of a modification of the formal structure of the enterprise to provide for workers, through their elected representatives, an opportunity to participate in the administration and government of the enterprise in varying degree. Shop floor participation involves a variety of different forms, all of which have the common feature of building into the worker's job elements of planning and supervision which would otherwise be performed by supervisors. Collective bargaining involves participation by workers through representatives who are part of the formal structure, not of the enterprise but of another organization (the union), by means of which workers participate in management from outside the enterprise, as it were.

While collective bargaining is not universally regarded as a form of workers' participation in management, it cannot be denied that in the absence of collective bargaining management would make decisions unilaterally. Each widening of the range of issues subject to collective bargaining has been contested by management as an invasion of managerial functions, and the historical trend has clearly been toward greater and greater penetration of areas of decision which would otherwise be taken unilaterally by management.

Representative integrative participation now exists in quite a few European countries, both through elected works councils and through representation on the governing board of the enterprise. One notable exception, Great Britain, is now considering legislation for representation of workers on the board and Ireland may also do so.

The trend is definitely toward extension of this form of participation, as some recent examples will show. The number of workers' representatives on the board is being increased (as in the Federal Republic of Germany). Board room participation initially introduced on a trial basis is confirmed permanently (as in Scandinavia). The rights of works councils to information are being extended (as in Belgium and the Netherlands), and the councils' consultative and decision-making roles are reinforced (as in the Federal Republic of Germany and Italy). In no country has this trend been reversed.

Shop floor participation in its various forms is not yet a major feature of the industrial landscape, but it, too, appears to be spreading in most European countries, despite many setbacks and false starts.

Collective bargaining continues to spread to categories of employees not previously covered, particularly among white-collar workers, technical and professional staffs, and the middle levels of management. More important for our purpose is its continuing penetration into areas of decision making traditionally regarded as the preserve of management, such as investment plans, major changes in scale of production, technological procedures, and methods of work organization. The 1974 legislation in Sweden may be regarded as the culmination of this trend, reversing, as it does, the traditional dominance of management over such decisions and proceeding on the basis that all managerial decisions are in principle negotiable. Without changes in the law, the de facto situation in Great Britain and Italy is similar, and the trend in other countries is in the same direction. (For example, some years ago the German metalworkers' union began to include limitations on the length of the work cycle in its collective agreements.)

In addition to the clear historical trend of each form of participation to extend, a tendency is observable for further forms of participation to be added in order to complement existing ones. Thus countries like Britain and Ireland, which have previously relied on participation through collective bargaining alone, are considering adding representative participation. The Federal Republic of Germany, after 25 years' reliance on collective bargaining and representative participation, is now starting to develop shop floor participation. Norway, after a period of concentration on shop floor participation, a few years ago returned to developing representative participation. Both the Biedenkopf Commission in the Federal Republic of Germany and a European Economic Community (EEC) commission have stressed the need for a

comprehensive structure of participation at all levels of the corporate
organization.[1]

The Participatory Enterprise as a Model of Organization

The concept of the participatory
enterprise contrasts sharply with the
concepts of classical organization
theory and with traditional managerial practice. Both classical
theory and traditional practice take
a "top-down" view of the enterprise, regarding the problem of
organization as essentially that of
establishing a technological or administrative system which determines the tasks to be performed by
the subordinates in the enterprise
and the conditions under which they
are to be performed.

When the enterprise is seen as a
technical system, designed according to engineering criteria, the
human beings in subordinate positions are seen as necessary only to
the extent that they are required to
fill the gaps between machines to
perform the necessary tasks. This
line of thought leads logically to the
creation of automated factories.

When the enterprise is seen as an
administrative system, the subordinates are thought of as a kind of
human extension of the managers,
carrying out the tasks which the
managers would perform if they
were omniscient and omnipotent. In
this view the machines are regarded
as extensions of the human beings,
helping them to carry out tasks
which they could not do at all other-

wise, or which would be more
arduous or more time-consuming
without the machines.

For both these classical concepts
of the enterprise the personnel
functions of management are regarded as existing essentially to
ensure that the subordinates in the
enterprise play their appropriate
part in the operation of the system,
while workers' responsibilities are
restricted to the diligent performance
of their allocated task.[2] This view can
only conceive of workers' participation in management as a cooperative
process.

The top-down view of the enterprise characteristic of classical organization theory is paralleled by
traditional managerial approaches
which also see the enterprise as
essentially unitary, an organization
in which all parties cooperate, sinking their individual and sectional
interests in a consensus and collaboration. The existence and significance of conflicts of interest
among the members of the enterprise are ignored by this approach.[3]

In fact, conflict is built into the
nature of enterprise organization.[4]

1. See *Mitbestimmung im Unternehmen:
Bericht der Sachverständigenkommission*
(Stuttgart, Berlin, Cologne, Mainz, January
1970); and Commission of the European
Communities: "Employee Participation and
Company Structure," *Bulletin of the European
Communities*, Supplement 8/75 (1975).

2. This basic tenet of the classical view
lingers on in some attempts to formulate a
participative conception of management. See,
for example, P. Hill, *Towards a New
Philosophy of Management* (London: Gower
Press, 1971), which speaks of the manager
guiding employees "to commit themselves
and their energies wholeheartedly to the objectives of the company and to the tasks
they undertake" (p. 44). The possibility that
workers might have objectives of their own
is ignored.

3. See Allen Fox, *Industrial Sociology and
Industrial Relations* (London: Her Majesty's
Stationery Office, 1966), Royal Commission
on Trade Unions and Employers' Associations, Research Papers No. 3.

4. As Simmel noted: "a certain amount of
discord, inner divergence and outer controversy is organically tied up with the very
elements that hold the group together," in

Subordinates have a certain "zone of indifference"[5] within which they are prepared to comply with the commands of their superiors. The width of this zone is determined by exchanges between superior and subordinate, resulting in what has been called an effort-bargain[6] or inducement-contribution balance.[7] At each moment of his working life, each member of a work organization contributes a certain proportion of his total energies and abilities to the organization and withholds a certain proportion. The balance between contribution and withholding is struck in the interaction between superior and subordinate in what is in effect, if not in appearance, a continuous process of bargaining.[8] Each time a supervisor gets a little more work out of the worker in return for the same pay, a new effort-bargain has been struck and the true price of labor has fallen. Each time the worker succeeds (through restrictive practices or other means) in putting in a little less effort, the effort-bargain has altered and the true price of labor has risen.

Thus, an enterprise is not a unitary but a pluralist system, "containing many related but separate interests and objectives which must be maintained in some kind of equilibrium."[9]

Enterprises viewed as pluralist systems contain people who not only have abilities to perform the tasks demanded by the functions of the enterprise but also possess personalities and economic and political interests as workers and citizens. In varying degree, they have needs to structure their own work situations and to control their own lives, at work as well as off work. In this perspective, the question is not whether workers shall participate in management, but rather how and to what extent.[10]

An important feature of the concept of the participatory enterprise is that it accommodates the possibility of conflictual, as well as cooperative, participation. Furthermore, participation in management can only be democratic in the context of the participatory enterprise; a unitary view of the enterprise is not consistent with industrial democracy, since it denies the existence of workers' independent interests.

Conflict (New York: The Free Press, 1955), pp. 17–18. Gross stated that: "One of the major advances of modern administrative thought has been an ever-widening recognition that conflict and co-operation are inextricably inter-twined in the life of any organization." Bertram M. Gross, *The Managing of Organizations* (New York: The Free Press, 1964), vol. 1, p. 265.

5. Chester I. Barnard, *Functions of the Executive* (Cambridge, Mass.: Harvard University Press, 1938).

6. Hilde Behrend, "The Effort Bargain," *Industrial and Labor Relations Review*, vol. 10, no. 4 (1957), pp. 503–15.

7. James G. March and Herbert A. Simon, *Organizations* (New York: John Wiley & Sons, Inc., 1958), ch. 4.

8. This point was made well before the writings of the organization theorists referred to in the last two notes by John R. Commons, *Industrial Goodwill* (New York: McGraw-Hill, 1919).

9. N. S. Ross, in *Human Relations and Modern Management*, ed. E. M. Hugh-Jones (Amsterdam: North-Holland Publishing Company, 1958), p. 121. A similar view is taken by E. Pusic (see I.I.L.S., "Workers' Participation in Management in Yugoslavia," *I.I.L.S. Bulletin*, no. 9 (1971), pp. 129–72). Michel Crozier, *The Bureaucratic Phenomenon* (London: Tavistock Publications, 1964), adopts an essentially similar approach.

10. This was the conclusion of a colloquium held in May 1976 to discuss the implications of the EEC's "Green Paper" on "Employee Participation and Company Structure." See European Institute of Business Administration (INSEAD), *The Reform of the Enterprise* (Fontainebleau, 1976).

CLARIFICATION OF CAUSAL RELATIONS

In controversy, workers' participation in management is approached from various perspectives, each of which carries with it expected (hoped for or feared) results. These perspectives and their corresponding expectations I have described in more detail elsewhere.[11]

The link between each perspective and the corresponding expected effect is, in each case, one or more assumptions about the operation of workers' participation in management practice. Thus, for example, those who view workers' participation in management from the perspective of democracy assume that in its practical operation workers will be able to exert real influence on managerial decisions. Those who see workers' participation in management from the perspective of reducing alienation assume that the form of participation they have in mind will, in practice, produce greater worker satisfaction and fulfillment.

Compared with the amount of ideological debate, the amount of research on workers' participation in management is pitifully small. It has, however, not been altogether negligible, particularly in certain countries,[12] and there are certainly sufficient well-established data to demonstrate that many of the assumptions made about the cause-and-effect relationships involved in participation are not necessarily correct, at least not in all circumstances.

It is clear from German research, for example, that representative integrative participation through works councils and workers' representatives on company boards has had practically no effect on the daily life of the worker on the job.[13] Thus, this type of participation does not serve the purpose of increasing workers' personal fulfillment in their daily work situations.

Research also shows that personal participation in a representative participatory body may contribute to or detract from fulfillment according to how well the participative body functions. For example, a Polish worker is reported as saying: "The self-management conference enables one to know the life of the undertaking better . . . a man considers himself as a worker of greater value."[14] Both Yugoslav and French research report frustration of members of participatory bodies which they considered not to be working satisfactorily.[15] Personal participation in decisions concerning the immediate work situation may not be related to satisfaction with the job, according to British research,

11. Kenneth F. Walker, "Workers' Participation in Management: Problems, Practice and Prospect," *I.I.L.S. Bulletin*, no. 12 (1974), pp. 3–35.

12. The conclusion of Clark and Heller that there is practically no field research on the subject seems to ignore the substantial body of research in the Federal Republic of Germany. See A. Clark and F. Heller, "Personnel and Human Resources Development," *Annual Review of Psychology*, vol. 27 (1976), pp. 4–9.

13. See Friedrich Fürstenberg, "Workers' Participation in Management in the Federal Republic of Germany," *I.I.L.S. Bulletin*, no. 6 (June 1969), pp. 94–148.

14. International Institute for Labor Studies, *Further Data on the Operation of Workers' Participation in Management in Poland* (Geneva, 1971).

15. See J. Obradovic, "Participation and Work Attitudes in Yugoslavia," *Industrial Relations*, vol. 9, no. 2 (February 1970), pp. 161–69, and M. Légendre, *Quelques Aspects des Relations Professionnelles* (Paris: Service d'Etudes pour le Développement et l'Animation, 1969).

although it may be related to labor turnover.[16]

Another widely held assumption in the controversies over participation is that representative participation increases workers' power over decisions, although certain union federations (notably the Confédération Générale du Travail in France) hold the opposite view of such participation under capitalism. Mulder's research[17] suggests that participation may reduce the power of workers, while that of Tannenbaum[18] shows the possibility that both management and workers may gain in power.

One of the most common expectations is that participation will increase cooperation and promote industrial peace; this goal may even be written into the legislation or collective agreements establishing the participative structure.

Experience indicates that whether, and how much, participation contributes to cooperation and industrial peace varies according to the total situation. Participative structures intended to promote cooperation may merely provide another area of conflict.[19] Descending participation in the form of work groups tends by its nature to be cooperative in character and effects, but conflict may arise between such groups,[20] and changes in work organization may raise issues that can provoke industrial conflict.[21] Collective bargaining, although based on an adversary principle, varies widely in the extent to which it is conflictual; in addition to the fact that in many cases negotiations proceed peacefully and in a constructive atmosphere, the trend toward continuous bargaining and the establishment of joint committees for the study of problems of mutual interest shows that many collective bargaining relationships have important cooperative dimensions.[22]

The expectation that participation will raise or lower efficiency is particularly difficult to test, mainly because of the problem of separating the effects of participation from those of other factors. Research so far suggests that participation is unlikely to have major effects, either positive or negative. In general, the hopes of advocates and the fears of opponents of participation appear to have been exaggerated.[23]

These examples suffice to show the need to test the veracity of assumptions as to causal relation-

16. J. A. Lischeron and D. Wall, "Employee Participation: An Experimental Field Study," *Human Relations*, vol. 28, no. 9 (1975), pp. 863–84, and N. Nicholson, T. Wall, and J. Lischeron, "The Predictability of Absence and Propensity to Leave from Employees' Satisfaction and Attitudes toward Influence in Decision-making," unpublished manuscript.
17. M. Mulder, "Power Equalisation through Participation," *Administrative Science Quarterly*, vol. 16 (1971), pp. 31–8.
18. Arnold S. Tannenbaum et al, *Hierarchy in Organizations* (San Francisco: Jossey-Bass, 1974).
19. As reported by Légendre, *Quelques Aspects des Relations Professionnelles*.

20. As reported in D. Gorupic and I. Paj, "Workers Participation in Management in Yugoslavia."
21. See, for example, J. Douard and J. D. Reynaud, "Union-Management Conflicts over Quality of Working Life Issues," ch. 26 in L. E. Davis and A. B. Cherns, eds., *The Quality of Working Life* (New York: The Free Press, 1975), vol. 1, pp. 393–404.
22. See, for example, A. Shirom, *Industrial Co-operation and Technological Change: A Study of Joint Management-Union Committees in American Industry*, paper submitted to International Industrial Relations Association, Second World Congress, Geneva, 1970.
23. This was the conclusion of the Biedenkopf Commission in the Federal Republic of Germany.

ships implicitly made in most ideological debate. The same needs to be said of the statements of some social scientists who continue to list psychological job requirements which are, by implication, attributed to all workers despite evidence that workers vary in their aspirations and in the criteria by which they judge their jobs.[24]

The task of the next 25 years will be to build on the research to date, which has shown the fallacies of dogmatism, either by practitioners or social scientists, to explicate the causal relations involved in the participative process.

PERENNIAL PROBLEMS IN THE OPERATION OF WORKERS' PARTICIPATION

Parallel to the conceptual clarification that has been emerging, actual experience in a variety of countries, both Communist and non-Communist, has revealed a remarkably similar set of problems in practice. This suggests that these problems are inherent to representative integrative participation and may be expected to recur, no matter what its form or in what economic, social, and legal context it may be set. In the evolution toward the participatory enterprise in the next 25 years, therefore, these problems may be expected to arise and to set limits to the realization of the concept of participation.

So far as representative integrative participation is concerned, it is clear that the placing in position of a structure intended to provide for workers' participation in manage-ment does not guarantee that such participation will be fully effective. Institutional arrangements for workers' participation in management may become either a living reality or a mere "petrifaction of a participation philosophy."[25] Legal prescriptions for participation may be observed in varying degree, and even when the law is observed, what happens in practice varies considerably from enterprise to enterprise.[26] The problems encountered include:

1. role-conflict of workers' representatives;
2. maintenance of effective links between workers' representatives and their constituents;
3. effective communication to the workforce about the operation of the participative institutions;
4. achieving living participation within participative structures.

In addition to these problems encountered in the operation of representative integrative participation, all forms of workers' participation in management appear to experience difficulty in extending participation throughout the work force generally. Experience in all countries, Communist and non-Communist alike, has revealed considerable difficulty in getting all workers to participate, no matter what the structures and the process of participation available to them.[27]

---

24. An example is F. E. Emery and M. Emery, "Guts and Guidelines for Raising the Quality of Working Life" in Doran Gunzburg, *Bringing Work to Life* (Melbourne: Cheshire, 1975).

25. A. B. Cherns, "Conditions for an Effective Management Philosophy of Participation," in C. P. Thakur and K. L. Sethi, eds., *Industrial Democracy: Some Issues and Experiences* (New Delhi: Shri Ram Centre for Industrial Relations and Human Resources, 1973), p. 95.

26. This occurs even in Communist countries. See, for example, I.I.L.S., *Further Data on the Operation of Workers' Participation in Management in Poland*.

27. Research in Communist countries shows that workers with greater education,

There are many reasons why it is difficult to obtain the participation of all types of worker, most of which have been documented by research. There is, first, the general tendency in human affairs for the majority to remain relatively apathetic while the active minority participates. Many workers may be more concerned with their lives outside of work. Workers at low levels in the hierarchy may take a cynical view of the possibility of influencing their immediate work situation through representative participative bodies, a view which may well be realistic since such participation may have relatively little impact on the factory floor. Workers also vary in personality traits, some being more amenable to authoritarian styles of management than to participation. Some types of worker are apathetic toward shop floor participation, resisting attempts to give them more interesting work and added responsibility or to make them participate in groups. The tendency of representative participation and, perhaps, trade union structures to become bureaucratic may also discourage workers from active participation.

Parallel to the problem of involving all workers in participation is the difficulty, experienced in Communist countries and in trade union enterprises as well as in market economies, of gaining wholehearted cooperation by all managers in the operation of participative bodies. Many managers who claim to practice participatory approaches do not believe that their subordinates possess the abilities necessary to

take part in managerial functions.[28] Variations in managerial attitudes have been found to have much effect upon the operation of participative bodies.[29]

A further practical problem experienced quite generally in the operation of participation is that workers (and their representatives) may lack the knowledge necessary to take part in managerial functions, or at least in certain functions. This problem points to the need for adequate training.

Once more, there is a parallel on the managerial side, where technical knowledge may be adequate, but deficiencies may exist in competence to operate effectively in a participative structure, on account of attitudes (as noted above) or habituation to more authoritarian approaches. Training is evidently required here, too.

The role of the time factor must also be taken into account in the operation of workers' participation in management. Neither workers nor managers may be able to adapt at once to a participative mode of working in the early stages—time may be needed to learn to participate.[30] Time may also work in the opposite direction—enthusiasm for participation may wane. (For example, improvements in absenteeism following the introduction of

28. See A. W. Clark and J. Wotherspoon, "Managers, Conflict: Democratic Management versus Distrust of People's Capacity," *Psychological Reports*, vol. 32 (1973), pp. 815–19.

29. See M. Montuclard, *La Dynamique des Comités d'Entreprise* (Paris: Centre National de la Recherche Scientifique, 1963).

30. The evolution of attitudes and practices through time are well documented by Montuclard, ibid., and by S. K. Chakraborty, "Joint Consultation in the National Coal Board (U.K.)," *Indian Journal of Industrial Relations*, vol. 7, no. 1 (1971).

technical expertise, and skill are over-represented in the participative bodies while unskilled manual workers, younger workers, and shorter service workers are under-represented. See ibid., and I.L.S., "Workers' Participation in Management in Yugoslavia."

shop floor participation have frequently worn off with the passage of time.)

Experience has also shown that the practical operation of any particular form of participation is much affected by the existence and functioning of other forms of participation. The growth of informal shop floor bargaining in Great Britain, for example, clearly contributed to the decline in joint consultation machinery. Participation through works councils and representation on company boards of directors would work quite differently in the Federal Republic of Germany were it not for the active support of the unions.[31]

Finally, account must be taken of the general economic, social, and political climate, from which various pressures arise, some favorable to participation and others unfavorable.[32]

FROM GLOBAL VISION TO SOBER REALITY

Research and experience to date both show clearly that participation has no magic but is, rather, an alternative form of enterprise organization which has its own problems of human interaction and relationships, as well as of operating efficiency. Participation does not remove problems—it changes their character.

It is also evident from research and experience that it is time to give up thinking of participation globally and move to a much more discriminating approach, distinguishing various forms, aims, operating problems, and effects of participation. It is necessary, too, to recognize that what happens in each case will vary according to differences in the human and situational factors and their interplay.[33] Further research and experience will illuminate the ways these factors operate and enable global visions of participation (favorable or unfavorable) to be replaced by increasingly precise operational models.

It must be recognized, however, that the nature of the participation process renders it logically impossible to specify the shape and character of the participatory enterprise in detail in advance. Participation is a living process, and if its outcomes could all be foreseen in detail it would not be truly free participation. Thus, there can be no final solutions in participation, only learning, development, and choice among a number of alternatives.

The emergence of the participatory enterprise will be conditioned by three needs which will have to be met in such a form of enterprise organization. Sufficient autonomy will have to be provided for managers in order to induce capable people to undertake this essential task. First, a role for enterprising leadership (of a non-authoritarian character) will have to be provided. Second, unions will have to be given a meaningful role; there is no long-term future for forms of participation which ignore or seek to counter union activities and responsibilities. Third, participation must provide workers with practical gains—it must make a significant difference to their work lives, or they will be apathetic toward it.

31. See I. L. Roberts, "The Works Constitution Acts and Industrial Relations in West Germany: Implications for the United Kingdom," *British Journal of Industrial Relations*, vol. 11, no. 3 (November 1973), p. 350.

32. See Walker, "Workers' Participation in Management: Problems, Practice and Prospect," pp. 19–20.

33. Ibid., pp. 12–18.

The participatory enterprise will, however, not function solely in the interests of its members (including the shareholders), but it will be required to meet community standards of social responsibility. This may involve means for the representation of the interests of various groups of stakeholders in the success of the enterprise. In this sense, the evolution of the participatory enterprise is an aspect of the wider issue of the reform of the enterprise, another theme that will increasingly engage our attention during the final quarter of the twentieth century.

Unions and Industrial Democracy

By ADOLF F. STURMTHAL

ABSTRACT: This article concentrates on the role of unions in a system of industrial democracy, which is interpreted as labor participation in managerial decision making. The Western industrial world is confronted with two conceptions of the role of unions in the plant: one, characteristic of the great majority of U.S. unions and a substantial part of organized British labor, sees unions as countervailing power to management; the other, predominant on the European continent, wants labor to take its place in management and to participate in both the privileges and the responsibilities of decision making. This analysis is based on a comparison of the institutional arrangements of West Germany, Great Britain, and Sweden. In each of these countries, unions have a different role in industrial democracy. At one extreme unions operate at top managerial levels; at the other they function largely at the workshop level. These differences are further complicated by the danger of a cleavage between collective agreements concluded for an entire industry or other comprehensive unit and the reality that exists in the plant, a distinction to which the British Donovan Commission drew public attention. Moreover, efforts to combat wage-push inflation tend to concentrate union power at the top, while industrial democracy is more vital the closer to the plant level it operates.

Adolf Sturmthal is Professor Emeritus of Labor and Industrial Relations at the University of Illinois. He received his Doctor rer. pol. from the University of Vienna and served on the faculties of Bard College, Columbia University, Cornell University, Yale University, the business schools of Columbia University and the University of Chicago, University of Montreal and Laval University in Canada, and the University of Aix-en-Provence. His published work consists of some 15 books and monographs and some 80 articles in scientific journals. He is also a contributor to the International Encyclopedia of the Social Sciences *and the* Encyclopedia Britannica.

The preparation of this paper was facilitated by a grant from the Ford Foundation.

BY FAR the most attractive attribute of the term industrial democracy is the infinite variety of meanings that can be read into it. The range is indeed bewildering. It reaches from workers' self-management via consultation and codetermination to collective bargaining, and in passing picks up such diverse notions as job enrichment and autonomous work groups.[1] It goes back in history to such utopian ideas as eternal social harmony, passes through various forms of industrial engineering designed to make workers accept the social status quo, and reaches to new devices for managing the inevitable conflicts that arise in the context of industrial relations.

"Basically," says the article on democracy in the *International Encyclopedia of the Social Sciences*, "industrial democracy is democracy within industrial plants. . . . In its ultimate form, industrial democracy calls for self-government by the workers in a plant. . . ." Although the author of the article fails to do so, he could have quoted a series of opponents of Karl Marx, such as Proudhon, Kropotkin, and other anarchists, or even the early Bolsheviks as adherents of this interpretation. The roots of industrial democracy in French syndicalism and British guild socialism are well known.[2] Alas, we have become less optimistic than these earlier theoreticians about the outcome of experiments of this kind, just at a time when the rising educational levels of large parts of the labor force in the industrially advanced countries bring closer the day when at least some forms of greater self-determination at the work place seem feasible, are often asked for, and frequently realized. Perhaps Harold Wilson, the accomplished politician, was sensing the trend of the times when saying: "The pressure for a greater degree of workers' democracy in whatever form—joint consultation, participation, works councils, and so on—is only in its infancy. There is little doubt that we are at the beginning of a social revolution in this sphere."[3]

Under the circumstances, any meaningful discussion will have to start with a process of elimination—excluding topics not to be discussed—and a process of concentration—that is, a list of questions to be explored and the context of the particular industrial relations systems in which they are to be studied. I shall disregard problems of job enrichment and autonomous work groups, on one hand, and all schemes of consultation, on the other hand,[4] and concentrate on an examination of the role of unions in industrial democracy. The examples on which I intend to draw are taken from Great Britain, Sweden, and West Germany, with one or two brief references to the United States and other countries.

1. Johannes Schregle, "Workers' Participation in Decisions within Undertakings," *International Labour Review*, vol. 113, no. 1 (January–February 1976), pp. 8–15.
2. See Adolf F. Sturmthal, "Industrial Democracy in the Affluent Society," *Proceedings* of the Seventeenth Annual Meeting of the Industrial Relations Research Association, 1964, pp. 270–79.
3. Quoted in John Horner, *Studies in Industrial Democracy* (London: Victor Gollancz, Ltd., 1974), p. 11.
4. Many experiments in industrial democracy are undertaken in order to stimulate higher productivity. While such changes may be a by-product of the institutional arrangements which we are considering, we are dealing here with those which aim at changes in the power structure of the enterprise concerned.

THE ROLE OF UNIONS

Perhaps the most fundamental problem of industrial democracy is to fit the union into the system. The British long ago coined the slogan "You cannot sit on both sides of the bargaining table," meaning that the union cannot at the same time represent the workers in a given plant and be part of the management. Attempts to do so, nevertheless, were—partly inadvertently—made in France during the first rush of nationalization measures after World War II and led to some of the most confusing results in the industrial relations systems of the enterprises concerned. One solution, which indicates how desperate the confusion was, consisted of the enactment of a law prohibiting representatives of interest groups in managerial functions to consider any other interest except the one they were supposed to defend.[5]

The basic difficulty arises from two circumstances. First, the union exists to defend its members' interests in conflict situations. Second, while industrial democracy appears to demand that power be moved as close as possible to the shop floor, other concerns, primarily the need to check wage-push inflation, require that power be shifted to the

5. Even though the Yugoslav system of workers' self-management is altogether different from any of the examples used in this paper, this experience shows some of the problems here discussed with—perhaps excessive—clarity. Thus, *Yugoslav Trade Unions*, no. 78 (September–October 1972), reports that an enterprise, ironically called "Tito's Mines," with about 11,000 workers, in drawing up a new statute "did not mention them [the Trade Union Confederation, the League of Communists, and the Youth Union] at all. . . . Simply, for one reason or another, certain organs seemed to 'forget' that they existed." This error was duly corrected when the "socio-political organizations" themselves protested.

upper ranks of the union hierarchy. In either respect, it is the role of the union in a system of industrial democracy which presents one of the central problems that reformers have to tackle.

Whoever refers to unions in relation to industrial democracy speaks in the first place of methods of managing industrial conflict. All talk about collaboration and common objectives notwithstanding, industrial relations consist of a mixture of conflict and cooperation. It is not simply a conflict over the distribution of revenue, but also the inevitable clash between those who have authority and those they have authority over. It is true, of course, that workers are interested in the well-being of the industry and the enterprise in which they are employed; but no public relations slight of hand can make us forget the tension between those who manage and those whom they manage. Any attempt at using devices labeled "industrial democracy" to make us overlook this element of conflict is— consciously or unconsciously—an act of deception.

Collective bargaining enters the area of industrial democracy in two ways. It can be an instrument through which the institutions of industrial democracy are established. In isolation, this is a rare case, if it exists at all. Usually, it is legislation which paves the way for the new institutions to come into being. In another role, collective bargaining, extended in scope, is itself the process by which participative management is implemented. Needless to say, in the latter situation the system of bargaining, indeed of industrial relations as a whole, is radically changed if the union participates effectively in decisions which traditionally have been regarded as management pre-rogatives.

Basically, collective bargaining is one of many ways of managing conflict. Although it does not always succeed in avoiding some forms of conflict settlement which are painful for society at large, it does succeed in the large majority of cases. Participation in managerial decision making represents another method of settling conflicts. A fairly new attempt consists of combining both methods. Examples for each of these three methods of managing industrial conflict can be found in the three countries which we shall examine.

THE BRITISH APPROACH

The purest form of collective bargaining cannot be found any more in the United Kingdom. Even though it is the homeland of this form of conflict management, the U.K. has departed from it and is probably going to deviate from it even more. The issue of whether the union should limit itself to the role of bargaining partner or seek some form of participation in management had long been hotly disputed in the British labor movement. Ernest Bevin and Herbert Morrison were, at one time, the leading spokesmen of the two sides in the discussion. Bevin was the advocate of union participation in the management of nationalized enterprises. Morrison defended the view that only experts—including those with industrial relations experience, such as former union officials—should be appointed managers. Morrison's views triumphed and continued to prevail for almost four decades. It was only when the steel industry was nationalized at the end of the 1960s that employee directors at area group level were appointed from among unionists in the industry. These were part-time appointments, and on assuming their positions the employee directors had to resign their union functions, though not their main jobs in the industry or their union membership. The 16 employee directors represented a new departure in another sense, too. Unlike former unionists who had been appointed to the boards of other nationalized industries, they came from the same industry they were to supervise and help manage.

The more recent attempts of the Labour party and the leadership of the Trades Union Congress to introduce a German type of co-determination in Great Britain run counter to a long tradition. It is, thus, not surprising that they have met with sharp resistance from some of the most powerful British unions that wish to retain their full independence from management and to continue to act as bargaining partners rather than as co-administrators.

Underlying these striking divergences of views of the role of labor unions in the enterprise are different conceptions of their task in society at large. Many, though not all, British (and American) unions see themselves as countervailing powers whose main or even almost exclusive assignment is to bargain with management. They refuse to accept any share of responsibility for the administration of the enterprise and expect that the bargaining process will establish a fair balance between their demands on behalf of the interests of their members and those of the owners of the enterprise. In this process, the interest of society at large—if there exists such a clearly definable interest—will also be preserved: in extreme cases by the intervention of the government, but in most cases by the simple fact that no single bargain is of sufficient gravity to have a substantial impact on the well-being of society. Industrial democracy, in this view, is limited in scope to bargainable issues. Since, however, almost any problem confronting the enterprise can, under certain circumstances, affect the interests of the union or of its members, no issue can definitely and persuasively be designated as not bargainable except where some issues are explicitly insulated from union influence (as was the case for a long time in Sweden). While acknowledging the right of management to manage, the unions reserve for themselves, in fact, the right to bargain on any managerial prerogatives if circumstances appear to require such procedures.

The locus of industrial democracy in this interpretation is to be as close as possible to the work place, where the impact of the union is most clearly felt by the rank and file. This is the approach of U.S. unions and of many British unions, even though the British Trades Union Congress (TUC) now seems to lean toward the high-level interpretation of industrial democracy. The picture in the U.K. is further confused by the substantial degree of independence from union control which shop stewards in many industries enjoy.[6]

CODETERMINATION: THE GERMAN ROAD

German unions conceive their area of work to be within the man-agement of the enterprise. They are, thus, at the opposite end of the spectrum from American and a substantial number of British unions. Instead of being a countervailing power to management they want to be a part of it. Their two main arguments in favor of union representation on the governing boards of industrial enterprises are: first— regardless of what unions do or say —they will be held responsible by public opinion for whatever ills befall the enterprise; and, second, they can discharge their responsibility only if they are fully informed about the problems, activities, and technical and economic conditions of the enterprise. Such information, the unions claim, can only be obtained by labor representation on the boards that decide enterprise policies.[7]

It is important to remember that the German codetermination concept was deeply influenced by the tragic end of the Weimar Republic and the horrors of the Nazi era. Two notable historical considerations played a particular role: one was the financial support that some elements of big business gave to Hitler, the other was the division in the German trade union movement under the Weimar Republic which weakened its power of resistance to the rising tide of Nazism.

To meet the first consideration, codetermination on a so-called parity scale was introduced in the iron, steel, and coal industries during the postwar occupation, with the approval of the then-existing British Labour government to monitor the political activities of German heavy industry. The second consideration

6. For instance: "Few unions trouble to prescribe for the processes that include election of stewards and convening of shop meetings." John Hughes, "Trade Union Structure and Government," *Research Papers*, no. 5, part 2 (Donovan Commission Research Documents), p. 59. See, also, W. E. J. McCarthy, "The Role of Shop Stewards in British Industrial Relations," *Research Papers*, no. 1 of the Donovan Commission, especially pp. 50 ff. and pp. 72 ff.

7. A good presentation of these arguments can be found in Ludwig Rosenberg, "Codetermination, Socialism, and Education," *Free Labour World*, no. 314 (July/August 1976), pp. 313–14.

was resolved by the merger between the formerly separate Socialist and Christian unions; but this required a program acceptable to both, and codetermination appeared to fill the bill. In their postwar role as guardians of political democracy, the unions assumed managerial functions, and even though the original consideration has long lost its importance, the concept of union participation in management has remained. Yet it creates about as many problems as it appears to solve.

The advantage, from the point of view of the union, is that the system permits it to settle labor-management conflicts often long before they reach the bargaining table or even become publicly known. Codetermination, as noted earlier, is an additional method of managing the inevitable conflicts between labor and management. Thus, one aspect of codetermination is that it provides a supplementary means—additional to collective bargaining—of settling disputes. Whether the low incidence of strikes in West Germany can be explained this way is doubtful, since the low levels also apply to industries in which only a modicum of codetermination exists. Some observers, including Chancellor Helmut Schmidt, have reasoned this way.[8]

Codetermination, however, is supposed to mean much more than an additional way of managing conflict. It is to be workers' participation in management in general. And this is the area in which it presents its most difficult problems. Elsewhere I have referred to unions who seek this kind of participation with the concomitant assumption of responsibility for the welfare of the enterprise as administrative unions.[9] The main issue in this respect does not really relate to the role of the labor members of the supervisory boards who, on the whole, create few problems. Rather, the really serious problem stems from the ambiguous position of the so-called labor director, a member of top management who is a guardian of the interests of the enterprise and at the same time a union man owing his well-paid position in almost every case to the union. To a considerably lesser degree, the same problem of divided loyalty arises for the members of the works council, who are in most cases union members of fairly long standing and owe their office to election by all employees regardless of union membership. It is reasonable to expect that the labor director will solve his dual loyalty problem in most cases by behaving as a member of the management team, and the empirical evidence available on this point appears to confirm this assumption. After all, it is not too difficult to identify the long-term interests of the enterprise with those of its employees.

However, for employees it is frequently their short-term interest that matters and if, apart from the crisis of 1969–1970, there has been no major manifestation of dissatisfaction with the existing institutions of industrial relations in West Germany, at least some part of the credit should go to the fortunate economic developments in the country. Still, "when people are questioned on the degree of personal satisfaction and asked, 'How well are you personally satisfied with co-

8. See Heinz Hartmann, "Codetermination Today and Tomorrow," *British Journal of Industrial Relations*, vol. 13, no. 1 (March 1974), p. 55. The excellent performance of the German economy may have played a more important role in maintaining industrial peace.

9. Sturmthal, "Industrial Democracy in the Affluent Society," p. 9.

determination? Did you get out of codetermination what you wanted personally?' there is a noticeable lack of enthusiasm."[10] Moreover, public opinion polls, even those taken in behalf of the trade unions recently, indicate almost invariably that an extension of codetermination does not rank at the top of the list of demands of individual union members.

On the negative side of codetermination, one must add that it operates at the top level of the company. And since until quite recently the German unions only rarely attempted to operate at the workshop level, leaving this area to the works council, the union is often said to be in danger of "operating in a void."[11] Even if this is an exaggeration, it contains more than a germ of truth. "Codetermination has long been a high-level affair."[12] The worker himself quite often does not even know the names of his representatives on the supervisory board. Nor have the unions made any sustained effort to achieve worker participation on the floor.

There are powerful reasons in an age of predominantly high employment levels and inflationary tendencies to justify a concentration of union influence at the top. They have mainly to do with anti-cost-push efforts, such as the German "concerted action" which has been remarkably successful. But there is no point in denying that high-level forms of industrial democracy do little to bring about genuine workers' participation and may, in fact, widen

10. Erich Potthoff, Otto Blume, and Helmut Duvernell, *Zwischenbilanz der Mitbestimmung* (Tübingen: J. C. B. Mohr, Paul Siebeck, 1962), p. 321.
11. Hartmann, "Codetermination Today and Tomorrow," p. 58.
12. Ibid., p. 62.

the gap between the worker and his union.

THE SWEDISH SOLUTION

It is this issue which the Swedish labor organizations have squarely faced in their attempt to introduce workers' participation. They have combined collective bargaining and industrial democracy at the plant level in a particular fashion designed to strengthen union influence both in the workshop and in national policy matters. Legislation in 1976 has paved the way for different forms and degrees of workers' participation to be made the subject of collective bargaining. In the first place, unions may delegate two members to the board of larger companies, those with more than 100 employees. So far, this has meant fairly little in practice and, in fact, has been used by unions in only about two-thirds of the applicable cases.

The main emphases of the Swedish unions have been on the extension of the scope of collective bargaining and shifting its focus to the plant. Practically every important management decision is henceforth to be open to bargaining, and the bargaining process is to involve the union in the plant. In effect, this practice will shift industrial democracy to the place where it is most meaningful for the worker, that is, the work place, and will avoid putting labor representatives in a schizoid position. At the same time, by transferring unsolved local disputes to negotiations at the national level, the system maintains the ultimate authority of the national union. Sweden thus seems to have devised a solution for what in other countries has appeared to be an insoluble problem—how to combine industrial democracy at the work place with collective bargaining and to give the union a status in the plant without compromising union independence. This is, at least at first sight, a very different formula from the division between unions and works councils in West Germany and unions and shop stewards in Britain.

To maintain separate organizations for bargaining and organizing work at the shop floor level and for the same or similar tasks at national or regional levels is likely to produce suspicion or at least tension between the two parts. Even if all members of the works council have a union affiliation, their dual loyalty must expose them to severe strains from time to time.[13] If it does not, then another danger appears: that of workers creating their own independent and informal organizations to which, at least for a period, their primary loyalty belongs. This seems to have happened during the great strike wave in Western Europe in the late 1960s and in the Italian rebellion against the *Commissione Interne* created after World War II.[14] To cite the fact that the great majority of works council members

belong to unions does not suffice as an answer. Indeed, it merely tends to focus our attention more clearly upon the danger of dual loyalty. In the Swedish case this issue was accentuated, in spite of the tremendous authority of the union leadership, by the ill-famed Article 32— originally Article 23 of the Basic Agreement of 1906 between the federations of employers and trade unions, which gave management full authority at the work place. One of the main reforms in the direction of industrial democracy was the nullification of Article 32 by the Swedish legislation of 1976, which now enables the union to negotiate on any issue of importance in plant operations and on individual workers' tasks and working conditions.

SOME GENERAL IMPLICATIONS

This means, of course, a radical change in the structure of unions and in the collective bargaining system. The great battle for union representation in the plant has to be won on two fronts: against union tradition and probably also against workers' refusal to pay higher union dues, since new union agencies will have to be created.[15] The second front is that of the employers who wish to keep union representatives out of the plants.

Collective bargaining will have to be changed to end the dual system of national and plant level bargaining, of which the Donovan Commission in Britain spoke in its 1968 Report. Enterprise or even plant agreements will have to become the rule rather

13. For example, in the Netherlands the simultaneous presence of works councils and shop stewards has at times led to strained relations between them, since their competencies overlap. See J. T. M. Andriessen, "Developments in the Dutch Industrial Relations System," *Industrial Relations Journal*, vol. 7, no. 2 (Summer 1976), p. 52.

14. ". . . what was new about the winter 1969/70 strike wave was not the resort to unofficial, and illegal, action but the strike's size and duration, and a much higher level of wildcat strikes thereafter than before. The Swedish unions' hold on their members' loyalty was evidently eroding, as elsewhere in Europe." Andrew Martin, "From Joint Consultation to Joint Decision-Making: The Redistribution of Workplace Power in Sweden," *Current Sweden* (June 1976), p. 6. This refers to events preceding the recent reforms.

15. Even if unions succeed in shifting their financial burden to the enterprise, the result for the individual worker is the same as if he had to pay higher union dues. Wages are reduced either way, since labor costs increase.

than the exception. Some movement in this direction is already under way in a number of countries. This, too, of course, adds to the costs of unionism.

More important than the relatively minor financial issue is a basic problem which this extension of union activity into the plant is likely to create. Where industrial unionism prevails as in Germany, problems of which union is to represent the workers in a given enterprise are relatively easily solved. The issue, then, is merely whether the all-embracing union confederation, as the agency of all organized workers, will also have some voice in any participation scheme. But where the structure is more fragmented, the difficulties will be correspondingly greater. Even in Germany, the existence of a separate and fairly small white-collar trade union occasionally presents problems. However, these become tremendously magnified when, as in Britain, a large number of unions can claim to be spokesmen for different groups of workers in the same plant. Even greater difficulties arise in countries in which two, three, or still more unions of differing ideological attachment and confederal affiliation dispute each other's right to represent the same group of workers.

However, while admittedly complicated and painful, these situations need not be regarded as insuperable hurdles. They have been handled, with tolerable degrees of success, in the elections of comités d'entreprise in France and in the corresponding institutions in Italy, Belgium, and elsewhere. If these have not always produced the desired results, it is partly because one ought not to expect eternal harmony between capital and labor and, in a more immediate sense, because until quite recently, these bodies were mainly consultative bodies only. Consequently, the workers attached only little, if any, significance to them. Organized labor can hardly be expected to accept responsibility for decisions which it cannot effectively influence.

Beyond these—admittedly serious —organizational and financial issues there remains a basic ideological one which no public relations campaign can cover up. The more the union becomes involved in management participation, the more serious the danger of syndicalism is likely to be. I am using this term in a special sense: a coalition of management and union directed against the consumer. Management accepts, to a large extent, union demands, with the more or less clear understanding that the two will cooperate in transferring cost increases—usually with an adequate increment for profit— to the consumer of the goods or services involved.[16]

Yet, as we have seen, separating the employees' organs of industrial democracy from the union is likely to lead to an alienation between the union and its rank and file. Indeed, it may create the kind of situation which the Donovan Commission in Britain so tellingly described—the coexistence of two industrial relations systems, one legal but fictional, the other real but often outside the control of the unions. What matters, therefore, is to avoid creating new institutions that are competitive with those of collective bargaining, but at the same time prevent management and union

16. A searching, but greatly exaggerated and one-sided version of this theme appeared as early as 1944 in Henry C. Simons, "Some Reflections on Syndicalism," *Journal of Political Economy*, vol. 52, no. 1 (March 1944), especially p. 23.

from exploiting the powerful position which such exclusivity gives them.

It is obviously dangerous for a society to have management and unions engaged in almost continuous warfare which powerfully contributes to the disintegration of society. It is almost equally harmful, in the light of a wider interpretation of social concerns, to permit excessively close collaboration between the two. A respectful distance, permitting both conflict and cooperation, seems to be best. This is partly a matter of attitudes about which outsiders may have little or no control; it is also a question of institutional arrangements. It is at this point that society, and perhaps also the social scientist, may have some influence. Neither the dream of eternal class warfare nor that of perpetual harmony is attractive when closely examined. Fortunately, they are both utopian.

Industrial Democracy and Industrial Relations

By JOHN P. WINDMULLER

ABSTRACT: Some of the changes which are transforming Western European industrial relations systems under the banner of industrial democracy are in reality serving to expand the scope of collective bargaining and to extend it structurally downward to include the level of the individual enterprise. Through employee representation on corporate boards of directors and enlarged rights of works councils, many issues formerly the exclusive prerogative of the employer are becoming subject to joint decision making. As a general rule, the new rights are being obtained almost entirely through legislation rather than collective agreements. They include, among others, a right to information about vital affairs of the enterprise which management is obliged to provide to employee representatives. Since the scope of collective bargaining in the United States has always been wider than in Western Europe and the individual enterprise is central to the North American bargaining structure, it is not readily apparent how worker participation in management would contribute to improved labor-management relations in the United States.

John P. Windmuller has been on the faculty of the New York State School of Industrial and Labor Relations at Cornell University since 1951. He has held Ford Foundation and Fulbright research fellowships and has lectured in several European countries. His principal interests are comparative industrial relations systems and international labor organizations. Among his publications are studies on comparative collective bargaining, labor relations in the Netherlands, U.S. labor and American foreign policy, the International Labor Organization, and international labor movements. He was special editor of volume 310 of THE ANNALS *(March 1957) which dealt with* Current Issues in International Labor Relations.

I N APRIL 1976 the Volkswagen
    Company of West Germany
decided to invest about a quarter
billion dollars in setting up an automobile assembly plant in the United
States.[1] The decision expressed a
determined effort to preserve the
company's North American market
in the face of rising production
costs at home and a declining
competitive position overseas. The
step also ended a long period of
bargaining inside the company over
the employment impact of setting up
an American manufacturing operation. Labor won a guarantee that
no jobs would be lost and that VW
employment levels in West Germany would be maintained over
the next 10 years.

What was remarkable about these
negotiations was neither the issue
nor the outcome—job security
has always been a primary union
goal, especially in Western Europe.
Rather, it was the fact that the
bargaining occurred inside the company's supervisory board, approximately equivalent to an American
board of directors, on which labor
at that time held one-third of the
seats outright. Other persons sym-
pathetic to labor's interests occupied several additional seats. (The
ratio of outright labor-controlled
seats has since been increased by
new legislation.) Thus, labor used
its legally mandated positions on
the company's highest policy-making body to extract concessions
that management might well have

rejected or even refused to discuss as bargainable items if the
union had demanded them in regular collective bargaining negotiations. By taking full advantage of
its insider position, labor demonstrated that control of a bloc of
employee representatives on the
board could be converted into a
de facto extension of the structure
and subject matter of collective
bargaining.[2] And in a wider sense,
the outcome demonstrated once
again that arrangements providing
for worker participation in management are capable of exerting important effects on industrial relations.

A caveat to begin with: the industrial relations effects of participation will vary considerably from
country to country. After all, even
if every country were to adopt
precisely the same kind of worker
participation scheme—which is not
very likely—it would impinge on
very differently constructed industrial relations systems and perforce
lead to different results. The fact
is, of course, that each country
is evolving a distinctive form of
worker participation, distinctive in
major components as well as nu-
ances. The overall effect, therefore,
may well be to increase—or at the
very least to maintain—the already
considerable differences among industrial relations systems rather
than bring them closer together.

Nevertheless, the differentiation
does not preclude certain common
consequences. As a general proposition, worker participation in the
several variants currently emerging
in Western Europe is tending to
bring about a closer integration of

1. *New York Times*, 24 April 1976. For
the background of this decision and for an
incisive discussion of the operation of codetermination inside the VW board of directors, see the excellent article by Alfred
L. Timm, "Decision Making at Volkswagen
1972–1975," *Columbia Journal of World
Business*, vol. 11, no. 1 (Spring 1976),
pp. 94–103.

2. See Johannes Schregle, "Worker Participation in Decisions within Undertakings,"
International Labour Review, vol. 113, no.
1 (January–February 1976), pp. 6–7.

certain components of national industrial relations systems. For example, the predominant practice of sectoral or industry-wide bargaining between national unions and employers associations is being increasingly articulated with negotiations at enterprise and plant levels. This is particularly the case in countries where the two usually separate organs of employee representation—trade unions and works councils—are moving closer together.

Some interesting changes in traditional roles and attitudes are part of this process. In most countries the law still imposes on works councils an obligation to cultivate a harmonious and collaborative relationship with the employer "for the good and welfare of the entire enterprise." For example, the West German works council law, as amended in 1972, provides that "the employer and the works council shall work together in a spirit of mutual trust, having regard to the applicable collective agreements and in co-operation with the trade unions and employers' associations represented in the establishment, for the best interests of the employees and the establishment."[3]

Yet by gradually becoming involved in plant level collective bargaining, many works councils are turning into more militant organs of employee interest representation. In some situations, this trend has even reached a point where occasionally a works council will nowadays assume a leading role in an industrial dispute, once almost unheard of. Unions, on the other hand, although expected to be more aggressive than works councils, are no longer quite so free to push the cause of their followers when union officials spend part of their time attending to the responsibilities of membership on corporate boards of directors. In fact, it is more than likely that this awkward duality of tasks will require unions to accept some sacrifice in militancy and perhaps even to soften their social criticism. The class struggle does not fit readily into the board room.

Although participation schemes can assume a variety of institutional forms, most of them can be subsumed under one of five categories: (1) the inclusion of employee representatives on corporate policy-making boards; (2) the integration of works councils or similar bodies into the managerial decision-making procedure at plant and shop floor levels; (3) the introduction of changes at the work place designed to improve the quality of working life; (4) the establishment of employee stock ownership plans or other forms of participation in enterprise capital or profits; and (5) the appointment of workforce-oriented managers to handle labor relations.[4] All five are potentially of considerable significance for industrial relations, but the discussion here will emphasize

3. International Labor Organization, *Legislative Series*, Federal Republic of Germany 1 (March–April 1972), p. 2.

4. Under legislation which at one time applied to only one sector of German industry but is now being extended with some modification to the others, a designated member of top management is to be responsible expressly for employee relations. In the coal and steel industries, where he is known as the labor director, his appointment and in due time the renewal of his contract require the approval of the employee members of the board. Contrary to expectations, this peculiar form of participation does seem to be practicable, but at least for the time being it has remained confined to West Germany.

the first two because they are currently most widely applied.[5]

THE STRUCTURE OF COLLECTIVE BARGAINING

Industry-wide bargaining between employers associations and national unions—whether for an entire country or only for a particular region—has been the prevailing practice in most Western European countries for a long time. In some countries, such as Sweden, Norway, and Holland, economy-wide negotiations between central federations of employers associations and trade unions have sometimes been superimposed on industry or sectoral bargaining, and when that happened the resulting agreement has become the framework establishing the limits for further bargaining at industry level. But whether fully or only partly centralized, the bargaining process has rarely moved in the opposite direction, that is, to the individual firm or plant, although here and there a few large enterprises (VW in Germany and Renault in France) have constituted an exception.

The reasons for the neglect of the individual enterprise, a neglect which is so markedly in contrast with the enterprise-centered bargaining structure in North America and Japan, have been explored at

length elsewhere.[6] On the union side, one must consider a combination of ideological preferences and organizational weakness. The priority that European labor movements accorded to class-oriented industrial unionism, with its accent on worker solidarity and on mass organization, usually left a vacuum at shop and enterprise levels. On the continent, it was filled by independent, statutorily created works councils and in Britain by shop stewards with uncertain and undefined ties to the union. Where unions forsook the individual enterprise for larger aims, employers were at least equally keen to limit bargaining relationships to an entire branch of industry or some other multiple of firms, for in this way they were best able to protect specific managerial and entrepreneurial prerogatives against union encroachments. Whenever challenged on this point—which was not too often—employers offered tenacious and, on the whole, successful resistance to union efforts to penetrate the enterprise and dealt instead with works councils or shop stewards.

It is conceivable, of course, that the macro-oriented European bargaining structure might at some indefinite point in the future have become more decentralized even without any explicit stimulus. In fact, in some countries a trend toward decentralized bargaining did get underway in the 1950s and 1960s. A notable example is Great Britain, where postwar full employment greatly strengthened the bargaining position of shop stewards vis-à-vis plant management. Yet, whatever

5. On the whole, empirical data about participation are still scarce. Only the West German experience with codetermination is of sufficiently long standing to represent an important body of experience. But even in that country, the amount of published empirical research constitutes just a minute portion of the enormous literature on codetermination. See Bernhard Wilpert, "Research on Industrial Democracy: The German Case," *Industrial Relations Journal*, vol. 6, no. 1 (Spring 1975), pp. 53–64.

6. See, for example, *Collective Bargaining in Industrialized Market Economies* (Geneva: International Labor Office, 1974), pp. 93–5.

organic developments along such lines might eventually have occurred, the recent development of formal schemes of industrial democracy, including worker participation in management, has enormously quickened the extension of the bargaining structure to the level of the enterprise.

The required presence of employee representatives on company boards constitutes an important expression of bargaining decentralization, especially when employee directors are sufficiently numerous to form a bloc of their own. Of course, not all issues coming before company boards for decision will henceforth be resolved through bargaining between employee and shareholder blocs, nor should one assume that unit voting will determine all policy choices. The lines of division will not always run automatically between shareholder representatives (or management) and employee representatives. Nevertheless, there is no question that bargaining will become a common form of resolving differences between blocs on many issues, including those that are of most immediate concern to employees and that are likely to impinge in some way on present or future terms of employment. Among them will be such items as plant location, the opening or closing down of entire operations, securing of investments, introduction of labor-saving equipment, employee and executive compensation policies, and other fundamental matters requiring top-level decisions. The submission of such items to a bargaining or quasi-bargaining process between more or less homogeneous blocs represents, in effect, a penetration of the collective bargaining process into the individual firm.

Another current development tending to alter the bargaining structure is the result of a changing orientation of works councils and similar bodies of employee representation. Regardless of the origins or the traditional functions of works councils, which do differ considerably from country to country, formal schemes of worker participation generally tend to promote the integration of works councils into the bargaining structure. They do so most frequently by allocating to the works councils explicit bargaining rights in certain subject areas or by entrusting them with responsibility for supervising the implementation at plant level of macro-type collective agreements concluded between unions and employers associations. They may, of course, do both. The eventual result of these developments could well be an "articulated" bargaining structure in which enterprise agreements concluded between plant managements and works councils become an integral element in a chain of coordinated bargains that extends from the individual plant at the base to the national economy at the top.

Several current developments are gradually leading in that direction. In some of the new legislation or drafts of legislation, works councils not only have gained recognition as bodies suitable for representing the interests of employees in the individual enterprise—a recognition which in most countries they have long enjoyed—but also are being granted a status equivalent to that of a U.S.-style bargaining agent. In effect, works councils are beginning to acquire a kind of legal authority to engage in adversary collective bargaining at the level of the individual enterprise.

This development constitutes a

sharp departure from traditional conceptions of the proper role of works councils. In the Netherlands, for example, which is, in this regard, representative of many other countries, the principal task of works councils since their establishment by law in 1950 has been the cultivation of a harmonious partnership between employer and workforce to promote their mutual interest in the prosperity of the enterprise. To underline that this was to be a cooperative rather than a conflictual relationship, the employer or his designated representative has by law sat as the chairman of the council, and that arrangement is by no means unique to the Netherlands. According to newly proposed amendments, however, the works council is to become first and foremost an instrument for the vigilant protection of employee interests per se, a watchdog over management, and an agency for plant-level bargaining over issues supplemental to the industry-wide agreement. In short, it is to resemble a union and may adopt an adversary posture vis-à-vis the employer. In this new conception of the role of the works council, there may still be a bit of room for formal cooperation between management and workforce, but that is to be subsidiary to the works council's primary tasks of closely monitoring management decisions and watchfully protecting employee interests. Of course, the employer will not only have to give up his role as chairman, but disappear from the council entirely.

CREATING NEW RIGHTS

Worker participation in management frequently establishes new power relations in the enterprise by conferring on employees, more particularly on their representatives, certain rights designed to enable them to share in areas of corporate decision making that previously were under the exclusive control of the employer or his representatives.

The specific character of the new bargaining rights is, of course, bound to vary. Some examples of the potential range will be given below. What most of them have in common is their statutory origin. The new rights at enterprise level are being obtained, or have already been achieved, almost entirely through legislation rather than collective agreements between unions and employers associations at national or industry levels. To be sure, that is in part the result of a general preference for national standardization, a preference which is much stronger in Europe than in North America. But it must also be recognized that in most European countries (Britain being an important exception) organized labor's efforts to expand the range of issues subject to joint determination—what is often termed the scope of bargaining—have been far more successful when labor has relied on its political strength than on its ability to extract concessions from employers in collective bargaining.

Even in Sweden, where labor's bargaining power at national level relative to the bargaining power of employers is greater than in most other countries, the recent statutory expansion of union bargaining rights at enterprise level—and the corresponding contraction of long established management rights—came about only when a labor-oriented government passed the necessary legislation. The alternative would have been a collectively negotiated basic agreement similar in form to other basic agreements that have led to important innovations in Swedish labor-management relations. That route, however, was effectively blocked by determined employer resistance. And so, after discovering that its bargaining strength was insufficient to achieve a significant degree of worker participation in operating management, Swedish labor exerted its considerable political leverage to secure by law a fundamental shift in the balance of bargaining power at the level of the individual enterprise.

Sweden's decision exemplifies developments elsewhere.[7] The new bargaining rights at enterprise level, as specified in legislation, are too detailed and comprehensive to be reviewed here except for a few major items. First, they include procedural rights, such as required meetings between works councils (or their counterparts) and management, the type and scope of information to be supplied by management, internal procedures for settling disagreements, and provisions for the use of outside agencies in resolving certain kinds of disputes. Second, they cover explicitly the substantive issues which have become mandatory subjects for bargaining at plant level, including working hours, vacation schedules, pension plan regulations, and health and safety provisions. There can be little doubt that these new items, which have become bargainable subjects, coincide very closely with the detailed substantive and procedural terms of collective agreements that are customarily concluded between local unions and plant managements in North America.

7. See "Swedish Codetermination at Work Act," *European Industrial Relations*, no. 31 (July 1976), pp. 19–24.

The parallel underlines a vital aspect of European worker participation schemes. Not only do they constitute a legislative-political redress of the balance of bargaining power in the enterprise, but they also seek to remedy the past organizational failures and neglects of unions at local and plant levels.

RIGHT TO INFORMATION: THE DISCLOSURE RULES

In most industrial relations systems based on collective bargaining, controversies are bound to arise from time to time over the obligation of employers or employers associations to provide the employee side with information relevant to the bargaining process. Nowadays it is not so much the principle of sharing information that is an issue, for that has been pretty well settled, but rather the nature, detail, and disposition of the information to be furnished. As a general rule, disputes over information sharing have been most acute in systems based on single-firm bargaining, not only because enterprise and plant-level agreements are almost by definition tailor-made to fit the circumstances of the individual enterprise, but also because in such systems a union's bargaining effectiveness depends to some extent on the specificity of the information at its disposal. In industry-wide bargaining, however, the outcome is likely to be a set of minimum standards rather than genuinely effective terms, and therefore the union's need to have detailed information about the economic and financial circumstances of each enterprise is considerably less acute. This important distinction helps to explain the construction in North America of a body of detailed administrative regulations specifying the employer's obligation to furnish bargaining-related data to the union and the absence of comparable rules in the bargaining systems of Western Europe.

More recently, however, institutionalized worker participation, with its emphasis on changing the balance of decision making in the individual firm, has been compelling Western European countries to become much more explicit and regulatory about this kind of information sharing. This again underscores the theme of this essay that participation in essential aspects, is an extension of collective bargaining to the individual enterprise.

Generally speaking, employee members who serve on corporate boards are entitled to receive the same information, in kind and volume, that is supplied to all other board members. This is the case even when some of the board members on the employee side are actually full-time union officials who directly or indirectly represent their organizations in negotiations with the same companies on whose boards they are serving or who at the very least will eventually negotiate agreements with employers associations to which these companies belong.

At the works council level, the legal requirements on information sharing are more often than not enumerated in considerable detail in the relevant legislation. Not only do the laws require the employer to report periodically to the works council or one of its committees on corporate financial policy, profits and losses, the state of the order books, production planning, and other vital data, but he must also supply detailed information on all items that have been designated as subject to joint employer-employee determination. Thus, in the Netherlands draft legislation now being considered specifies pension plans, profit sharing, employee savings plans, working hours, vacation schedules, compensation plans, job evaluation, health and safety rules, contemplated acquisitions of other firms, spin-offs of subsidiaries, plant closings, mergers, production cutbacks or expansion, plant relocation, organizational changes, and related matters. Comparable statutes in other countries are nearly as detailed.

Wherever legislation on worker participation makes the execution of management initiatives contingent on the consent of the works council or at least on prior consultation with it, the employer must supply information sufficient to enable the works council to make an informed judgment. There is very little difference in principle between this rule and the detailed administrative prescriptions of the National Labor Relations Board in the United States defining the employer's obligation to bargain in good faith.

A difference does exist, however, in the subsequent treatment of such information. Whereas in the United States there has been relatively little concern about the problem of protecting the confidentiality of bargaining-related information supplied by an employer to a union, in European systems the employee members of corporate boards and the members of the works council are legally required to safeguard privileged information made available to them. Indeed, some laws provide for stiff penalties where a breach of confidence can be proven. Nevertheless, it would be unrealistic to expect such a rule to be effectively enforced, particularly in cases where employees are represented on corporate boards by union officials who in another context represent the bargaining interests of their members. In practice it is to be expected, therefore, that in most instances detailed information about the affairs of an individual enterprise will become available to the research departments of the unions in due course. That is not necessarily a deplorable consequence, considering that other outsiders such as banks have long had access to supposedly confidential corporate information by virtue of their widespread representation on boards of directors.

It is still an open question, however, what use unions will make of the information acquired through worker participation. West German experience indicates that the unions have so far made no effort to use the multiple board memberships of their officials as a means for establishing a central depository of information through which to oversee a particular industry, not to mention the economy as a whole. Nor does information sharing seem to have made them noticeably more aggressive in their bargaining. Indeed, it is at least conceivable that possession of detailed information on the economic status and prospects of individual enterprises will moderate instead of sharpen a union's bargaining expectations.

IMPLICATIONS FOR THE UNITED STATES

The spread of information about current developments in industrial democracy in Western Europe is bound to raise the question of whether the United States, too, will move in a similar direction.

The foregoing analysis suggests that some of the main purposes of worker participation in management have already been achieved in the United States through an enterprise-centered system of collective bargaining. Part of what is being sought in Western Europe under the banner of industrial democracy—that is, joint decision making on issues of vital importance to employees, information sharing, adequate procedures for disputes settlement in the enterprise, and related goals—has long been an integral part of the American industrial relations system. In a thoughtful review of American labor's position, Thomas Donohue of the AFL-CIO explained at a conference on industrial relations in May 1976 that "because American unions have won equality at the bargaining table, [they] have not sought it in corporate board rooms."[8] Perhaps, then, the question one should really ask is whether the European model of worker participation in management is not, in substance, a reasonable facsimile of the American pattern of decentralized collective bargaining, as adapted to the historically different circumstances of the Western European countries. It would appear so.

In any event, it is quite certain that Donohue's rather negative appraisal of participation ("it offers little to American unions in the performance of their job unionism role") and his rationale for that appraisal ("We do not want to blur in any way the distinctions between the respective roles of management and labor in the plant") are shared by an overwhelming portion of American unions. And yet, there is

8. *John Herling's Labor Letter*, 7 August 1976, p. 1.

a point to be made on the other side of his argument which leads straight back to the case of the Volkswagen Company mentioned at the start of these observations. If labor's spokesmen in the United States are justified in their complaints that American workers have suffered a serious loss of jobs and income through the capital and technology exports of U.S.-based multinational firms, and if neither labor's application of considerable political pressure to change the permissive terms of present legislation nor the practice of adversary collective bargaining is capable of securing adequate relief, control of a bloc of seats in corporate board rooms might be an alternative worth considering.

ANNALS, AAPSS, **431**, May 1977

New Focus on Industrial Democracy in Britain

By ANDREW W. J. THOMSON

ABSTRACT: Industrial democracy in Britain has traditionally operated through the process of collective bargaining, but since 1973 the Trades Union Congress has pursued the objective of giving workers' representatives parity on company boards of directors with shareholders' representatives. This approach was adopted in the Labour party's election manifesto for the current Parliament, but the government, somewhat uncertain as to how to implement this objective, has appointed the Bullock Committee to investigate the issue. The committee's report is expected to be broadly favorable to the TUC viewpoint, but most employers and some unions want a more flexible approach to worker participation. Any government legislation in the near future is likely to be threatened by time constraints and a declining majority in Parliament, but there is general agreement in all the political parties about the need for some further development in participation, even if not about the precise form that it should take.

Andrew W. J. Thomson is Senior Lecturer in Applied Economics at Glasgow University, and is presently visiting Associate Professor of Industrial Relations at the University of Chicago Graduate School of Business. He did his undergraduate work at Oxford and received M.S. and Ph.D. degrees from the New York State School of Industrial and Labor Relations at Cornell University. He has written books on grievance procedures and the 1971 Industrial Relations Act in Britain and is currently working on collective bargaining in the public sector and the twentieth-century history of labor in Britain.

THE ISSUE of industrial democracy is in a state of flux in Britain at the present time, and a watershed in its development appears imminent. Industrial democracy is, of course, a term which covers a variety of different concepts, but for reasons of space this paper will concentrate mainly on the issue of most immediate relevance, namely worker representation on the board of directors.

BACKGROUND UP TO THE 1970s

The major industrial relations legacy from the nineteenth century to the twentieth was a solid commitment to trade unionism and collective bargaining as the primary focus of worker self-expression, although the nineteenth century had seen a number of socialist and anarchist theories and experiments, including self-governing cooperatives and Owenite communities, none of which flourished except the retail cooperative movement. The first quarter of the present century saw the growth of a much more explicit political orientation through the emergence of the Labour party and also a sudden mushrooming of more radical ideas based on syndicalism and guild socialism, with nationalization becoming the practical focus of aspirations toward industrial democracy. In the discussions of the time, nationalization was often taken to involve some form of workers control, but over the next 20 years opinion within the Labour party moved in favor of the public corporation, in which there would be a conventional management structure but with some interest group representation on the board, as the primary vehicle for implementing nationalization. This approach was duly incorporated in the post-World War II nationalization legislation without much opposition; a sprinkling of unionists were put on the industries' boards of directors, but not in any dual capacity which might compromise their responsibility to one side or the other. Little thought was given to the private sector.

Parallel with these developments was the consolidation of the role of the trade union as the primary representative of the workers. With the exception of the short-lived World War I period, there was no plant-based challenge to the status of the national union and the industry-wide collective agreement, and its eventual emergence in the late 1950s in the form of informal bargaining by shop stewards and stewards' committees merely served to underline the formal status of the union even if the reality was that unions frequently lost control of plant level activity. By the 1960s, it could be said that unions had already achieved effective participation through the limitation of management discretion in most large and medium-sized companies in Britain.

This essentially pragmatic position was perhaps best rationalized by Hugh Clegg.[1] His approach was to take an analogy from the democratic political pluralism of government and opposition and argue that industrial democracy is best obtained by having two opposed sides, management and unions. He advocated three basic principles whereby this concept of industrial democracy might be perceived: "The first is that trade unions must be independent both of the state and of management. The second is that

1. Hugh Clegg, *A New Approach to Industrial Democracy* (Oxford: Blackwell, 1960).

only the unions can represent the industrial interests of workers. The third is that the ownership of industry is irrelevant to good industrial relations."[2] Such a situation is, of course, perfectly compatible with capitalism; indeed, it conveniently justified the status quo and the predominance of collective bargaining and as such reflected a majority view at the time within the Labour movement. Even at the present it remains an important strand of thinking.

In the middle 1960s, however, a new dissatisfaction with the state of industrial democracy arose. Best represented on the left by the Institute for Workers Control,[3] it drew on the growing power of shop stewards within industry and within the union movement while also reacting against the bureaucratic structure of the nationalized industries, which it perceived as state capitalism. The swing of the unions to the left as the state attempted to exert controls on collective bargaining through law and incomes policies was a further factor in arousing interest in new forms of industrial democracy. Within the Labour party itself, a working party on industrial democracy was set up in 1967,[4] but in spite of endorsing the general principle, it was unable to recommend a blueprint for participation which covered the various situations and issues in different sectors of the economy.

However, the most influential voice of the 1960s came from the Royal Commission on Trade Unions and Employers' Associations (the Donovan Commission),[5] which carried out a thorough review of the British system of industrial relations in its report in 1968. The commission thought that its proposals for the reform of collective bargaining would adequately cover developments at plant level and intermediate level, and a majority felt unable to recommend the appointment of workers' directors to the boards of companies, although a group of three thought that experiments should be facilitated, and two others (not union representatives, incidentally) wanted mandatory arrangements. In its White Paper *In Place of Strife*,[6] which resulted from the Commission's Report, the Labour government merely noted that it favored experiments with worker directors and intended consultations as to how this might best be achieved. It also, like the Donovan Commission, took the view that collective bargaining "represents the best method so far devised of advancing industrial democracy."

NEW DEVELOPMENTS IN THE 1970S

The issue, however, remained a topical one, and indeed spread well beyond the Labour movement to other political parties and bodies. A particular impetus was given by Britain's entry into the European Common Market in 1973. The Liberal party produced proposals similar to the German framework, and the Conservative government promised, although it did not actually produce, a discussion paper on the subject. The key occurrence, how-

2. Ibid., p. 21.
3. See Ken Coates and Tony Topham, *The New Unionism: The Case for Workers' Control* (London: Peter Owen, 1972).
4. The Labour party, *Industrial Democracy* (London, 1967).

5. *Report of Royal Commission on Trade Unions and Employers Associations* (London: Her Majesty's Stationery Office Cmnd 3623, 1968).
6. *In Place of Strife: A Policy for Industrial Relations* (London: Her Majesty's Stationery Office Cmnd 3888, 1969).

ever, was a paper produced initially by the research staff of the Trades Union Congress (TUC) in 1973 which broke sharply with the rather xenophobic tradition of the unions by proposing what was, in considerable part, the European framework of industrial democracy. This paper made a major issue of board level representation, although it reaffirmed the primary significance of collective bargaining.[7] Not only was the paper accepted by the unions at the 1973 Congress, albeit without great enthusiasm or even discussion of its implications, but more importantly the subject became one of the focal points of discussion between the TUC and the Labour party in the development of a Social Contract.[8] The Social Contract was a wide-ranging set of promises by the Labour party in exchange for voluntary wage controls by the unions, and when the party took office in March 1974, it became the centerpiece of economic and political policy. After the passage of the first two of the three promised pieces of industrial relations legislation, the Trade Union and Labour Relations Act of 1974 and the Employment Protection Act of 1975, industrial democracy came to the forefront of attention. However, the government, although largely committed to the TUC scheme, was uncertain about how to implement it, and therefore announced a committee of inquiry in August 1975.[9]

7. Trades Union Congress, *Industrial Democracy* (London, 1973). The document was reissued in a slightly amended form in 1974.
8. The Labour party itself produced a document which made proposals similar to that of the TUC. (*The Community and the Company*, London, 1974).
9. The setting up of the committee was hastened by the introduction of a private member's bill on board representation in the House of Commons, sponsored by Giles Radice, M.P.

The terms of reference of the committee were extremely narrow, leaving little room for any fundamental appraisal of the underlying issues:

Accepting the need for a radical extension of industrial democracy in the control of companies by means of representation on the board of directors, and accepting the essential role of trade union organisations in this process, to consider how such an extension can best be achieved, taking into account in particular the proposals of the Trades Union Congress report on industrial democracy as well as experience in Britain, the EEC and other countries. Having regard to the interests of the national economy, employees, investors and consumers, to analyse the implications of such representation for the efficient management of companies and for company law.

The restrictive terms of reference created difficulty in finding an adequate chairman and membership, but a team of suitable weight was duly assembled under Lord Bullock, the Oxford historian. The Bullock Committee was also restricted to the private sector, and a separate working party was set up under Alan Lord of the Treasury to investigate similar issues in the public sector. We will first look at the private sector.

THE POSITION OF THE TUC

As expressed in the TUC's major policy document of July 1973:

The traditional British trade union attitude to schemes for "participation" in management of private industry has been one of opposition. It has been considered that the basic conflict of interest between the workers and the owners of capital and their agents prevents any meaningful participation in management decisions. The reasoning behind this opposition has varied from the claim that the trade unions' job is simply and solely to negotiate terms and conditions, and not to usurp the function of management, to the proposition that trade unions should not be collaborationists in a system of industrial power and private wealth of which they disapprove.[10]

However, although the TUC made a number of recommendations about the scope for improving industrial democracy based on the strengthening of union organization and the widening of the scope of collective bargaining, it now saw the need for something more:

. . . it is clear that this leaves a wide range of fundamental managerial decisions affecting workpeople that are beyond the control—and very largely beyond the influence—of workpeople and their trade unions. Major decisions on investment, location, closures, takeovers and mergers, and product specialisation of the organisation are generally taken at levels where collective bargaining does not take place, and indeed are subject matter not readily covered by collective bargaining. New forms of control are needed.[11]

The TUC's basic proposal to achieve this objective in the private sector was that there should be a new Companies Act, to be introduced in stages, initially applying to the 600–700 enterprises employing more than 2,000 workers. In the companies covered, there would be a two-tier board structure with supervisory boards that would be responsible for determining company objectives and for appointing the management boards. One half of the supervisory boards should be elected through trade union machinery, but the new provisions would only become operative in unionized firms. Representation of workers on boards could

only be through bona fide unions choosing to exercise this right. Finally, the change in structure should be reflected by a statutory obligation of companies to have regard for the interests of working people as well as shareholders.

This pattern was in keeping with, and was undoubtedly influenced by, other European developments. But another element of European practice, the works council, was emphatically rejected by the TUC which argued:

An attempt to introduce a general system of works councils in British industry would lead to one of two things. Either they would duplicate existing structures at plant levels, in which case Works Councils would clearly be superfluous; or they would displace and supersede existing trade union arrangement; this latter approach would be even more unacceptable to the trade union movement.[12]

In its evidence to the Bullock Committee, the TUC based its major submission on the document already discussed, but added a supplementary memorandum to expand on certain issues. The only point of change was that as a second best to giving union members half the seats on supervisory boards, the TUC might accept equal voting rights with other directors on unitary or single-tier boards. This alternative envisaged that union directors might be outnumbered by shareholders' representatives and executive managers, but the TUC was prepared to accept it, provided the managers had no vote. On other issues the TUC argued that: the legislation should not specify how elections of union representatives should be conducted, for this should be decided by the union organization,

10. Trades Union Congress, *Industrial Democracy*, p. 14.
11. Ibid., p. 34.

12. Ibid., p. 38.

typically a shop stewards body; nonunionists should be excluded from participation because, in the large companies with which the TUC proposals were concerned, the majority of employees are union members; parity of representation would not necessarily lead to deadlock because neither side need vote as a block, or the chairmanship (with casting vote) could rotate or an independent chairman could be appointed; there should be no consumer representation, since there would be no definable constituency to which representatives would be accountable; where unions decided not to participate in the new system, the structure should operate but the workers seats would remain unfilled; the reason for the claim to 50 percent of the seats was that only in this way could union representatives be expected to feel any sense of collective responsibility for board decisions; and finally, equal responsibility would not mean identical responsibility, since the primary responsibility of union members would be to their constituents, and they would thus be workers' representatives on the board rather than worker directors.

OTHER UNION VIEWS

Although the TUC has carried its viewpoint at its own congresses, there is far from unanimous acceptance of its proposals within the union movement. For example, the Engineering Workers Union has argued that supervisory boards could act in opposition to the development of collective bargaining; such boards, like works councils, would duplicate or supersede the growth of collective bargaining at company level, and they could well degenerate into the rubber stamps of management

boards, creating the illusion of power without the reality. For this union, the desirable alternative is the unlimited extension of collective bargaining into areas such as pricing, investment, location, forward planning, sales, and profitability. The Electricians Union, from a much more right-wing political stance than the engineers, has argued along similar lines: the essential need is for unions to maintain their independence; there is a danger that management could coopt the union, which might lead to an alternative representation at the place of work; it is not the responsibility of working people to manage the enterprise, nor can union directors accept responsibility for managerial decisions and still represent workers who feel they must oppose them. The General and Municipal Workers Union has indicated that a general mandatory obligation should be placed on managements to negotiate with unions on a number of issues, including those which might be decided at board level, such as forward decisions on investment, reorganizations, mergers, and changes in product lines. While parity of union representation on supervisory boards might be one way of achieving such joint control, the union has commented that TUC policy did not provide for equivalent compulsion on negotiations where the unions concerned did not opt for this type of board.

THE EMPLOYER POSITION

Employer submissions to Bullock were almost universally critical of the TUC proposals. The Confederation of British Industry (CBI) pronounced itself in favor of participation, but argued that there was no suitable standard system: larger companies with over 2,000 employees should be required by law to reach participation agreements within four years, failing which there would be an arbitrated solution; medium-sized companies might be brought within the law on participation agreements later, and in the meantime should be encouraged to extend participation voluntarily; small companies with under 500 employees should be encouraged to set up company councils. Employee representation at board level would not generally be suitable; where they were favored they should be solidly based on other arrangements below board level; and any suggestion that employee participation necessarily involves employee delegates on the board was seen as irrelevant and unacceptable. In addition, the CBI rejected the TUC principle of single-channel representation which excluded nonunion employees, especially among manual workers, and also the proposal that there should be participation only when this was desired by trade unions. The participation agreements, which were the keystone of the CBI approach, were to come within certain guidelines, including ratification by all employees in a secret ballot, joint arrangements where more than one union was participating, no conflict with collective bargaining or recognition arrangements, and, perhaps most important, no interference with the executive function of management or its legal responsibility for discharging its third-party obligations. The actual participation in decision making would thus be extremely limited. Company councils for smaller companies (which were generally ignored by the unions) would consist entirely of employee representatives with the chief executive as chairman.

Most employer and independent evidence similarly stressed the need for flexibility, although in doing so it was bound to fall short of the TUC claim for parity on the board. Another theme running through the employer evidence was the need to build up participation from the bottom rather than impose it from the top if commitment from employees was to be achieved. There were many other criticisms of the TUC's proposals on grounds of democracy and accountability, but perhaps most of all there was criticism of the impact on efficiency of the TUC proposals, which had suggested that board representation would decrease workers' resistance to change and thus increase overall efficiency. Rather, the feeling was that there would be delays in reaching decisions, not infrequently deadlock, and that a great deal of extra time would be consumed; boards would become an arena for political maneuver and conflict rather than a forum for making realistic decisions. Finally, apart from anything else, there would be great difficulty in obtaining suitable people.

POLITICAL AND OTHER PERSPECTIVES

The Conservative party has said little of substance about methods of representation. A recent party pamphlet merely noted:

The appointment of worker-directors is not the first or the most obvious way of achieving real participation involving the whole of the labour force. A Conservative government will encourage the implementation of schemes which fully involve all employees in the operation of their companies. Schemes for financial participation will also be encouraged.[13]

The Liberal party also rejected key parts of the TUC proposal, in particular the emphasis on union domination. They accept two-tier boards, but want directors elected by shareholders and employees who would have equal voting rights. The party also wants workplace councils which would have to approve certain decisions jointly with management.

The government has naturally been reserving its position while the Bullock Committee has been sitting, but a speech in May 1976 by the responsible minister, Edmund Dell, the secretary for trade, suggested that, except for the fundamental principle that some form of employee representation on the boards of companies should be introduced, all options were open. But he also stressed that any government initiatives would have to be "compatible with improved industrial relations, the efficient management of companies, and an increasing level of investment of risk capital."[14] Britain, he added, "could not afford the luxury of radical change if the result is not to be greater efficiency."

There is no space to do justice to the large number of other views, but one which must be mentioned is the National Consumer Council (NCC). Their main point was quite different from those mentioned so far, but very clear:

. . . such a carve-up between labour and capital in a modern version of the corporate state could not be in the interests of consumers . . . we cannot but fear that, if labour and capital were locked together in one organizational combine, the push for security would become strongly underpinned and the tendency to monopolistic limitation to new entrants to a trade enhanced.[15]

The NCC therefore has suggested, although with little hope of success, that there should be consumer directors.

THE PUBLIC SECTOR

So far we have dealt with the private sector of industry, but the issue of industrial democracy also applies to the public sector in which there are two main types of situation. The nationalized industries are reasonably similar in their structure to private sector companies, and there the TUC proposed similar arrangements, that is, a two-tier board with a 50 percent trade union representation on the first-tier board. But it also wanted direct involvement on managerial boards at lower levels. There have already been some developments in this sector: the British Steel Corporation, for example, has had worker-directors on divisional boards since the late 1960s, but this experiment has not generally been regarded as a success in spite of some restructuring of the scheme in 1972;[16] the Post Office has also already agreed that there will be union representation on its board, possibly in a two-tier structure which would be echoed at regional and lower levels. As in the private sector, however, views are far from uniform. A report on the structure of the electricity industry unequivocally rejected equality of numbers on the board. It argued that such a board could not have a common purpose, and the unions in the industry strongly supported this

13. Quoted in *The Times*, 5 July 1976.
14. Quoted in *The Financial Times*, 19 May 1976.

15. Quoted in *The Times*, 25 March 1976.
16. See Peter Brannen et al., *The Worker Directors: A Sociology of Participation* (London: Hutchinson, 1975).

position. At the other end of the spectrum, the National Union of Mineworkers has put forward proposals that each colliery should be directed by a team of 12 persons elected by the employees for a three-year period. The team would appoint the professional managers.

The public services, primarily central and local government, present much more difficult problems because of the role of Parliament and the local authorities as representatives of the electorate. However, without being explicit, and accepting that the machinery might need to be different, the TUC has argued that "in principle the case for giving public services trade unions due and timely opportunities to contribute the views of their constituents is as valid as the case for a greater measure of industrial democracy for the rest of the working community."[17] By this, the TUC means "a satisfactory degree of representation on the main decision-making operational bodies." But which bodies and what kind of representation are difficult issues, which, like all the issues in the public sector, have not been adequately ventilated in public. The Lord Committee has operated in private, there has been no provision for outside views to be heard, and there is unlikely to be any published report.

THE PROBLEMS FOR POLICY

The foregoing views and issues present both philosophical and technical problems for policy determination. Most of them can only be listed rather than discussed. But one key issue deserving at least a brief discussion is how far unions can or must accept responsibility for the deci-

sions taken at board level. In its 1973 document, the TUC tried to detach the sharing of power from the sharing of responsibility, and even though the TUC General Secretary Len Murray accepted the need to share responsibility at the 1976 congress, it is precisely for this reason that many unions have preferred to pursue other ways of exercising power. As already noted, unions in Britain generally can already exercise power through participation in the process of management via collective bargaining, and there is considerable fear not only that collective bargaining will be diluted, but also new challenges from below will appear to conflict with the formal union organization. It seems likely, indeed, that any emerging possibilities of board level representation will not be taken up in a number of companies where unions wish to preserve their independence. For employers, the problem is the obverse: will the changes merely take bargaining into the boardroom without achieving the objective of cooperation in implementing company policy? Beyond this central issue, a list of some of the more significant problems which Bullock and the government will have to face up to is as follows:

—Should there be a two-tier structure of boards of directors, and if so how should powers be divided between the two?
—Should worker directors be solely the representatives of trade unions or should they also cover nonunionists? Can worker representation be equated with trade union representation? What about representation of managers, few of whom are unionized in the private sector? What about nonunionized companies?

17. Trades Union Congress, *Industrial Democracy* (1974 version), p. 43.

—What proportion of worker-directors should there be?

—What arrangements should be made in regard to decisions below board level?

—Should worker directors be elected directly or indirectly, or appointed?

—Should there be powers of recall of worker-directors in certain circumstances?

—What should be done with multi-plant company structures, multi-nationals, and holding companies?

—What should be the responsibilities of worker-directors?

—How should the workers themselves be involved, given obvious dangers of remoteness from their representatives?

—How should the system of collective bargaining operate if the board has overall responsibility for industrial relations policies?

—How will enough suitable worker-directors be discovered, trained, and serviced by their unions?

—How can difficulties associated with secrecy and confidentiality of company information be overcome?

—What should be the authority of the shareholders' meeting?

—Should there be differences between the public and private sectors?

—Should there be differences in sizes of companies?

—Should the system be mandatory or voluntary?

—How quickly should any new scheme be introduced?

—What should be done to reconcile disagreements in setting it up, including differences among unions in a system of multiple union representation?

OTHER DEVELOPMENTS IN INDUSTRIAL DEMOCRACY

While the central focus of attention to new systems of representa-tion in decision making is on the Bullock and Lord Committees, there have been other developments of significance in recent years. Those in the nationalized industries have already been mentioned. British Leyland, recently brought under state control through the National Enterprise Board, has introduced an elaborate three-tier participation structure after a good deal of advance preparation. The base of the struc-ture consists of more than 30 plant-level joint management-union com-mittees. From these, the stewards elect representatives to divisional middle-level joint committees, and in turn these bodies send 15 stewards to the car council chaired by the chief executive. However, it is fundamental to the scheme that management retains the ultimate right to make all decisions. The structure is designed to allow the workforce to contribute to problem solving and the formation of future plans, but it precludes negotiations and codetermination. Somewhat similar schemes have been intro-duced in other large companies such as Chrysler and Ferranti; it is noteworthy that these, like Leyland, are companies which have recently received large public subsidies.

A very different dimension of industrial democracy has been the experience with various forms of cooperatives. There has been a long history of producer cooperatives, most of them members of the indus-trial Common Ownership Move-ment, but unlike their retail counter-parts, they have been small in scale and significance. There have also been copartnerships, such as the John Lewis Partnership, but again, they have been very much the exception.

The early 1970s saw a consider-able number of factory occupations, mainly in protest against closures, and some of these led to work-ins and cooperative ventures.[18] The work-in at Upper Clyde Shipbuilders was the best known, but there were several other smaller ones. However, the major institutional developments came with the new Labour government of 1974 which inherited a number of closure problems. Wedgwood Benn, secretary of state for industry, after considerable arguments within the government, offered public aid to finance worker cooperatives in the N.V.T. motorcycle factory at Meriden, the Fisher-Bendix plant at Kirkby, and the *Scottish Daily News*. Another separate aspect of industrial democracy is experimentation with various forms of job enrichment or improvements in the quality of working life,[19] but while such experiments do exist, it is probably fair to say that in this respect Britain lags behind other countries.

Finally, there have also been, or are pending, other governmental measures which can be said to contribute to industrial democracy;[20] indeed elements of significance for industrial democracy are scattered through various pieces of legislation. The Employment Protection Act of 1975 and the Trade Union and Labour Relations Act of 1974 were both major pieces of legislation extending individual and union rights; perhaps the most significant provision was the right to disclosure

18. See Ken Coates, ed., *The New Worker Cooperatives* (Nottingham: Spokesman Books, 1976).
19. See Department of Employment Manpower Papers No. 7, *On the Quality of Working Life* (London: Her Majesty's Stationery Office, 1973).
20. For a review of this legislation, see A.W.J. Thomson and P.B. Beaumont, "The British Labor Government's Industrial Relations Program," *Cornell International Law Journal*, vol. 9, no. 2 (May 1976), pp. 159–90.

of information given to unions in the Employment Protection Act. Beyond these, the Health and Safety at Work Act of 1974 provided for unions to request and participate in safety committees and to have safety representatives with designated powers. The Industry Act of 1975 created the possibility of voluntary planning agreements in which unions would be expected to be consulted and also created rights of information disclosure going beyond those contained in the Employment Protection Act. Also within the Industry Act, the National Enterprise Board (and its sister bodies the Scottish and Welsh Development Agencies set up under separate legislation) was given the task of promoting industrial democracy in undertakings which it controls. The government is also planning to bring in legislation to give unions 50 percent representation on pension scheme management bodies.

THE NEXT STAGE

The publication of the Bullock Report is expected in mid-January 1977, but there has already been a good deal of informed speculation about its contents. It seems likely that the whole committee will accept the principle of worker-directors, including the employer representatives, which may create difficulties for the CBI in its present opposition to this principle. There is likely to be a recommendation for a single-rather than a two-tier board (on this issue the TUC and the CBI have changed sides), which would be divided into three parts. Shareholder and union representatives would comprise the largest (and equal) groups which would then together nominate the smaller third group. Worker-directors would be elected through the union machinery, and only company employees would be eligible; an external union official could, however, come in as part of the third group. The machinery would be brought into operation by a ballot of the whole workforce, with the employer having no say in the decision. The employer representatives on the Bullock Committee are, however, expected to dissent on two points: they would prefer a two-tier board, and they do not want so many places to be given to the workers. The report as a whole will, nevertheless, generally endorse the TUC position.

However, this will be far from the end of the story. Although the government is largely committed to the TUC viewpoint and has included industrial democracy in its legislative program for 1976–77, it may well find it necessary to interpose another stage of discussion, such as a Green or White Paper. In any case it will have difficulties in pushing through early legislation on industrial democracy because the coming parliamentary session is likely to be dominated by the issue of devolution to Scotland and Wales, and time considerations may prevent its passage. There is also likely to be a major battle in Parliament, since employers and the Conservative and Liberal parties are unlikely to accept the government proposals. Moreover, the government is likely to lose some of its parliamentary support through defeats at by-elections, and already at the time of writing its majority is a precarious one. A general election is indeed a distinct possibility well before the government's full period expires. Therefore, legislation in the form the TUC and the Labour party would like is by no means assured. However, the general principle looks certain to advance in one form or another. All the political parties are committed to some conception of industrial democracy, and there will also be some pressures arising from Common Market obligations.

West German Experience with Industrial Democracy

By FRIEDRICH FÜRSTENBERG

ABSTRACT: The prevailing forms of industrial democracy in West Germany and the proposals for its further development cannot be encompassed in a single integrated system. There are few basic issues of industrial democracy which do not contain a complex interlocking of regulative norms, contractual relationships, and cooperative activities. A genuine German development is codetermination or Mitbestimmung. In order to evaluate its proper significance it is necessary to differentiate between shop floor and board levels, between the institutions of works councils, labor directors on management boards, and worker representatives on supervisory boards. The greatest achievement in industrial relations, largely due to the works councils, is perhaps the establishment of a reasonably well functioning grievance and negotiation machinery within the individual plant and the larger corporation. Codetermination in supervisory boards has not undermined profit orientation as a criterion of performance, but employee representatives have been able to obtain proper consideration of the social aspects of work. There are limits in a system based mainly on statutory measures. More personal involvement and more self-government at workplace level might be on the agenda for the near future.

Friedrich Fürstenberg has been Professor of Sociology at Johannes Kepler University in Linz, Austria, since 1966. He received a doctorate in economics in 1953 at Tübingen University, and in 1953–54 was a member of the Human Relations Research Group at the New York State School of Industrial and Labor Relations, Cornell University. During 1957–58 he conducted research on joint consultation in Britain, being affiliated to the London School of Economics. He is currently President of the Austrian Industrial Relations Research Association and a member of the Executive Committee of the International Industrial Relations Association.

THOUGH there is much agreement about the need for more democratic participation within the world of work, opinions differ widely as far as content and scope of industrial democracy are concerned. This also applies to the case of West Germany where the prevailing forms of industrial democracy and the proposals for its further development cannot be encompassed in a single integrated system. They reflect, rather, a pluralism of possible interpretations of basic concepts and, within these limits, of historically established areas of consensus in terms of working solutions.

Public attention usually focuses on codetermination, especially at supervisory board level. But one must realize the complex meaning even of this key concept and its interrelation with other practices of industrial democracy in contemporary West Germany. In order to get as clear a picture as possible of the present situation and of the forces working to maintain or change it, the basic approaches to problems of industrial democracy in West Germany must be briefly analyzed.

BASIC APPROACHES TO INDUSTRIAL DEMOCRACY

In a society based on democratic principles, the structure and operation of enterprises require legitimization by consent. In order to serve this purpose three models are used in West Germany.

First, industrial democracy can be fostered by state regulations which offer a framework for the articulation and consideration of various interests. Such legal provisions are fundamental prerequisites for the form and content of industrial relations.

Second, the contractual model offers the parties concerned an opportunity to settle their problems in free negotiations leading to agreed compromises that are limited both in time and scope. Industrial relations at sectoral and regional levels of industry usually follow this pattern.

Finally, we also encounter the application of a cooperation model which is characterized by joint participation in problem-solving processes and which offers to the representatives of employees varying degrees of information, consultation, and codetermination. It is this model especially which has strongly influenced industrial relations within the West German enterprise.

There are few basic issues of industrial democracy in West Germany which do not contain a complex interlocking of regulative norms, contractual relationships, and direct cooperative activities. But in specific situations the different models are unevenly applied and promoted by the various interest groups. This becomes quite clear when one considers the main viewpoints that usually emerge in any major discussion of issues in industrial democracy. There are always groups aiming to enlarge the basic rights of the workforce in order to improve the quality of working life. However, there is often a clear distinction between those advocating the improvement of basic individual rights and those aiming at greater collective rights. In practice, individual rights usually focus on the conduct of individual contracts of employment and problems of the individual career as well as on issues of social and employment security. Collective rights are the basis for most activities within the area of codetermination and will be discussed in more detail later on.

The contractual element, of course, prevails in collective bargaining, though it is also based on relevant legislation (that is, the law on collective agreements). But contractual elements can also be found in codetermination activities. For example, negotiations between works councils and management often result in individual plant-level agreements.

More participation in order to foster industrial democracy is usually claimed by the unions within their concept of codetermination, covering the whole area of industrial relations from workplace levels to issues of the economy in general. Arguments in this direction usually focus on representative participation. Arguments for direct participation by individuals and work groups are usually brought up either by syndicalist groups within the trade union movements or, from a quite different viewpoint, by advocates of industrial partnership models. Some employer groups aiming at social reform are strongly recommending a type of industrial democracy based on both participative management and employee stock ownership plans.

Before turning to a discussion of the different attitudes and the underlying interests which shape the dynamics of industrial democracy, we shall analyze the framework for the type of industrial democracy which is a genuine German development: codetermination (or Mitbestimmung).

THE FRAMEWORK FOR CODETERMINATION

Codetermination in West Germany is based on worker or employee representation. In varying degrees, it extends to both shop floor and board levels as far as private industry is concerned. Three fundamental laws determine its functioning: the Works Constitution Act (Betriebsverfassungsgesetz) of 1972, which covers all enterprises with at least five employees; the Codetermination Act (Mitbestimmungsgesetz) of 1951, as amended in 1955, which covers only the coal and steel industries; and the new Codetermination Act (Mitbestimmungsgesetz) of 1976, which covers corporations with more than 2,000 employees. In the public sector, the Personnel Representation Act of 1974 provides codetermination rights similar to those granted by the Works Constitution Act.

In order to evaluate the proper meaning of codetermination, it is necessary to differentiate between shop floor and board levels,[1] between the institutions of works councils, labor directors on management boards, and worker representatives on supervisory boards.

WORKS COUNCILS AT SHOP FLOOR LEVELS

1. Works councils are elected by all employees of the enterprise, but separately for blue-collar and white-collar workers. They are formally independent of the unions.

2. Works councils cannot call a strike, but they have the right to sue management for alleged breach of contractual or legal rights. In

1. West German companies are governed by two strictly separate boards: the Supervisory Board (Aufsichtsrat), usually convening once quarterly to decide general matters of company policy, and the Management Board (Vorstand), whose full-time members are appointed by the Supervisory Board and who actually run the business.

such cases, which are rare, remedial action has to be sought in the specialized labor courts. More usually, failure of management and works council to agree leads to referral of the issue to an arbitration tribunal.

3. The law grants works councils a broad range of rights to information, consultation, and codetermination. For example, the Works Constitution Act of 1972 grants codetermination rights to works councils in respect to the shop rules, the regulation of daily working hours and rest periods, temporary short-time or overtime work, the time and location for wage payments, the preparation of the vacation schedule, the installation of devices for controlling employee performance, safety regulations, the administration of welfare services in an individual plant, the assignment of company housing, the determination of job and piece rates, the formulation of wage determination systems, the introduction of new methods of remuneration, and the determination of principles for the operation of suggestion schemes. Codetermination rights are also granted to cover the introduction of any technological changes affecting the work place, work flow, or work environment. In such cases the works council may demand appropriate measures to take into account considerations based on ergonomics. There is also an important right to codetermine in the issuance of guidelines for personnel selection and in the administration of vocational training. In the event of major operational changes within the enterprise, management and works councils are mandated by law to conclude an agreement which pays due regard to the balance of interests involved; and in case economic disadvantages result for employees, they are to introduce adequate measures of social planning.

Thus, the legal rights of works council members in West Germany by far surpass the rights of equivalent bodies in other countries. Nevertheless, the system of works councils creates certain problem areas which limit the effectiveness of participation. Each works council operates within a social tension field comprising its employee constituency, management, and the union. The relations between the works council and its constituency are largely shaped by the problem of proper representation. Employees in modern plants are divided into numerous formal and informal groups, each having its own goals. It is difficult to reflect the complexity of this structure in the composition of the works council. Usually some groups are underrepresented, for example female employees,[2] shift workers, or foreign workers. The evidence also shows that among blue-collar workers those in the higher skill grades have a better chance than others to elect their candidates.

As a rule, a newly elected works council has to contend with a certain amount of employee antagonism toward, and lack of interest in, its work. In larger plants, the unavoidable bureaucratization of works council activities intensifies the existing alienation. The appointment of union stewards for each workshop and office often helps to facilitate two-way communication between works council members and their constituents. Research has shown that the chairman of

2. In West Germany 15 percent of works council members were female in 1975.

the works council tends to be assured of regular reelection, thus making this office a quasi-professional function.[3] Likewise, the diversified activities of the works council require increasing specialization on the part of its members in order to negotiate effectively with management experts. As a result, a wide range of special committees has come into existence, the most common ones being committees for problems of wage rate setting, accident prevention, white-collar employees, female workers, young workers and apprentices, social welfare, and physically handicapped workers. Thus, a properly functioning works council usually has quite a complex structure. The better equipped it is to match management's qualifications in negotiations, the more its members are professionalized, thereby creating a social distance between themselves and the average employee.

The practice of holding plant assemblies during working hours has not proved sufficient to neutralize oligarchic tendencies within the works council. Most employees are not interested in detailed reports on works council activities. Though by law such assemblies must be held four times a year, empirical research in the West German electrotechnical industry has shown that actually they take place quite irregularly. In a group of 104 plants, they were held only once in 19 plants, twice in 33 plants, three times in 35 plants, 4 times in 15 plants, and not at all in 2 plants. There was also a noticeable trend toward a steady decrease of employee participation in the assemblies.[4]

The relations between works councils and management are decisively influenced by the problem of integration. At least once every four weeks, council and management representatives are required by law to meet in joint conferences. These are often organized by the personnel manager. Of course, management usually attempts to utilize the works council's functions for its own purposes and to integrate them into the existing social system of the factory. This is usually done by inviting the works council members to assume functions and to organize activities holding out the prospect of some tangible advantage for employees. The administration of company-financed social institutions, the control of working conditions according to the provisions of law, and especially the selection of workers for layoffs in periods of work scarcity are examples of works council activities supporting the personnel department.

Besides areas in which a works council can be used, in effect, as an executive organ of management policy, there are also conflict areas. The greater the difficulty of agreement between management and works council, the more the negotiations become formalized. In cases where they are conducted in a formal and legalistic manner, management is aided by its own legal department, while the works council largely depends on experts provided by the union. Though there are some cases where works councils still identify themselves wholeheartedly with management's policy, there are other cases where the works councils show a high degree of militancy

3. See Friedrich Fürstenberg, *Die Anwendung des Betriebsverfassungsgesetzes im Hause Siemens* (Munich: Siemens AG, 1970), p. 11.

4. Ibid., p. 10.

toward management. In the long run, the works council can operate successfully only when it is not closely identified with either management or the union.

The relationship between works council and union poses the problem of solidarity. In spite of the legally autonomous status of the works council, works council members are usually union members and often hold positions as union officers. To be a member of a works council can be an important step in a career that may ultimately lead to full-time office in a union or even to political office. There are strong informal organizational ties between the works council and the union. Newly elected works council members are trained in union-sponsored courses, and the union also provides them with specialized information and advice necessary for their work. In dispute situations, the unions are the only organizations which can back up the works councils in their dealings with management. On the other hand, works councils must also be able to act successfully within the enterprise by taking into consideration worker interests as well as management objectives. Therefore, issues may well arise where a certain company-mindedness by the works council comes into conflict with union policies aimed at achieving uniform terms of employment for an entire industrial sector. Although the unions hold a key position in elections to works council membership through their ability to enter slates of nominees, they do not completely control the composition of the works council. For example, in the 1968 elections in the Siemens Company, 41 percent of the newly elected works council members were not organized. However, shortly after the election most of them became union members.

Generally speaking, harmonious relations between employer associations and unions and the maintenance of full employment tend to facilitate the effective functioning of works councils. By the same token, conflict in society at large or in a particular industrial sector will adversely affect the works council by creating instability. Perhaps the greatest achievement in industrial relations attributable to the works councils is the establishment of a reasonably well functioning grievance and negotiation machinery within the individual plant and the larger corporation. Open conflicts, such as strikes, only rarely involve the works councils.

PARTICIPATION IN MANAGEMENT BOARDS

At the level of management boards, so-called labor directors were introduced in the West German mining and iron and steel producing industries by the Codetermination Act of 1951. They are appointed in the same way as other members of the management board, but they cannot be appointed against the wishes of the employee representatives in the supervisory board who usually initiate the appointment. As a rule, the labor directors have the confidence of the unions. While it is their special responsibility to administer the personnel and labor relations policies of the company, they also participate fully in the decision making on company policies in general, for these must be made jointly by the members of the management board acting as a group. Under these circumstances, a basic dual loyalty is inevitable:

the labor director is responsible both for effective management performance in general and for effective representation of the employees' point of view. In 1960 about two-thirds of all labor directors were in charge of the entire personnel administration apparatus of their firms, but only between one-third and one-half of them played an actual part in the firing and dismissal of staff members not covered by collective agreements.[5] This group usually consists of the higher level employees and of academically trained employees in the enterprise.

Experience has shown that the labor director can handle his difficult marginal situation only by attempting to become fully integrated in the management structure and socially accepted by his colleagues on the board. This is, of course, a matter of both competence and tact. Usually, labor directors are not recruited from the ranks of works council members or union officials. They tend to be persons of high technical or intellectual qualifications, experts in their field of competence rather than skillful politicians. From the employees' and the unions' point of view, their main function is the development of personnel and social or labor policy within the enterprise in a way that reconciles the company's economic and social requirements. In practice, this task amounts to introducing modern methods of personnel management. Thus, the labor director's role has generally been one of counterbalancing the points of view of the technical and financial experts on the management board.

5. See E. Potthoff, O. Blume, and H. Duvernell, *Zwischenbilanz der Mitbestimmung* (Tübingen: J. C. B. Mohr, Paul Siebeck, 1962), p. 102.

The recently introduced general codetermination law in West Germany departs from the long-established rules for the coal, iron, and steel industries by specifying only that a labor director shall be appointed in firms with 2,000 or more employees—in other words, by omitting the additional requirement that the labor director's appointment have the endorsement of the employee members of the board. In consequence, there will be no direct representation of employee (and union) interests on the management boards outside the mining, iron, and steel producing industries.

WORKER REPRESENTATION ON SUPERVISORY BOARDS

Regarding worker participation on the supervisory boards of German firms, two types of legal provisions must be distinguished: minority representation and parity (or equal) representation. Minority representation applies to firms subject to the Works Constitution Act. It provides that in joint stock and limited liability companies having more than 500 employees, one-third of the members of the supervisory board shall be employee representatives nominated by the works council but elected by the employees. Obviously in such situations the employee members cannot, as a rule, prevail against the will of the shareholder representatives on the board.

Full parity representation has so far been achieved only in the mining and steel industries. There the Codetermination Act of 1951 prescribes parity of capital and labor representatives, the former being designated by the shareholders' meeting and the latter by the works councils and unions. Both parties select by cooptation one neutral person. The recent Codetermination Act of 1976 has now extended this system to all companies with more than 2,000 employees, but with two restrictive provisions: (1) at least one employee representative must be designated by the group of so-called Leitende Angestellte (employees exercising managerial functions); and (2) in impasse situations, the chairman, who is always designated by the shareholders, casts the deciding vote.

In order to evaluate the functioning of worker representation in supervisory boards, one has to take into account the proper meaning of these institutions in West Germany. The legal function of supervisory boards is mainly the appointment and control of the management board. In practice, especially during periods of flourishing business operations, the actual activities of supervisory boards do not amount to much more than policy coordination and advice and formal ratification of decisions already made by the managing board. Supervisory boards usually convene not more than once every three months. Thus, their activities are rather remote from day-to-day management operations.

In terms of actual power relationships, minority representation of employees in supervisory boards ought to be seen as a means of improving internal consultation and the flow of information. Interestingly enough, works council members who simultaneously sit on supervisory boards have an advantage over their counterparts in plant management, who often get their information secondhand and rather late at that. Though employee representatives on the board have no decisive veto rights, their consent is usually considered useful by share-holder representatives. That usefulness at times enables them to obtain some concessions for the workforce. A typical case occurred when the supervisory board of a large German automobile manufacturing firm decided to raise the dividend. The employee representatives objected to this decision until a large bonus payment for all employees of the firm was approved at the same time.

The interests of employee representatives focus, of course, particularly on measures which are likely to affect employment conditions, such as changes in products and production. Timely information on plans in these areas may help the works councils to take appropriate measures.

The functioning of parity codetermination in the coal mining and steel producing industries has been the subject of several empirical studies, the most recent one being the so-called *Biedenkopf Report* of 1970.[6] The report, widely considered to be authoritative, found that parity on supervisory boards had not led to revolutionary changes in company policy. Moreover, the boards functioned smoothly, and unanimity in decision making was the rule.[7] The favorable result has been fostered by the already mentioned fact that decisions in the supervisory boards very often amount to no more than an endorsement of plans already discussed in detail at management board levels. Therefore, decisions by actual voting are less important than informal consultations beforehand. Such consultations usually take place between the works council members and union officials represented on the

6. *Mitbestimmung im Unternehmen* (Bundestags-Drucksache VI/334).
7. Ibid., p. 36.

supervisory boards, on the one hand, and shareholder representatives and members of the management board, on the other hand. The neutral member on the supervisory board usually does not cast the deciding vote. Instead, his role is that of a mediator.[8]

The decisive problem for supervisory boards is setting long-term goals for company policy. Under West German codetermination, profit orientation as a guide to policy has not really been questioned. No major projects planned by management have been prevented by employee representatives, as shown by analyses of corporate merger proposals and the controversial issue of pit closings in coal mining. However, employee representatives have often been able to obtain proper consideration of the social and labor aspects of such situations. Thus, supervisory boards have become more involved not only in the technical and financial but also in the social planning of company operations. This holds especially true for the social effects of investment and organizational restructuring. The Biedenkopf Commission did not find any evidence that there had ever been a severe breach of confidence or a deliberate act directed against the well-being of the enterprise by employee representatives.[9] On the contrary, the rather difficult restructuring of the West German coal mining industry proceeded without any major strikes, due largely to worker participation in all major decisions.

We would summarize by noting that the present provisions for employee representation on supervisory boards do not amount to real codetermination in all managerial affairs. Rather, the very structure of supervisory boards and the legal framework within which they operate offer indirect but very real opportunities for influencing the decisions in the management board. And it is this board which decisively shapes the technical, economic, and social reality of the enterprise. The authority of management decisions has not been questioned by this system of representation, but the basis for its legitimacy has changed.

CURRENT ISSUES OF INDUSTRIAL DEMOCRACY

Industrial democracy is less a state, characterized by legal and contractual provision, than a constant process that changes its focus according to differential participation and goal setting. This observation applies also to the case of West Germany. Public opinion, parliamentary debates, and discussions among both union members and managers clearly show that the current framework has many built-in tensions.

The new Codetermination Act of 1976 embodies many features of a fragile compromise. For instance, the German Federation of Trade Unions (DGB) does not regard the law as an adequate expression of parity codetermination because, in case of a tie vote, the chairman of the board (who is elected by the shareholder representatives) has the deciding vote. For its part, the Confederation of German Employers Associations fears that the new law might shift the balance of economic power decisively in favor of the unions.

The present and foreseeable practice of codetermination places de-

8. Ibid., p. 40.
9. Ibid., p. 54.

cisive power in the hands of representative oligarchies. Empirical research shows, however, that the rank and file of employees often have quite different notions of codetermination, their focus being on direct action at shop floor level.[10] Similarly, the still existing legal obligation of works council members to cooperate with management in mutual confidence and to avoid open conflict sometimes causes unrest on the shop floor, as articulated by unofficial work group spokesmen. Some left-wing unionists, therefore, are demanding new forms of interest articulation—for example, by strengthening the role of the union stewards (following the model of shop stewards in Britain and the United States). Such development would obviously run counter to the dual structure of industrial relations in West Germany under which unions are excluded from plant-level negotiations. Nevertheless, more direct participation in codetermination by the workers at shop floor level is still an unsettled problem.

Generally, the unions have had to face some opposition from certain members who object to the growing importance of cooperative forms of industrial democracy. These groups would prefer to return to labor relations patterns requiring less union involvement in managerial affairs.[11] The quest for a more militant union movement is often advocated also on the grounds that otherwise the membership might fade away or that the emancipation of workers is being sacrificed for greater privatization of affluent employees.

By contrast, there are many ongoing activities aiming at the introduction of participative management, possibly combined with profit sharing and property formation by employees. Such models often appeal to more highly skilled employees. The fact that the number of production workers is gradually declining and the number of white-collar workers is rising certainly will have an impact on future strategies for more industrial democracy and on relevant ideological justifications.

We may conclude this survey by noting that the present West German system of industrial democracy, based as it is mainly on legally secured codetermination, has some specific limits. More personal involvement and more self-government at work-place level might be on the agenda for the near future. At the same time, unions are mustering all their political strength to achieve a social partnership in public affairs designed to improve the quality of life of the working population. Industrial democracy in West Germany is still an issue with a considerable dynamic of its own.

10. See, for example, Friedrich Fürstenberg, *Die Soziallage der Chemiearbeiter* (Neuwied-Berlin: Hermann Luchterhand, 1969).
11. See, for example, F. Deppe, ed., *Kritik der Mitbestimmung* (Frankfurt/M.: Suhrkamp Verlag, 1969); also J. Bergmann and W. Müller-Jantsch, "The Federal Republic of Germany: Cooperative Unionism and Dual Bargaining System Challenged," in *Worker Militancy and Its Consequences, 1965–75,* ed., Solomon Barkin (New York: Praeger, 1975), pp. 235–76.

ANNALS, AAPSS, **431**, May 1977

The "Reform of the Enterprise" in France

By YVES DELAMOTTE

ABSTRACT: In France, the "reform of the enterprise," a more common term than "industrial democracy," became an acute question in 1974–1975 with encouragement from President Giscard d'Estaing. He appointed a commission chaired by Pierre Sudreau to investigate the matter and make appropriate recommendations. The commission's report was published early in 1975. This essay is divided into four sections. First, it provides a brief outline of the most relevant institutions in the labor field to set the framework for examining the problem of the reform of the enterprise. The second section outlines germane developments prior to the appointment of the Sudreau Commission and notes that, before 1974, reform of the enterprise consisted mainly of a steady enlargement of the functions of plant committees (comités d'entreprise). The third section summarizes the chief proposals of the Sudreau Report. The final section reviews the still very modest follow-up to the report.

Yves Delamotte was until recently the Director of the French National Agency for the Improvement of Working Conditions (Agence Nationale pour l'Amélioration des Conditions du Travail). He studied at the Sorbonne and the Ecole Nationale d'Administration. He has been an official of the Ministry of Labor and has taught in universities in France and other countries. Currently he teaches labor law at the Conservatoire National des Arts et Métiers and is the author of monographs and articles on industrial relations, including a study on the functioning of the grievance procedure in a large American firm.

IN FRANCE the term "reform of the enterprise" is in much more common use than the expression "industrial democracy." Generally it refers to initiatives by government rather than spontaneous developments or understandings reached jointly by the parties in industry. Historically, reforms in France have been expected to come through new laws and through state sponsorship of new institutions, for it is generally assumed that only in this way can their general implementation be ensured. That explains why the president of the republic, Giscard d'Estaing, took the initiative in 1974 to put the reform of the enterprise on the national agenda. Before examining the issue more closely, we must first indicate the basic institutional and political context in which the problem has been posed. We shall do so by outlining first the organizations of unions and then the system of employee representation at the plant level.

THE BACKGROUND

The General Confederation of Labor (CGT) is the oldest and most influential labor federation. The bulk of its membership are manual workers. Some of its leaders are members of the Communist party, and for the CGT the exploitation of the working class will cease only with the advent of collective control of the means of production. For the CGT, long-term objectives do not necessarily exclude specific short-term demands, particularly for higher wages and improved job security, but the prospect of reform of the enterprise within capitalist society is considered an illusion.

The French Democratic Confederation of Labor (CFDT), which holds second place in terms of membership, does not accept capitalist society either. It differs from the CGT, however, in its profound distrust of collective and bureaucratic models based on authority from the top down. The principle of industrial self-management which the CFDT espouses expresses its intent to preserve for workers a certain freedom and spontaneity against the encroaching pressures of institutions and political parties.

Three additional confederations are more reformist in orientation: the so-called Workers' Force (FO), with members mainly in the civil service; the very small Confederation of Christian Workers (CFTC); and the larger but occupationally limited General Confederation of Supervisors and Technicians (CGC).

Employees are free to join the union of their choice or not to join. The choice depends mainly on personal beliefs. The overall rate of unionization is low compared with most other industrialized countries.

Local unions with a sufficient number of members are entitled to recognition as representatives of employees in an enterprise. They may play an active role when a dispute occurs, but unlike American unions they very seldom negotiate collective agreements at the individual enterprise level because the customary unit for collective bargaining is an industrial sector or branch at national or regional level.

The system of employee representation in the enterprise is based mainly on institutions which are legally distinct from the unions. Shop stewards (délégués du personnel) are elected annually by all employees. Their task is to take up grievances with management. The plant committee (comité d'entreprise) consists of the employer and representatives elected biennially by all employees. It has essentially an advisory role. The employer is required by law to provide the committee with certain information, such as balance sheets and profit and loss statements and projected innovations or reorganizations, and to entertain the committee's advice. When plant committees were established by law in 1945, the main objective was to encourage cooperation within the enterprise and to develop a form of participation in management. We shall note below to what extent this aim has been met.

The existing plant-level institutions do not depend on the presence of unions. However, where unions do function in an enterprise, they are each entitled to put up lists of candidates in elections for shop steward positions and plant committee membership. The seats are then allocated among candidates of the different unions in proportion to the votes cast for each list.

Following the events of May 1968, the unions gained the establishment by law of a new plant-level institution, namely union stewards. These union stewards, which are not to be confused with the much older institution of shop stewards, are directly designated by the several unions represented in the enterprise rather than being elected by all employees. Their task is essentially to ensure a union presence in the enterprise, to collect union dues, distribute union literature, arrange for union meetings, and similar union-centered activities.

Seen as a whole, the system of plant-level representation is varied and complex; it is the result of a juxtaposition of institutions created by successive laws rather than the outcome of a global and coherent conception. The question is, of course, frequently posed whether it should not be simplified, but that would be a difficult undertaking.

REFORM IDEAS PRIOR TO 1975

Between 1945 and 1974, the idea of reforming the enterprise inspired occasional management initiatives and, of course, occupied the thoughts of various individuals and organized groups. It even stimulated some government activities. Two phases may be distinguished. The first scattered efforts in the years immediately following liberation from German occupation tended to turn on the association of capital and labor. This association, however, usually did not go beyond employee profit-sharing plans. The plans actually implemented lost their originality with the passage of legislation on profit sharing in 1959 and in 1967, especially the latter which instituted compulsory profit-sharing plans, as mentioned below.

The second phase, which started in 1972–1973, resulted from the realization of certain employers that there was a certain urgency attached to making improvements in the quality of working life of their employees. In reaction against the former application of the ideas of scientific management, they began experimenting with new forms of work organization which sought to enrich rather than to simplify individual tasks or which made possible the establishment of work groups able to organize their work themselves and to negotiate production standards with management. The experiments showed that the reform of the enterprise did not necessarily have to be achieved solely from the top down but could also come from the base by giving workers more autonomy, more responsibility, and more influence over their environment.

Of all the writings on reform during these years before 1975, we mention here only the one which examined the issues most profoundly, *Pour une réforme de l'entreprise*, published in 1965 by François Bloch-Lainé, a high civil servant known for his ability and imagination.[1] He proposed, among other ideas, a new type of employee representation, the creation of a genuine grievance procedure (joint examination of grievances and possible recourse to arbitration), and minority participation of employee representatives in a supervisory board to which management would have to submit periodic reports. In its own time, Bloch-Lainé's work unfortunately did not lead to any immediate results, but in 1975 the Sudreau Report incorporated the last of these ideas.

During the pre-1975 period, the government took the initiative in two fields: in the name of participation it instituted profit sharing and it also enlarged the functions of plant committees.

Regarding profit sharing, a first decree in 1959 created an optional system which was seldom used. A second decree in 1967 established a compulsory system which is still in force and affects all enterprises with more than 100 employees. Profit sharing as a form of participation was largely the idea of General de Gaulle. After the events of 1968, he began to emphasize the need for forms of participation that had to go beyond profit sharing, but he

left the presidency in 1969 without explicitly elaborating his ideas.

The second line of government action was pursued more consequentially. Between 1966 and 1973, various laws defined and increased the functions of plant committees in areas of job security, industrial safety, working conditions, vocational training, and related matters. Regarding job security, to mention only one example, the kind of information now required from an employer who plans to effect a major retrenchment in his workforce is extremely detailed, and the period of required advance notice has been made very specific.

It is rather remarkable that the legal extension of the functions of the plant committee was in practice achieved by prior agreement between employers and unions. The explanation is that management now considers it necessary to provide employees with accurate information about a variety of problems. Also, since the introduction of union stewards in 1968, employers have acquired a more favorable opinion of the plant committees, for they are institutions based on plant-wide elections among all employees and thus less susceptible to external influences than the union stewards.

For the unions, the plant committees are a most important source of information. For instance, when a mass layoff is envisaged, the period between the first receipt of the information and the effective date can be used to make counterproposals, to appeal for help to government agencies, and to mobilize public opinion. This enables the unions to pressure management into reversing its plan, and at the same time helps them to avoid the appearance of involvement in a

1. François Bloch-Lainé, *Pour une réforme de l'entreprise* (Paris: Editions du Seuil, 1965).

decision which they don't want to seem to have approved. Thus, management and unions both recognize the value of plant committees but for quite different reasons. The consensus remains somewhat ambiguous, and one author has referred to the kind of participation generated in the plant committees as adversary participation.

The period 1945 to 1974 may be summed up as follows:

1. The two major unions (CGT and CFDT) opposed direct involvement of employee representatives in management responsibilities.

2. In an adversary context, the most natural way of participation was one that developed within the plant committee and that allowed employee representatives to exercise some measure of control over certain decisions of management.

3. The main changes took the form of a continuing extension of the functions of the plant committees. Proposals for radically restructuring or simplifying the complex system of representation met with no success.

4. Toward the end of the period, it had become ever more clear that reform of the enterprise had to be sought not only in institutional terms, but also at the level of the workers themselves so as to improve working conditions and increase employee influence over the work environment.

THE SUDREAU REPORT

A few months after his election to the presidency of the republic in May 1974, Valéry Giscard d'Estaing, who throughout his campaign had emphasized the need to renew French society, asked the government headed by Jacques Chirac to draft a number of reform proposals, including a reform of the enterprise. Since it was not self-evident what reform measures would be acceptable both to employers and unions and since it seemed that a preliminary investigation might help to answer that question, the president established a "Commission for the Study of the Reform of the Enterprise" in July 1974 consisting of 11 persons under the chairmanship of a former cabinet minister, Pierre Sudreau. The CGT and CFDT, which in the elections had opposed the candidacy of Giscard d'Estaing, refused to join the commission.[2] However, a former head of the CFDT did become a member in his private capacity.

The Sudreau Committee sat from September 1974 to January 1975. It heard evidence from the National Council of French Employers (CNPF), the five main labor federations (CGT, CFDT, CGT-FO, CFTC, CGC), and individual experts. It set up 12 working groups, each one in charge of a specific aspect of potential reform. The report was presented to the president of the republic on February 7, 1975, and was distributed a few days later.[3]

2. According to the CGT and the CFDT, a genuine reform of the enterprise can only take place if there is a change in the economic and social system. These two confederations are demanding a considerable enlargement of the prerogatives of the plant committees and of union representatives, even to the extent of giving them power to stop work on machinery considered dangerous. The Sudreau Report did not go that far.

3. *Rapport du Comité d'Étude pour la Réforme de l'Entreprise*, chaired by Pierre Sudreau (Paris: La Documentation Française, 1975). (An English translation of the report has been published under the title *The Reform of the Enterprise in France* by the University of Pennsylvania, The Wharton School, Industrial Research Unit, Philadelphia, 1975).

The report is divided into two sections. The first one is entitled "The Background." It contains a statement on the general philosophy which underlies the specific proposals in the second section, and it makes clear that the objective of the report is not to propose a single reform of the enterprise but rather a variety of reforms which take into account the diversity of corporate structures. The authors chose deliberately not to emphasize labor-management relations in the enterprise, nor the role or power of the unions and employees, but rather to deal with these questions in conjunction with others of generally greater interest to employers and shareholders than to employees.

This choice is made particularly clear in the second section which contains the specific proposals. They are divided into 10 chapters: (1) transforming day-to-day activities in the enterprise; (2) redefining the position of employees; (3) adjusting certain provisions of corporation law to the contemporary situation; (4) strengthening the rights of shareholders; (5) improving the operation of employee profit-sharing plans; (6) enacting new legislation on business; (7) encouraging the creation of new types of enterprises; (8) preventing problems in industry and helping firms to face up to them; (9) updating current procedures to settle labor disputes; (10) integrating the objectives of the enterprise with those of society.

It is not possible even to summarize here all the proposals. We shall only mention those which particularly affect the position of employees and their representatives in the enterprise. These can be grouped into three main categories: (1) the employees, (2) representative institutions, (3) company law.

The improvement of working conditions is given a position of top priority. Such improvements are not to be limited merely to the prevention of accidents or to purely physical facilities. They must also aim to give workers more varied and challenging tasks as well as increased responsibility.

The report suggests that each employee should have the opportunity to express himself on the content and the conditions of his job. This proposal is based on the positive results of experiments undertaken in enterprises where workers in the same department met regularly with their foremen to discuss improvements in work organization and setting. Underlying these suggestions is the idea of upgrading manual work, an idea derived from the fact that in France the position of manual workers is materially and socially still inferior to that of manual workers in other industrialized countries. The upgrading is to occur both in the enterprise and in society.

Some proposals aim at achieving a more representative and differentiated composition of plant committees. It is also proposed that multinational corporations designate a representative to make annual reports on overall corporate strategy to the plant committees of their French affiliates. Other proposals are designed to furnish employee representatives serving on plant committees with more precise and concrete information so as to enrich the social dialogue. The suggestion is also made that economic subcommittees with 5 to 12 members be created in enterprises employing more than 1,000 persons. These subcommittees would be attached to the plant committees. Their task would be to scrutinize thoroughly the economic information which management is legally required to provide to the plant committees. The Sudreau Report also recommends that each enterprise prepare certain social indicators (on the wage structure in the enterprise, weekly working hours, absenteeism and turnover, industrial accidents, vocational training and advanced training, and so forth). These data, constituting a kind of social balance sheet or social audit, would be given each year to the plant committee. The purpose would be to provide a statistical base for dialogue between management and employee representatives, to emphasize areas in which further action is necessary, and to assess the effect of measures already taken.

The report further proposes that company law should be amended to allow experimentation with new corporate arrangements, such as firms administered by a system of participative management under which employees would own stock entitling them to a share in profits and to representation in management. However, the most innovative proposal aims to set aside one-third of the seats on corporate boards for representatives of the employees.[4] The idea is not to institute co-management but rather a form of joint supervision. Employee representatives would still be in a minority on the boards. In any case, French boards of directors do not usually intervene actively in operating management. Various formulas have been proposed to pick the employee representatives; for example, election by the plant committee or by the employer or appointment by the unions.

4. Most French corporations have a supervisory board or board of directors. Its chairman is also, as a rule, the chief executive officer.

Joint supervision would allow employee representatives to be informed about decisions without necessarily being involved in making them. Furthermore, as the Sudreau Report puts it, "the representatives of the employees could exercise their right to abstain when the decision at issue would seem to them to pertain to the field of management and not to [policy] supervision."

IMAGINATION AND REALISM

Although it was denounced by the CGT as a political maneuver, the Sudreau Report was quickly recognized to have two major qualities: imagination and realism. Its imagination manifests itself in the multiplicity of the proposals, of which we have examined only a few. Its realism is inherent to the substance of the proposals and the suggestions for their implementation.

By and large, the proposals are designed to cause the least possible resistance from management and unions. Extending the prerogatives of the plant committees responds to frequent union demands, as does the suggestion to employers to accept the trade unions as genuine partners. No effort has been made to simplify or clarify the very complex system of representation within the enterprise, for the unions are strongly attached to the multiplicity of institutions and to their acquired positions. There is even less intention to circumscribe the right of the unions to propose candidates for election to the various bodies of representation in the enterprise.

The expansion of the prerogatives of the plant committee affects an essentially advisory institution, and the report underlines the necessity for continued strong leadership and authority in the enterprise. As compared with co-management, joint supervision through employee membership on corporate boards is likely to appear to employers as more tolerable. It also respects the desire of French unions not to assume management responsibilities; these are to remain in the hands of a top manager or a management group. If the supervisory board were compelled to make a decision impinging directly on management, the employee representatives could always abstain.

Considering that France is a country where the viewpoints of the employer side and the major unions are very far apart, the authors of this report have framed their proposals so that they should be acceptable to both parties. The realism of the report also shows through in the measures envisaged for the implementation of the recommendations. The report suggests that, to begin with, joint supervision should only be instituted where employees and shareholders agree. The proposal for a social audit presupposes a period of experimentation in order to determine the social indicators that would be appropriate. Each enterprise is to decide for itself how to implement the rights of employees to express their views.

Recognizing the wide diversity of individual enterprises, the authors of the report suggest that many of their innovations should first be tested and that the parties themselves ought to determine how the experiments are to be conducted. This pragmatic approach, which might also have the secondary effect of promoting more collective bargaining in the enterprise, is most remarkable since in France the main tendency in labor relations has al-

ways been to have recourse to legislation.

IMPLEMENTATION

At the time of writing (October 1976), more than 18 months have passed since the publication of the Sudreau Report, and some progress has been made in implementing its proposals. A Fund for the Improvement of Working Conditions was created in July 1976. This fund, with a budget for 1976 of 24 million francs, will provide financial assistance to those enterprises that submit model programs for the improvement of working conditions. Parliament now has before it a bill on industrial safety which represents a significant advance over previous legislation in that field. The upgrading of manual work, the need for which was underlined in the report, has become one of the main concerns of social policy. A high level government post to deal with working conditions of manual workers was created in January 1976. A new law passed in December 1975 allows manual workers who have held certain kinds of strenuous jobs for five years (continuous production flows, assembly line, foundries, construction) to retire on full pension at age 60 instead of 65. Another act of July 1976 provides that workers who have done considerable overtime work are entitled, in addition to premium pay, to compensatory time off with remuneration.

Among measures still in the planning stage is a bill to amend the company laws to authorize supervisory boards of enterprises with more than 2,000 employees to coopt employee representatives into membership. An awkward legal obstacle could thus be avoided, and the boards would still be free to use the option or not. Another bill in preparation deals with the social audit. It will specify the data which employers are to submit annually to the plant committees.

The government expects that economic subcommittees envisaged in the report will be established in enterprises with more than 2,000 employees. Employers and unions are to determine jointly the organization and functioning of this new body. In large corporations with several subsidiaries, the creation of corporate-wide employee representation committees will be encouraged. These group committees will include representatives of the several plant committees from the subsidiaries and will be entitled to scrutinize the consolidated financial statement of the corporation.

In considering all these issues and recommendations, the government has adopted the pragmatism of the Sudreau Report. Instead of immediately preparing new laws, it is encouraging industry to experiment. Once the results are in, laws might then be prepared. This flexible and rather loose concept of reform has enabled the government to bring under the umbrella of reform a considerable number of measures that have already been taken to improve working conditions.

However, if one were to insist on a more restrictive and more rigid concept of reform, that is if one were to define it in terms of industrial democracy, the measures taken up to now would seem meager indeed in comparison with the many recommendations of the Sudreau Report. As yet, the government is obviously determined not to impose by law such ideas as establishing economic subcommittees or forming consolidated plant committees for large corporations. A bill to modify the company law to enable corporations to coopt employee representatives for membership on the boards of directors has been announced, but no specific date for enactment has so far been mentioned.

This go-slow policy is probably due, at least in part, to recent economic and political changes. Opposition to the reformist ideas of President Giscard d'Estaing has been openly expressed in some major political parties. Besides, the current priority objectives of government are reducing unemployment and controlling the rate of inflation. The situation is thus quite different from what it was in February 1975 when the Sudreau Report appeared.

National elections are due to be held in March 1978. In the meantime the present government will certainly continue to push for improvements in working conditions and will seek to upgrade manual work, but it is difficult to foresee what the government will do for the reform of the enterprise in the narrower sense. No doubt political considerations will strongly influence the pace of developments.

Industrial Democracy in Scandinavia

By BERNT SCHILLER

ABSTRACT: In the 1930s industrial relations in the Scandinavian countries changed from conflict to cooperation. This change laid the basis for the negotiated establishment after World War II of consultative plant committees. The limitations inherent to the operation of such committees led, in the 1960s, to demands for more sweeping changes in industrial decision making, including demands for employee codetermination. All three Scandinavian countries have granted to their employees legal representation on company boards, but the unions have stressed that such representation will have only limited value if it is not simultaneously accompanied by the introduction of democracy on the shop floor. To that end experiments with semi-autonomous work groups have been carried out in Norway. In Sweden a law on codetermination in 1976 has made decision making at all company levels subject to collective bargaining. Moreover, in Denmark and Sweden labor has demanded a share in future corporate capital growth through employee stock ownership, and bills designed to achieve this objective have been drafted but not yet enacted in Denmark and Sweden. In general, these developments point to an increasing integration of trade union leaders in management functions and more government intervention in economic policy and labor relations.

Bernt Schiller, Ph.D., is Professor of History at the Roskilde University Center, Denmark. He was formerly on the faculty of the University of Gothenburg, Sweden, where he published his dissertation on the 1909 Swedish General Strike (1967) and other studies of labor relations and industrial democracy. He is also the principal author of the first Nordic handbook of statistics for historians and has written articles on the methodology of contemporary history. At present he heads a research project on Interest Organizations and Internationalism, supported by a grant from the Bank of Sweden Tercentenary Foundation. In 1975 he was a visiting professor at the University of Massachusetts.

THE study of industrial democracy is an integral part of the study of relations between capital and labor and the role of the state in that relationship. Here the term industrial democracy will be used to mean both worker participation in decision making (sometimes referred to as work-place democracy) and sharing in the company's capital or profit or both (sometimes referred to as economic democracy). The two aspects are related to each other, particularly in Scandinavia.

The trade union struggle to democratize the work place has historically been directed toward restricting the employer's prerogatives to hire and fire and to direct the work process. Its aim has been to increase employment security and to obtain influence on management. Influence could mean the right to be consulted or to take part in decisions. Whatever the degree of influence, it might be applied at different levels in the company: on the shop floor, at the top management level, in the company's board.

In this discussion, four questions will be asked:

1. What aspect of industrial democracy has been emphasized in Scandinavia?
2. What is the degree of influence on decision making?
3. What levels in the company are involved?
4. What is the structure of profit or capital sharing?

These questions will be set in the context of the development of relations between capital and labor in order to determine to what extent different components of industrial democracy are emphasized under certain conditions. Three phases of development may be distinguished. We shall call them conflict, cooperation, and integration. We shall test in particular the propositions which hold that over time the interest in work-place democracy has shifted from employment security to influence on management, from consultation to codetermination, and from the shop floor to executive board levels, while the approach to economic democracy is said to have shifted from an individualistic to a collectivistic one.

THE CONFLICT PHASE: FROM THE BEGINNINGS TO THE 1930s

In Scandinavia the existence of an unusually large rural middle class made a fairly smooth transformation from agrarian to industrialized societies possible. The trade unions were soon accepted by employers, and collective bargaining early became widespread. Collective agreements were local (only later industry-wide) and the trade unions were correspondingly decentralized. By prevailing standards the unions were well organized, but compared to the present period the membership ratio was low. The social democratic parties embarked early on the path to reformism, but they had no real access to power before the end of World War I. Employers' prerogatives were well protected, and the only concessions were some inadequate safeguards against dismissals of shop stewards.[1]

1. For a general background in English of labor relations in Scandinavia, see Walter Galenson, *The Danish System of Labor Relations* (Cambridge, Mass.: Harvard University Press, 1952); by the same author, *Labor in Norway* (Cambridge, Mass.: Harvard University Press, 1949); *Labour Relations in Norway* (Oslo: Norwegian ILO Committee and the Ministry of Foreign Af-

The question of industrial democracy was first brought up for public discussion immediately after World War I in the revolutionary tide of that period. Workers councils were to be given a role in the socialization of the means of production demanded by the revolutionary wing of the labor movement. The proposals set forth by government committees in the Scandinavian countries were influenced by British guild socialism, but they were mainly intended to ward off genuinely revolutionary aims. The revolutionary situation passed quickly, however, and had disappeared already by 1920.

A trait common to all the proposals laid before the several parliaments was that the competence of the proposed workers councils was to be strictly advisory. Even this went too far for the employers but, of course, not far enough for large sections of the labor movement. The problem for the future was set more precisely by the question posed during the first half of the 1920s: could real influence be assigned to the trade unions while preserving their traditional role in a capitalist society? Some employers during this time became interested in raising productivity through different schemes of voluntary profit-sharing plans, so as to link the economic motivation of workers to the interests of the company. Such schemes, however, were without lasting importance.

fairs, 1975); T. L. Johnson, *Collective Bargaining in Sweden* (London: Allen & Unwin, 1962). A more recent survey also covering the subject of this article is given by Walter Galenson, *Current Problems of Scandinavian Trade Unionism*, Conference Paper, American Enterprise Institute, February 1975.

THE COOPÉRATION PHASE: 1930s TO 1960s

From the Great Depression on, the labor movement increasingly turned to cooperation with the employers. The militants on both sides were suppressed, organizational structures were accommodated to centralized bargaining, and an ideology based on cooperation and the welfare state was developed. Social democratic parties, sometimes in coalition with liberal or farmer parties, soon became the largest parties and the ones most frequently in government. Social democratic dominance became most pronounced in Sweden, next in Norway, and least in Denmark.

Another world war was to occur before the time was ripe to carry out the moderate proposals of the 1920s. In the meantime, the strength of the labor movement increased further, and the new spirit of cooperation with the employers was symbolized by the conclusion of basic agreements in Norway and Sweden in 1935 and 1938, respectively.

After World War II, radical visions of socialism, as after World War I, had to be reconciled with employers' interest in stimulating productivity to promote the task of reconstruction. Agreements establishing plant committees with equal representation for management and employees (white-collar workers were also now included) were negotiated in 1945, 1946, and 1947 in Norway, Sweden, and Denmark, respectively. The committees, however, soon aroused dissatisfaction for being weak and having only an advisory function. Even the information flow to employees, which was intended to be the major vehicle for workers' motivation and participation, seemed irregular and insufficient.

At the end of the 1960s, new collective agreements in the three Scandinavian countries gave employees the right to exert an influence, sometimes equaling that of management, on safety rules, plant welfare arrangements, and long-term personnel policies. Equal importance was also attached to improved protection against arbitrary dismissals and a stronger position for shop stewards. These concessions were obtained gradually and were not tied to any unusual peaks of interest in industrial democracy as such. It should be noted also that the achievements up to this point generally came through negotiations between labor and employer organizations, not through legislation, even though the threat of legislation was invoked on occasion.

THE INTEGRATION PHASE: THE 1970s

In the mid-1960s, the rights of private ownership and labor's traditional fear of becoming hostage to a shareholders' majority on company boards still seemed to block any decisive trade union advancement into the sphere of management. But then the tide changed under the impact of two major developments.

First, the historical record shows that industrial democracy has had a particularly strong appeal in times of deep-going changes in social values, as for example after the two world wars. At the end of the 1960s, another wave of unrest and revolutionary change in both West and East brought with it an upheaval in prevailing value systems. The structural changes in industry which had taken place during the thrust of ex-

pansion in the late 1950s and early 1960s now began to produce a host of side effects. Dislocation of industries, regional unemployment, and a deterioration of the industrial milieu in Scandinavia as elsewhere in Western Europe led to radical claims for control of working conditions by the employees themselves.

Second, while the Scandinavian countries remained capitalist in economic structure, they developed large public sectors and increasing degrees of economic intervention by the state. Limited labor resources and the continued need to compete on the world market forced private industry to finance economic growth through huge capital investments. On one side, this led to large concentrations of capital in private hands, and, on the other, the difficulty of raising funds in the necessary amounts made industry increasingly dependent on public funds. At the same time, industry came to rely on government-supported incomes policies to keep consumption in check. This proved difficult even when social democratic governments were in power and used their influence inside the trade unions to enlist support for incomes policies. The problem was aggravated by the recession of the early 1970s, especially in Denmark. Inflation and taxes ate up wage increases, and the high rate of wage increases became itself one of the sources of inflation. The labor movement thus found itself frustrated in its traditional wage policy and looked to a new policy of industrial democracy for compensation.

LEGAL SYSTEMS OF REPRESENTATION

An early illustration of the spirit of integration between capital and labor is the Norwegian joint research project (Cooperation Project) set up in 1962. Significantly, personal remembrances of wartime cooperation between industrialists and labor leaders are said to have facilitated the undertaking which the state later was asked to finance. The employers were interested in increased productivity to prepare industry for eventual entry into the Common Market. An important motive for the Trade Union Confederation (LO) was pressure from the Left. The Socialist People's party, which had split from the Social Democratic party, had successfully made industrial democracy part of its platform in the 1961 elections. The bourgeois parties also showed a positive interest in workers participation, and thus the LO had to come up with direct proposals of its own. That occurred in 1963 and 1965 through the Aspengren Committee. This committee proposed that the development toward industrial democracy should follow three lines: (1) expanded consultation among employers, shop stewards, and plant committees; (2) education of workers to prepare them for participation; (3) and changes in company organization in order to enable workers to take part in decision making.[2]

These three principles were all realized during the following decade. The first one was included in the revised Basic Agreement of 1966, which also contained provisions for a Council on Cooperation. An agreement in 1970 between the LO and the national employers federation further widened the scope of education and research by establishing an Education and De-

velopment Fund which also took over the funding of the Council on Cooperation. The state was brought into the agreement as the collector of funds through the National Insurance Institution. For 1973 the total contribution of the private sector amounted to 25 million Norwegian crowns (U.S. $4.5 million at 1975 exchange rates). The LO that year financed 9,000 one-week courses for shop stewards.[3] The most interesting portions of the educational apparatus have been the experiments carried out by the Cooperation Project. Their findings imply that management should relinquish its decision-making power to semi-autonomous work groups in the company. The experiments have spread throughout Norwegian industry and have also influenced Swedish developments.

However, the proposal to change the internal company structure so as to give employees legal representation in decision making met fierce resistance from the employers. The sociologists Fred. E. Emery and Einar Thorsrud, who conducted the Cooperation Project, noted in their initial report in 1964 that worker representatives on company boards would be caught in the dilemma of dual loyalty. Such representation would have only limited value if democracy were not increased at the same time on the shop floor. The LO accepted this idea of making legal representation conditional on other measures to increase democracy. The idea of establishing a corporate assembly, proposed by the Aspengren Committee, left the question of board representation to the decision of the employees in the enterprise.

The necessary provisions of the

2. E. Thorsrud and Fred E. Emery, *Mot en ny bedriftsorganisasjon* (Oslo: Tanum, 1970), pp. 9–12.

3. *Industrial Democracy* (Oslo: NFTU/LO, 1975).

Company Act were not passed by Parliament until 1972. They came into force in mining and manufacturing in 1974 and in construction, transportation, and the service sectors in 1975. Any company with more than 200 employees was to have a corporate assembly of at least 12 members, two-thirds being elected by the shareholders and one-third by the employees. The corporate assembly may make recommendations to the company board on any matter. Employees are entitled to not less than two members on the boards of companies as long as there are more than 50 employees. A board on industrial democracy, with representatives from the central organizations of industry and labor and the state, supervises the law and may grant exceptions to its provisions.[4]

About the same time, that is in 1973–74, the trade unions in Sweden and Denmark also obtained through legislation the right for employees to appoint two members to company boards. In Sweden the legislation was intended to be provisional. In Denmark the use of employee representation was left to an employee vote. The figures show that in about 70 percent of the companies the employees have used their rights, and only in a few cases has there been an outright rejection of board representation.

The cautious attitude of the trade unions in all three countries is re-flected in the nonmandatory character of the legislation. It is left to trade unions to invoke implementation of the legislation. Also, the unions have stressed the importance of pushing for industrial democracy simultaneously at different levels in the company.

THE ATTACK ON THE SWEDISH EMPLOYERS' PREROGATIVES

In searching for an approach to industrial democracy that was congruent with traditional trade union policy, the Swedish trade union federation (LO) has dramatically increased the scope of collective bargaining. Growing discontent during the latter half of the 1960s focused on the well-known and long-standing Article 32 in the statutes of the Swedish Employers Confederation. The article laid down the employer's exclusive right "to direct and distribute the work," and was literally sacred to the confederation. Ever since the confederation had begun to engage in collective bargaining, Article 32 had been written into most agreements. But if it were to be removed, what should replace it? To fend off radical claims temporarily, the LO appointed a committee, in 1969, which after much deliberation presented a new scheme elaborated by an expert in labor law, Sten Edlund. Its report on industrial democracy, which was adopted by the 1971 LO congress, made the new scheme the core of a package that also included improvements in employment security and provided for employee representation on company boards.[5]

4. For detailed accounts of the experiments in Scandinavia, see Gerhard Bihl, *Von der Mitbestimmung zur Selbstbestimmung. Das Skandinavische Modell der selbststeuernden Gruppen* (Munich: Goldman, 1973). On the corporate assembly in Norway, see Åke Anker-Ording, "Industrielle Demokratie in Norwegen," *Industrielle Demokratie, Menschenwürde im Betrieb 2,* ed. Fritz Vilmars (Hamburg: Rowohlt, 1975), pp. 116–27.

5. *Industrial Democracy. Program Adopted by the 1971 Congress of the Swedish Trade Union Confederation* (Stockholm: LO, 1972), and Bernt Schiller, *LO, paragraf 32 och företagsdemokratin* (Stockholm: Prisma, 1974), pp. 84–105.

The last and most important part of the new scheme, a law on code-termination, was passed in 1976. Decision making on all company levels was made subject to collective bargaining, and employees acquired the right to strike over codetermination questions even after an agreement on wages had been concluded. The employer was required to negotiate before making decisions on important matters, such as reorganizations, expansions, or shutdowns. In case of disagreement, the trade unions were accorded the right to impose their own interpretation concerning employee obligations to work and the meaning of the provisions of agreements on codetermination, and that interpretation was to be binding until the labor court makes a decision.

PROFIT SHARING AND INVESTMENT FUNDS

The schemes of work-place democracy outlined above for giving employees an increased role in decision making at different levels of the company have all been enacted by law or have emerged from collective bargaining. The profit sharing proposals we shall consider next are currently in abeyance, and their adoption depends on the prospects for political change. Thus, the Danish proposal for profit sharing was set forth by the trade union congress of 1971 and by the Social Democratic government in 1973, but the 1973 election produced an overwhelmingly bourgeois majority which is not likely to enact the scheme. The proposal has three aims: (1) to give employees a stake in future capital growth and investments in industry; (2) to increase employee influence over company policies through stock ownership; and (3) to increase the rate of capital formation.

An "Employee Investment and Dividend Fund" is to be set up, financed from a payroll tax which is paid by employers only and which is to rise stepwise until it reaches 5 percent of total payroll. Every full-time employee, regardless of age and wage, will have the same share in the fund. The individually owned shares are not to be negotiable for seven years. Two-thirds of the contributions from the larger enterprises (more than 50 employees) are to remain in the enterprise as employee-owned shares, while one-third will become risk capital of the fund which can be invested in other companies. The steady growth of the employees' shares remaining in the company will give the wage earners an ever greater vote in general meetings of the shareholders. Had the proposal been enacted in 1974, the fund would have accumulated by the 1980s between one-tenth and one-third of all Danish share capital.[6] The fund is to be governed by a board which, according to the latest (December 1975) Social Democratic and trade union proposal, is to have 120 members, of which 40 will represent the trade unions, 40 will come from other employee organizations, and 40 are to be appointed by the state.

The scheme is characteristic of the views of Danish Social Democrats about the relations between capital and the state. It assumes that under welfare state conditions the private sector is no longer capable of generating a rate of savings necessary to maintain full employment. Yet the continued existence of

6. *Co-ownership, Co-determination: The Danish Government Bills on Economic and Industrial Democracy* (Copenhagen: LO, 1973).

capitalism itself is not to be challenged. Employee shares are not permitted to exceed 50 percent of total shares issued. The individual employee will become a small shareholder in the fund, not in his particular company, and the rights of disposal of the shares will be circumscribed. Investments are to be encouraged in a way which favors larger enterprises.

The Danish proposal has met criticism from the left which has described economic democracy as a kind of first aid for crisis-ridden monopoly capitalism. On the other hand, the idea of establishing a fund and the composition of the board to oversee the fund have been criticized by employers and by the bourgeois parties as a form of socialization of the economy and an expression of the excessive pretensions of trade union power.

THE SWEDISH EMPLOYEE INVESTMENT FUNDS

In Sweden a draft proposal for employee investment funds was adopted by the 1976 LO congress. It was drafted by a committee chaired by the trade union economist Rudolf Meidner. A government commission to prepare the necessary legislation was appointed by the Social Democratic government before it lost the 1976 elections after having been in power for over 40 years, but the prospects for action on the commission's work are, at least for the duration of the present Parliament, rather bleak.

Under the proposed system, 20 percent of the profits of all privately owned larger companies would each year be converted to employee shares which will remain in the company. The dividends paid on the shares will go into a Central Clearing Fund to be collectively owned and managed by the trade unions. Its revenues are to be spent to promote trade union activities. The basic aims of the LO proposal are said to be three: (1) to support the long-standing solidaristic or egalitarian wage policy; (2) to countervail the concentration of private capital; and (3) to reinforce work-place democracy.

Regarding the first point, the solidaristic wage policy, under which the differentials between high and low wage groups are to be narrowed, has required restraints to be imposed on workers in profitable industries and has had no mechanism for preventing the so-called unutilized scope for wage increases from increasing the returns to the owners in the more profitable industries. The fund is supposed to provide the solution for this problem.

The continuing demand for huge investments and the high degree of self-financing has led to a concentration of large amounts of capital. To transfer part of the profits to funds controlled by the trade unions would counteract private capital concentration and force the present owners to share economic growth with their employees. This is now the dominant motive, according to Meidner. Through the conversion of profits into employee shares, the majority of a company's shares and the right to vote them would in the long run be transferred to funds controlled by wage earners' organizations.[7]

Unlike the Danish proposal, there would be no withdrawal of capital from the company, for this would only lead to higher consumption and reduce employee power in the company. Consequently, there is no

7. "Employee Investment Funds" (mimeographed summary, LO, 1976).

place in the Swedish system for individual share certificates. Employee ownership would be collective. No limits are set on the growth of employee-owned stock. In these respects, the Swedish proposal is definitely more far reaching than the Danish one and reflects differences in the structure and power positions of the two labor movements.

The employer organizations have drafted a counterproposal to channel 1 percent of yearly wages into decentralized funds. The income would be invested in industry, but after 5 to 10 years employees would have the right to cash in their shares. The voting rights of the employee shares are to be restricted. The proposal in some respects resembles an employers' version of the Danish economic democracy proposal. It differs from that of the Swedish LO in its emphasis on individual instead of collective ownership; and, in advocating decentralized funds instead of collective ownership, it differs from the proposals of both the Swedish and the Danish trade unions. Their preference for centralization, according to the two trade union centers, is motivated by solidarity with workers in less profitable industries, but to an even larger extent it is regarded as a necessary means of achieving employee power over industry and society.

The Meidner report goes so far as to state that the remnants of class society will be eliminated only when the wage earners become the owners of large parts of Swedish industry, but the sponsors of the "Employee Investment Funds" are not very interested in labeling the coming social order either a mixed economy, socialism, or corporatism. They are pragmatic but also aware of the changing role of

the trade union movement. Gunnar Nilsson, president of the Swedish LO, pointed out to the 1976 LO congress that in a modern society the trade unions cannot be limited only to the conventional type of representation of their members' interest. He said: "With or without Employee Investment Funds, an inexorable change is taking place in the part to be played by trade unions."[8]

CONCLUDING OBSERVATIONS

At the outset, we suggested that the content of worker participation and the structure of profit sharing could be expected to change in certain directions as relations between capital and labor go through successive phases of development. To what extent have these expectations been confirmed?

There has been no clear shift in emphasis from employment security to influence on management as anticipated. It is true that employee efforts to exert influence on management were minimal before the end of World War II and hardly aroused profound interest in the 1950s and 1960s. Since only the most recent demands for worker participation have emphasized influence on management, it can be said that the shift has taken place. On the other hand, the far-reaching Swedish legislation of 1973 and amendments of the Danish and Norwegian basic collective agreements to strengthen employee protection against layoffs indicate that the trade union movement has not lost interest in job security.

One can be more certain about the second proposition. The expectation that labor would escalate its

8. "News from the 1976 LO Congress" (mimeographed, LO, 1976), pp. 16–17.

demands for influence from consultation to codetermination as capital-labor relations move from the cooperation to the integration phases has been substantially confirmed. Increased competition for export markets and a long period of labor shortages strengthened labor's position. It therefore became possible for labor to press for a much stronger role than the consultative status granted to the plant committees. The plant committees reflected older forms of production and power relations between capital and labor. New models, capable of assuring participation at all levels of a company's hierarchy, had to be constructed.

These very developments show that demands for codetermination have not shifted from shop floor to executive board levels, as our third proposition suggested they might. On the contrary, the demands have been applied to all levels in the company simultaneously. If anything, the greatest emphasis has been on the shop floor level, as in the Swedish law on codetermination and in the Norwegian experiments with semi-autonomous groups. In contrast, labor has been quite hesitant in entering the board room in all these countries. Thus, a gradualistic approach in which industrial democracy is built up from below has been preferred, with great emphasis placed on the need for education to back up this development.

While the demand for influence at all levels of the corporate hierarchy is the most important characteristic of the Scandinavian drive for industrial democracy, it also accelerates the process of integration. Labor's representatives will meet with those of capital in job design on the shop floor, in the for-

mation of policy in personnel administration and in overall enterprise decisions in the company assemblies or board rooms. Considerably more negotiation will go on everywhere in the company, with the radical expansion of the scope of collective bargaining in Sweden leading the way.[9] In all these respects, labor representatives will become more fully integrated into management functions. This creates the possibility that trade union leaders might become absorbed as new elements in corporate leadership. Employees in general may benefit from such a development, but there is also a risk that they could be left to the mercy of an all-powerful coalition of management and trade union leaders.

Finally, the anticipated shift from individualistic to collectivistic forms of profit sharing has taken place, on the whole, as suggested in our fourth proposition. To be sure, the Danish proposal, unlike the Swedish one, retains individual shares in a restricted form. However, the discretion and influence which the ordinary stockholder derives from his ownership will, in several respects, not be available to the employee owner, for under the Danish plan the funds are to be administered collectively by a combination of trade union and state appointed representatives, and under the Swedish plan they are to be completely controlled by the trade unions.

All the new arrangements here discussed have been introduced through legislation or are awaiting legislation. This is in marked con-

9. In some respects, counterparts are to be found in British and Italian industries. See "Employee Participation and Company Structure," *Bulletin of the European Commission*, Supplement 8/75.

trast to previous periods when issues of industrial democracy were settled through negotiations and collective agreements. The reason for the change may well indicate that stronger efforts were necessary to override employer opposition to admittedly more radical goals. The use of legislation to break the resistance of the employers does not necessarily imply that a new period of conflict will now prevail, but there is no question that legislation has noticeably increased the bargaining strength of labor in the triangular relationship between labor, capital, and the state.

The new role of the state in legislating on relations between employers and employees is a result of the fact that the state itself has undergone a fundamental change through the sharp expansion of the public sector and increasing intervention in the structure of industry, regional policy, and national economic planning. At the same time, the state as the largest employer has itself become subject to reform and regulation. In the future, this development may increasingly open up the possibility for employee organizations to claim that decisions made by the state bureaucracy should be subject to codetermination just like decisions in private enterprise. This prospect creates entirely new problems of balancing the public interest against the interests and rights of public employees, problems which are not present in the private sector. Codetermination and trade union representation at all levels of public enterprises and administrative agencies not only blur the line between employees and employer but also between organizations and the state, and they do so in a way which justifies raising the question of whether we are moving toward a corporate state. It is partly in this context that the development of industrial democracy in Scandinavia must be assessed.

ANNALS, AAPSS, **431**, May 1977

Between Harmony and Conflict: Industrial Democracy in the Netherlands

By WIL ALBEDA

ABSTRACT: Important changes are taking place in the industrial relations system of the Netherlands, and it is not clear yet whether the long established pattern of stable and peaceful relations can be preserved. The Catholic and socialist labor federations have merged into a single organization whose left wing is rethinking the issue of industrial democracy. The relatively new legislation of the early 1970s, which enlarged the rights of works councils and opened corporate board membership to representatives of employee interests, was still based on ideas generated in the 1960s. But the new structures which resulted from this legislation are already considered insufficient by some sections of the trade unions, although they command the support of the separate Protestant labor federation and of the expanding unions of white-collar employees. The two principal viewpoints are based on different models or concepts of industrial relations, with the older one relying on an essentially cooperative relationship while the new groups tend to think in terms of permanent conflict or adversary relations. Historically, the Netherlands has had an integrative industrial relations system. It remains to be seen how strong this tradition remains.

Professor Wil Albeda studied economics at the Rotterdam School of Economics (now part of the new Erasmus University). He worked for 15 years as an official of the Federation of Protestant Trade Unions (CNV). Since 1966 he has taught industrial and labor relations in the Faculty of Social Sciences of Erasmus University, and since 1973 he has also taught in this area at the Foundation for Business Administration in Delft. He is a member of the First Chamber of the Parliament of the Netherlands and the author of several books and many articles on labor relations and related subjects and has also functioned as a mediator in labor disputes.

MODERN industry was a latecomer in the Netherlands. For a long period, Holland was a country thriving on intensive agriculture and the commerce and traffic that was the result of the geography and the colonial history of the country. Before the Second World War, industry was small scale and family owned, though with some notable exceptions (Unilever, Philips, Royal Shell, partly the fruits of the colonial empire). As in some other Western European countries, the trade union movement was from the beginning split between a social democratic federation (Nederlands Verbond van Vakverenigingen—NVV), a Catholic federation (Nederlands Katholiek Vakverbond—NKV), and a Protestant federation (Christelijk Nationaal Vakverbond—CNV). Whereas the NVV based its activities on the ultimate goal of socialism and a moderate class-conflict ideology, the two "confessional" trade unions propagated cooperation between the different groups in society, hoping for a more organic organization of society through workers' participation in decision making, especially on issues of importance to the national economy as a whole or to an entire industry.

In the first half of the century, the three tendencies in the trade union movement found it difficult to cooperate. As a consequence, the movement was weak and divided. The style of management was paternalistic, and as in most continental European countries, labor relations did not include a trade union presence within the enterprise. In time, an interventionist government helped employers and trade unions to develop modern industrial relations. It is important to consider this background when discussing worker participation in the Netherlands. In more than one sense, this country represents a special case.

Not surprisingly, the pre-1945 discussions about granting workers some form of codetermination (medezeggenschap) focused more on proposals to create bipartite or tripartite bodies to govern each industry than on changes in the structure of the individual company. It is a symptom of the rapid modernization process that the country has undergone since 1945 that, by contrast, the discussions after 1950 began to focus on the internal organization of the company.

In the years after the second World War the preexisting trend toward strong centralization in Dutch labor relations was carried to its logical conclusion in the domain of national wage policy, carried out by the government in cooperation with the central organizations of employers and trade unions. The national wage policy was remarkably successful until the development of the Common Market, the pressure of inflation, and the completion of post-war reconstruction led to its disintegration. Centralization, however, has remained an important element in the Dutch industrial relations system. In order to create a forum for dialogue among government, employers, and trade unions, the legislature established a Social-Economic Council. This official advisory body consists of 45 members, 15 appointed by the employers' federations, 15 by the trade unions, and 15 independent members appointed by the government on the assumption that they will represent the general interest. The Social-Economic Council must be consulted on all important legislative bills in its area of jurisdiction. As a consequence, both trade unions and employers organizations have acquired an important say in matters of national policy. It should also be noted that the position of the trade unions in this consultative process has been strengthened as a result of a considerable softening of their historic differences. The NVV has kept its social-democratic outlook but abandoned the class-struggle ideology and the belief in the necessity of extensive nationalization. For their part, the Christian unions have shed their traditional fear of government interference in the private sector.

The first postwar measure to deal with industrial democracy was a law on works councils (1950) that sought only to develop a form of consultation and information sharing within the enterprise. The "independent position of the employer" was to remain unimpaired, and only in the so-called social field (which in the Netherlands includes personnel policies and company benefit programs) was a modest form of actual participation in the decision-making process introduced. The trade unions' role within the works council was to be very limited. They had preferential rights to submit lists of candidates for election as works council members, but unorganized lists were also acceptable. As a consequence, and especially where a large percentage of the workforce was white collar, many works councils included among their members a large minority and sometimes even a majority of unorganized employees.

In 1966 the Dutch Productivity Council, a subcommittee of the tripartite Social-Economic Council, published the results of an inquiry into the attitudes and opinions of employers and workers with regard to the functioning of works councils.[1] It is interesting to note that on general issues both sides seemed to express rather positive judgments. For example, there seemed to be a consensus on the usefulness of the works council. At the same time, however, the inquiry revealed a rather critical attitude toward the actual functioning of works councils. The more important findings may be summarized in these terms:

1. Both employers and works council members thought that the qualifications of works council members and the amount of information given to them were inadequate.

2. Communications between employees and the works council seemed to be weak. Through lack of interest and understanding, many employers had no clear idea of the tasks and functions of the works council.

3. Employee representatives felt that the powers of the works councils were too restricted, an opinion that was not shared by the employers.

4. Blue-collar workers in particular expressed the wish that the works councils should more clearly and more directly represent employee interests.

In the course of the 1950s and 1960s, two new trends became visible. First, the trade unions realized increasingly how weak their position inside the enterprise had remained. In a modern industrialized country, they simply could not afford to accept their traditional exclusion from the shop floor. Consequently, they developed a strategy for the penetration of the enterprise (bedrijvenwerk).

1. P. I. D. Drenth and J. C. van der Pijl, *De Ondernemingsraad in Nederland* (The Hague: C.O.P., September 1966).

Second, within the universities and the trade unions, a wide-ranging discussion got underway with regard to the process of decision making in the company, which led the government to appoint a commission to investigate the structure of the enterprise. The commission's report (1965) proposed minority representation of workers on corporate boards of directors and enlarged rights for works councils. Near the end of the 1960s, these recommendations resulted in specific proposals for new legislation concerning both works councils and boards of directors.

The preparation of the legislation concerning the composition of boards of directors affords particularly useful insights into the workings of the Dutch industrial relations system and the legislative process. The debate was rather confused. Three elements played a role:

1. The Protestant Federation of Trade Unions (CNV) and some important groups within the socialist trade unions (NVV) wanted to establish a system of worker representation on the board not very different from that of West Germany's.
2. The employers rejected the idea of worker representation on the board, but agreed that within the board expert knowledge of social affairs should be more adequately represented in the future.
3. Left-wing groups within the NVV and NKV (the Catholic Trade Union Federation) were afraid that direct representation of workers on corporate boards would enmesh the trade unions too strongly in the capitalist enterprise.

When the government asked the Social-Economic Council to draft a proposal for legislation, the above three viewpoints were, of course, brought forward. J. W. de Pous, the chairman of the council, then proposed an ingenious compromise: the board of directors would appoint its own new members through cooptation, but both the shareholders and the works council were to have the right to submit and veto new nominations. This compromise was taken over by the government in its own bill and made applicable to all companies with a workforce of more than 100 and a capitalization of more than 10 million guilders. An exception was, however, made for international companies, that is, those having more than 50 percent of their employees serving abroad.

The new law came into force on July 1, 1973. It allowed companies three years to adapt their by-laws. One of the early problems encountered by works councils was the lack of availability of qualified candidates for board membership. As one newspaper put it, the long practice of close contacts between works councils and managements had limited the number of potentially acceptable directors, that is, of persons not so far to the right politically as to be unacceptable to the workers and not so far to the left as to be unacceptable to the employers. The point has also been made that as a consequence of manipulative techniques works councils tend to accept nominees proposed by management and generally leave the initiative to the employer. Finally, the trade unions in general have not been successful in instructing their members on works councils to act more independently.

With regard to the revision of the separate legislation on works councils, a similar procedure was followed. The government asked the Social-Economic Council for advice, an imperfect compromise was reached, and on the basis of this advice a bill was introduced and enacted into law by Parliament. The main elements in the new legislation, passed in 1971, are the following:

1. It affords the elected members of the works council (meaning everybody except the chairman, who by law must be the employer or his representative) more possibilities to function independently. Elected members now have the right to hold preparatory meetings, or caucuses, before they meet with the chairman. In this way, they have more opportunity to reach agreement among themselves without excessive pressure from the employer. Further, they now have the right to obtain assistance from experts outside the enterprise.

2. The emphasis in the new law on greater independence for the elected members is reflected in a redefinition of their role as representatives of the explicit interests of employees in the enterprise. In the original law, the role of works councils had still been defined in terms of furthering the interest and well-being of the enterprise.

3. The new law also accorded several important new rights to the works council. First, it now is entitled to be informed in advance of important company decisions, for example the appointment of a new member of top management, and major economic and financial developments. Second, the works council now has the right to be heard before a decision is made on important matters. This means, for instance, that the board of directors cannot make a final decision on the annual report, including the distribution of dividends to shareholders, before the works council

has had an opportunity to examine and discuss the underlying documents. Decisions vitally important to the enterprise, such as mass layoffs, shutdown of the firm or of an important part of the firm, takeovers or amalgamations, require prior discussion with the works council. Moreover, in the so-called social field certain important decisions now require the consent of the works council, among them regulations concerning holidays, shiftwork, overtime, and profit-sharing.

Although the laws of 1971 and 1973 were based on a consensus of the social partners, new proposals were soon brought forward for additional changes. The background of the new proposals is to be sought in the still evolving development of trade union views on industrial democracy. Two elements in particular have played an important role in shaping the new attitudes. During the 1960s the trade unions experienced more and more strongly the disadvantages of the Dutch industrial relations system, which traditionally has had no place for trade union activities on the shop floor. In a country where the terms of the collective agreement are applicable to nonmembers as well as members of unions, this state of affairs could easily endanger the existence of the trade unions or at least seriously weaken their effectiveness. The danger was that a well-developed structure of relationships between trade unions and employers at the level of each industry, and between these two entities and the state at the level of the nation as a whole, would eventually collapse because it had been erected on the feeble basis of nonexistent or at best irregular and intermittent relations at the grassroots level. This anomaly could lead, and in fact did lead, to the loss of trade union membership and wildcat strikes, for example in 1969 and 1970.

On the basis of these considerations, the trade unions developed new strategies for trade union activities on the shop floor (the so-called bedrijvenwerk). Elements in this strategy were the organization of trade union structures within the firm, the explicit distinction between workers' interests and the interests of the firm, and an increased emphasis on the content and conditions of the individual job. From time to time the new trade union presence came into conflict with works council members who tended to continue working on the assumption of a genuine convergence of the interests of workers and the firm rather than on the assumption of an inevitable conflict. In addition, the trade unions reacted to the loss of membership (or at least to a rate of membership growth that lagged behind the development of the labor force) by taking an ideologically more radical and organizationally more militant attitude. The new attitude was reinforced by the penetration of neo-Marxist and new left ideas into segments of both the socialist trade unions (NVV) and the Catholic trade unions (NKV). These two trade union centers recently decided to form a new superfederation (FNV, Federation of Trade Unions in the Netherlands), in which the two constituent bodies will retain, for the time being, a certain measure of their own identity. The new superfederation came into existence in January 1976.

Whereas the Protestant trade unions (CNV) have retained their traditional reformist and integrative attitudes, the FNV tends to be more aggressive, and some of its affiliated unions even espouse a rather polarizing position. If carried to its logical conclusion, a polarizing attitude would, of course, lead to a rejection of the more integrative elements of industrial democracy, including the existing works councils and the presence of employee representatives on company boards of directors. Some radicals, though only a small minority, have even proposed replacing the works council entirely by a trade union presence within the firm.

THE NEW LEGISLATION

In an effort to cope with the serious economic difficulties that arose in the early 1970s, the government and the trade unions concluded a package deal at the end of 1974 in which the trade unions accepted a form of wage controls and the government promised to introduce further revisions in the legislation on works councils and a new law on capital gains sharing (the so-called Vermogensaanwasdeling). In promising new legislation, the government coalition of two socialist and two Christian-Democratic parties put itself into a very difficult position, for the socialists in the government tended to support the more radical position of the FNV while the Christian-Democratic coalition parties were at least in part closer to the views of the more moderate CNV.

The FNV proposal envisaged a works council consisting only of elected members, that is, without the presence of the employer as chairman. As already noted, the FNV is apprehensive that the presence of a management representative may lead to the manipulation of works council members who in general have less education and invariably less information than management. In the view of the FNV, the works council should be guided exclusively by considerations of employee interests and not allow these to be diluted by the broader interests of the enterprise as a whole. Therefore, works council rights should include the right to monitor management decisions, including the exercise of a veto power, rather than the right to participate in the decision-making process. On the other hand the Protestant unions, whose view is shared by many white-collar unions, the new third force in the Dutch trade union movement, want to maintain the existing orientation and organization of the works council.

The current Minister of Social Affairs Jaap Boersma, a former research director of the Protestant trade union federation, made a heroic attempt to combine the two positions in a bill that at this writing has not yet been passed by Parliament. The main elements of the bill provide, first, that the works council shall consist only of elected members and that the chairman may be chosen by the works council itself rather than being imposed on it by law. To this extent, the proposal follows the FNV position. Next, the bill proposes that a new institution be introduced, a consultative plant assembly, or joint meeting, where management can exchange views with the works council. Joint meetings are to take place at least six times a year under the chairmanship of the employer. In addition, the works council may demand at any time a joint meeting, and management must accept the demand within two weeks. Such a meeting is to be chaired by the chairman of the works council, an elected member.

The rights of the works council are to be extended in the following respects:

1. The works council is to be consulted before the appointment of a member of top management. In practice this will mean, of course, that it will be extremely difficult to appoint a manager who is not acceptable to the works council.

2. Important decisions that in the future cannot be taken without prior consultation with the works council shall include decisions on new investments.

3. All decisions in the area of social affairs are to be considered as subjects on which management has to get the prior approval of the works council.

It should be noted that the rights of the works council may be further extended by collective agreement, or by management alone if the works council approves. In case of disagreement over important decisions, the works council has the right to appeal to the courts.

Taking into account the fact that the existing works council already has, and in practice uses, the right to meet independently, that is, without the chairman, the changes proposed in the membership, chairmanship, and procedure of meetings are not particularly impressive. Certain other rights of the works council are to be extended, but the right to joint decision making is limited to social affairs. The new right of judicial appeal in case of important decisions might in practice turn out to be quite a nuisance if an employer is confronted with a difficult works council.

The question has been raised, not

only by employers but also by advocates of industrial democracy,[2] of whether the draft bill, based upon a too obvious compromise, really means progress. The new works council has more independence from management in the sense that its views and decisions may be prepared without a management presence. However, the law stipulates that the final decision of the works council should be taken only after "management has been heard."

An interesting confirmation of the doubts that have been expressed about the bill occurred when a number of works councils, among them some from large firms like AKZO and Unilever, proposed that the works councils of Dutch enterprises should come together to form a national body for the purpose of expressing the joint views of all works councils on the proposed new law in Parliament. The idea drew the disapproval of the trade union federations who claimed that it had been inspired by members of separatist white-collar unions.

DEVELOPMENTS AT THE SHOP FLOOR LEVEL

At the shop floor level, two recent developments must be stressed. One, already mentioned earlier, is the introduction of the new trade union strategy of establishing a presence on the shop floor. The other concerns experiments in shop floor democracy. It is beyond the scope of this article to describe the new trade union activities' inside undertakings in detail.

In principle, the trade unions—or at least several of them—are

2. As, for instance, Prof. H. J. van Zuthem, "Herziening van de Ondernemingsraad," *Economisch-Statistische Berichten*, 18 August 1976, p. 778.

setting up their own plant-based structures within the firm. The in-plant trade union organization is expected to become both a base for plant-oriented action, such as channeling employee grievances to the unions or to the works councils or preparing a strike, and a part of the external organizational structure of the trade unions. Members of the various executive bodies of the unions are increasingly being elected with the participation of the plant union organizations and the older, geographically based local and regional bodies.

Insofar as the union's in-plant organization is willing to cooperate with the existing decision-making structures within the firm, especially the works council, it can serve as a "constituency for the works council" and thereby strengthen its own ties with employees. In some cases, however, the in-plant organizations are more and more becoming a form of permanent opposition to management. In consequence, conflicts between unions and works councils may well develop where the latter choose to follow their own approach.

In the case of Hoogovens, the large steel-producing company, the in-plant organization of the union has adopted the practice of committing those of its members who serve on the works council to abide by the decisions of the in-plant section of the union. This decision, of course, makes the smooth functioning of the works council more difficult, for no decision can now be made without the consent of the in-plant section of the union. Considering the well-known apathy of the majority of union members, an internal union can easily fall under the domination of militant activists, including some on the left who look upon every form of cooperation with the employer as a form of class betrayal. As a result, the works council at Hoogovens is sometimes split between the moderate members of the Protestant blue-collar union and the several white-collar unions, which tend to be supported by the unorganized members of the works council, and the radical members of the socialist union, supported half-heartedly by their partners in the Catholic organization.

INDUSTRIAL DEMOCRACY BETWEEN HARMONY AND CONFLICT

Dutch industrial relations have always been characterized by a low level of labor unrest. Since the war, strikes have become even more infrequent than before. However, between 1969 and 1974 there was a sudden upswing of industrial conflict. In 1969 and 1970 wildcat strikes involved workers in several industries. In 1971, 1972, and 1973 the trade unions successfully took the initiative in several major conflicts to show their members that they had not grown as soft as their left-wing opponents suggested. Yet the new labor unrest took a rather heavy toll. Trade union strike funds were severely depleted, especially by strikes involving demands for greater narrowing of wage differentials. Consequently, in 1974 and 1975 labor unrest sank to the lowest levels ever reached, although a kind of verbal unrest developed in several firms, centering on the ambivalent attitude of works councils which were being pulled in different directions by conflicting viewpoints.

One might thus conclude that since open conflict was too expensive for the trade unions (and for the national economy as well), the trade unions transferred their aggressiveness to matters internal to the enterprise. The effects of this change include more emphasis than heretofore on issues that divide employees and employers. However, the national debate over the proper course to be followed is still continuing. The basic question remains whether a form of codetermination should be developed that would involve workers and their representatives in some formal way in the decision-making process or the trade unions should resist such integration until the country has adopted a form of genuine workers' control.

The debate places employers in an uneasy dilemma, for neither solution seems very attractive to them. The government, too, is not in an easy position. Should it accept the views of the Protestant unions, knowing that the new structures will in many cases not be able to function because of trade union resistance? Or should it rather accept the conclusions, and thus the consequences, of the left wing in the superfederation, FNV, which could frustrate the operation of the economic system as a result of ever greater polarization? The first view represents the official position of the Protestant unions and of many individuals and even some unions in the socialist-Catholic superfederation. The second reflects the views of the more powerful unions in the superfederation. A wise government would perhaps wait till the trade unions can reach a consensus. However, the promises inherent in the package deal of 1974 make procrastination an awkward policy for the government to adopt.

ANNALS, AAPSS, **431**, May 1977

Collective Bargaining: The American Approach to Industrial Democracy

By MILTON DERBER

ABSTRACT: Collective bargaining is the American route to industrial democracy. Some unionists and others, however, have advocated a widening and deepening of the participative role of workers and unions in managerial decision making. Examples of union-management cooperation outside of the conventional collective bargaining boundaries can be found as far back as the 1920s. But only a small number of cases have survived to the present day. Since 1970 the federal government has encouraged joint union-management committees and autonomous work group experiments to improve productivity and the quality of working life. A National Center for Productivity and Quality of Working Life has been established by Congress. A number of companies have, independently or in cooperation with unions, introduced job enrichment programs, flexible work schedules, and semi-autonomous work groups. Many companies have taken advantage of tax law benefits to adopt profit-sharing and employee stock ownership plans. Union leaders have generally been suspicious of such management schemes as well as productivity plans unless safeguards are provided for worker job security and employment conditions. They have rejected the German codetermination system of worker-directors. There appears to be little prospect of dramatic change during the foreseeable future although collective bargaining may gradually extend worker participation in managerial decision making.

Milton Derber has been Professor of Labor and Industrial Relations at the Institute of Labor and Industrial Relations, University of Illinois, since 1947. Prior to that date he was in the federal civil service for seven years with the Bureau of Labor Statistics, the Office of Price Administration, the National Labor Relations Board, and the War Labor Board. He received his Ph.D in 1940 at the University of Wisconsin. He has written extensively in the fields of collective bargaining, labor relations history, and industrial democracy.

IN CONTRAST to European developments, the theme of industrial democracy has evoked relatively little discussion in the United States in recent decades. This condition is not attributable to a lack of interest on the part of unionists or weakness in the labor movement. It is due, rather, to the predominant view that industrial democracy in the United States has been widely achieved through the system of collective bargaining. Imperfections and limitations of collective bargaining are recognized, but only a small minority of labor activists call for new routes to industrial democracy, such as German codetermination, Yugoslav workers councils, or Scandinavian autonomous work groups.

COLLECTIVE BARGAINING: THE AMERICAN ROUTE

The American idea of collective bargaining as industrial democracy is the product of more than a century's experience. Since I have treated this evolution in a book-length analysis,[1] I shall not attempt even a short sketch here. It is important to note only that the collective bargaining system emerged out of fierce competition with numerous alternatives: individualism; socialism; profit-sharing, stock-ownership, co-partnership; company employee representation plans; syndicalism; producers cooperation; scientific management; and others.

The essence of collective bargaining as industrial democracy is as follows: (1) employees have the right to form, belong to, and govern labor organizations of their own choice without employer interference; (2)

1. Milton Derber, *The American Idea of Industrial Democracy* (Urbana: University of Illinois Press, 1970).

employers and their managerial staffs have the right to form their own representative organizations and to manage the operations of their enterprise; (3) wages, hours, and other terms and conditions of employment are codetermined through the process of collective bargaining, and the agreement is reduced to writing in a signed and legally enforceable contract; (4) employee grievances and complaints over the implementation of the contract and claims to fair treatment are subject to due process through a formal grievance procedure specified in the contract; (5) neither the managers nor the union officers may discriminate against an employee (or potential employee) because of race, sex, age, national origin, or religion; (6) the strike or lockout is a legitimate tool in the determination of the contractual rules governing the relationship, although the parties may voluntarily abstain from or relinquish its use; (7) in the resolution of grievances the strike is generally replaced by binding arbitration; (8) the personal dignity of all employees, whether part of a minority or majority group, is respected, their freedom of speech is protected, and they are treated as equal citizens with equal opportunities at the work place and in their union.

This model of industrial democracy, like the counterpart model of political democracy, is rarely achieved in its entirety and is often seriously abused. The federal and some state governments have sought through legislation, administration, and adjudication to safeguard and promote its principles.

BEYOND COLLECTIVE BARGAINING

Since the 1930s, most trade unionists and their leaders, as well as most large employers, have been content to work and live under the collective bargaining system. Some, however, have desired to extend the scope of union-management interaction beyond its conventional boundaries. In particular, they have advocated a widening and deepening of the participative role of workers and the union in managerial decision making. This approach was epitomized several decades ago by a work entitled *Organized Labor and Production: Next Steps in Industrial Democracy*,[2] jointly authored by Philip Murray, then head of the Steel Workers Organizing Committee and vice-president of the Congress of Industrial Organizations, and Morris L. Cooke, a well-known consulting engineer and advocate of scientific management. The imaginative work envisaged a comprehensive integration of unionism and scientific management in the enterprise and the industry, the full sharing of business and industrial information, and even the seating of one or more union officials on company boards of directors. At the national level, unions, management, and government would cooperate in close harmony to achieve a stable and growing full-employment economy based on collective bargaining, civil rights for employees, and scientific control of industrial relations.

Although the Murray-Cooke dream of industrial democracy was largely ignored, a small minority of unionists and managers did develop schemes of union-management cooperation outside the normal collective bargaining boundaries. Examples[3] can be found as far back

as the 1920s in the railroad and garment industries, but the best-known programs developed just before and after World War II are the Tennessee Valley Authority joint cooperative committees to eliminate waste, increase efficiency, stimulate training, safeguard health, and generally improve employee morale, and the Scanlon Plan, a system of joint worker-supervisor suggestion committees combined with a cost-saving plant-wide bonus. In both cases, the cooperative arrangements were carefully kept separate from the collective bargaining process.

During World War II, some 5,000 joint management-labor production committees were set up under government sponsorship to help increase productivity and to boost morale, but only a few hundred were estimated to have made any significant contributions to productivity and virtually all of them disappeared after the war.[4] In the late 1950s and early 1960s, several major union-management agreements revived interest in developing new collective bargaining institutions for the furtherance of productivity, the protection of employee job rights, and the enhancement of cooperative relations. Among these were the Armour Automation Plan (1959) in which Armour and Company and the then two major meat packing unions attempted to ease the displacement effects of a major company reorganization involving the shutdown of about a dozen obsolete plants and the opening of several new plants in

2. (New York: Harper & Row, Publishers, 1940).
3. See Harry M. Douty, *Labor-Management Productivity Committees in American Industry* (Washington, D.C.: The National Commission on Productivity and Work Quality, May 1975).
4. Dorothea de Schweinitz, *Labor and Management in a Common Enterprise* (Cambridge, Mass.: Harvard University Press, 1949).

different geographical locations; the Mechanization and Modernization Agreement of the West Coast Longshore Industry (1960), in which the Pacific Maritime Association bought out a complex of restrictive work rules with work and income guarantees; and the Basic Steel Human Relations Committee (1959), which was an outgrowth of the 116-day steel strike and which established joint union-management subcommittees to study problems and potential conflict issues during the period between contract negotiations. All three of these programs and most of the others like them had a limited life but made important contributions during their existence.[5]

THE NATIONAL CENTER FOR PRODUCTIVITY AND QUALITY OF WORKING LIFE

A new stage in the evolution of methods to extend union-management relations beyond traditional collective bargaining limits was presaged by the establishment of the National Commission on Productivity by President Richard M. Nixon in July 1970.[6] As its name indicates, the original purpose of the commission was to revitalize a slackening productivity and to "achieve a bal-

5. See James J. Healy, ed., Creative Collective Bargaining: Meeting Today's Challenges to Labor-Management Relations (Englewood Cliffs, N.J.: Prentice-Hall, 1965).
6. This commission offers a striking contrast to the National Commission on Technology, Automation, and Economic Progress, established by Congress and appointed by President Lyndon Johnson in 1964. The latter was based on the assumption of an accelerating automation which, many feared, would displace workers and create extensive social and personal dislocations and hardships. See Report of the National Commission on Technology, Automation, and Economic Progress, Technology and the American Economy, vol. 1 (February 1966).

ance between costs and productivity that will lead to more stable prices."[7] In December 1971, an amendment to the Economic Stabilization Act (Public Law 92-210) gave the commission statutory recognition and enlarged the scope of its functions and responsibilities, including encouragement and assistance in the establishment of "labor-management-public committees." In 1973, when the Stabilization Act expired, the Senate passed a bill that would have expanded the commission's objectives to include "to help improve the morale and quality of work for the American worker." It was also proposed to change the name of the agency to the National Commission on Productivity and Work Quality. This bill was disapproved in the House, objections being voiced to its $5 million cost, and only by executive order was the curtailed commission able to survive as the Office of Productivity under the Cost of Living Council.

In the spring of 1974, however, the House reversed its earlier vote and a new law was enacted and signed on June 8, 1974, establishing the National Commission on Productivity and Work Quality under the chairmanship of Vice-President Nelson Rockefeller with a one-year appropriation of $2.5 million. In November 1975, still another law was passed (Public Law 94-136) which repealed its predecessors and transferred the staff and functions of the commission to a new National Center for Productivity and Quality of Working Life. The center was to be governed by a board of directors composed of 27 members, appointed by the president, from labor, business, the general public, state

7. First Annual Report of the National Commission on Productivity, appendix A, (March 1972), p. 21.

and local government, and the federal government. In addition to its prior functions of fostering productivity and work quality, it was directed to work closely with federal departments and agencies to help improve their productivity. It was given an appropriation of $6.25 million for the period to September 30, 1976, and $5 million for each of fiscal 1977 and 1978, thus assuring a continuity of nearly three additional years. The word "center" instead of "commission" was apparently intended to emphasize the agency's continuing role.

This brief, rather erratic experience was reflective of two incongruent forces. On the one hand, there was a widespread feeling in many influential circles (the media, academe, and segments of industry and government) that American workers were becoming increasingly discontented with work and work relations and that the productivity of American producers was falling behind that of their competitors in Europe and Japan. This sentiment, whether wholly accurate or not, was fostered by the widely publicized strike of General Motors workers at the company's new and highly automated assembly plant at Lordstown, Ohio, in early 1972; by the report of a Task Force of the Secretary of Health, Education, and Welfare published in December 1972 under the title, *Work in America*; and by a spate of American and European publications and conferences on worker alienation, the "new working class," job enrichment and enlargement, and humanization/democratization of the work place.

As a brake on the over-zealous proposals of some proponents of a new industrial order, spokesmen for organized labor expressed reservations and conditions. In cases such as Lordstown, they noted that the factors involved were no different from those in disputes of prior years over the speedup and other unsatisfactory working practices. On the productivity front, they reaffirmed a long-held position that productivity gains must not be made at the expense of worker employment, pay levels, or conditions of work. At the same time, they made it clear that if steps were to be taken to spur worker productivity and to humanize the work place, they wanted to be consulted.

The intended consequences of these dual forces were, as noted above, a continued and ultimately successful pressure for the establishment of a permanent center and a readjustment of the objectives and structure of the center (1) to balance employer interests in greater efficiency and competitiveness with labor interests in improved working conditions and (2) to assure that programs stimulated or assisted by the center would be based on union-management agreement and, where feasible, joint committees. In the course of these developments, the boundaries of the system of industrial democracy, based on collective bargaining principles and procedures, were enlarged.

It is too early to try to evaluate the contributions of the center and its predecessors since 1970 to American industrial democracy. Moreover, both before and since 1970, some of the more progressive corporations, occasionally in cooperation with unions, have conducted autonomous experiments and developed innovative programs without the commission's or center's involvement. Some illustrations from both categories may illuminate the paths for possible future development.

COMMISSION/CENTER HIGHLIGHTS[8]

The principal contribution of the commission was to encourage and support joint committee programs through publicity in the media, the issuance and distribution of popularly-written reports and pamphlets, and union-management conferences. Supplementing these efforts on a very limited scale, the commission helped to initiate and sometimes to finance joint committee systems as well as some experiments in autonomous work groups.

Among the plans which the commission widely publicized were the Employment Security and Productivity Committees established in the basic steel industry as a result of the collective bargaining agreement of 1971; the relatively long-established Scanlon Plans and the joint cooperative committees in the Tennessee Valley Authority (TVA); the Jamestown, New York, community program begun in 1971; several labor-management cooperation arrangements developed through the initiative of the Federal Mediation and Conciliation Service (FMCS) and utilizing its Relations by Objectives (RBO) technique;[9] the national joint labor-management committees in the retail food and interstate trucking industries fostered by the Cost of Living Council and the FMCS; the quality of work demonstration project at the Cleveland plant of the Eaton Corporation; and the autonomous work group experiment at the Rushtown Coal Mine of Philipsburg, Pennsylvania. In addition to these largely private sector plans, the commission/center has focused attention on the use of joint committees in the federal and local governments.[10] The origins, objectives, and procedures of these plans varied significantly. A brief description of three of them may indicate the range of thinking and practice.

In the steel industry, for example, the 10 major corporations and the United Steelworkers of America agreed in 1971 that in order to improve the international competitive position of American steel and thereby to protect jobs and profits, joint labor-management employment security and productivity committees would be set up at the plant level. The committees were to be composed, for the union, of the local union president, the chairman and secretary of the grievance committee, and the grievance committeemen most concerned with the agenda problems to be discussed, and for management, of the plant manager, the superintendent of industrial relations, the plant industrial engineer, and the area superintendent. Although final decisions on operations changes were left to management, the latter often adopted union ideas. When they did not, they discussed with the unionists the reason for not acting.

8. See National Center for Productivity and Quality of Working Life, *Recent Initiatives in Labor-Management Cooperation*, February 1976, 62 pp. and appendices.

9. RBO is a technique devised by the FMCS to resolve deeply imbedded union-management conflicts that have reached crisis proportions for the parties. It involves separate and joint sessions in which union and management officials are led to define what the other party should do to improve relations, what each party should do itself, what "action steps" should be followed to achieve each of a mutually accepted list of objectives, and a timetable for implementation.

10. Only limited information is available on these governmental committees. See, for example, James E. Martin, "Union-Management Committees in the Federal Sector," *Monthly Labor Review*, vol. 99, no. 10 (October 1976), pp. 30–2.

According to the National Center report, some 250 plant committees had been established by 1975 with widely varying results. Workers in some plants continued to be suspicious that productivity gains would be at the expense of speedup and job loss. On the other hand, examples of successful committees were cited to illustrate that by reducing costs and improving quality, job security was enhanced and worker morale was strengthened. Union President I. W. Abel credited the committees with contributing to more mature collective bargaining relationships throughout the industry. There were dissenters in the union, however, who thought the workers' interests had been sacrificed.

The Jamestown, New York, program illustrates a community-wide effort to restore economic health to a depressed and conflictful industrial city through union-management cooperation. The initiative came from the mayor with the assistance of a representative of the Federal Mediation and Conciliation Service. About two years after the Jamestown Area Labor-Management Committee had been established and had demonstrated notable progress in increasing productivity and reducing strife in its 36 member enterprises, it received financial assistance from the National Commission on Productivity and Work Quality and the Economic Development Administration of the U.S. Department of Commerce to intensify its program at the plant level. A full-time professional coordinator was appointed to get plant union-management committees started or restarted, to help implement skill development training of workers and managers, and to extend committee activities to work redesign, communication, grievance handling, and safety. No attempt was made to standardize in-plant committees. The parties in each plant determined their own structure, procedures, and problem priorities. In some plants, the committees almost failed because of insufficient or ineffective communication with rank and file workers. But overall, the leaders of the program felt that substantial progress had been made.

Perhaps the most far-reaching experiment sponsored by the National Commission was the autonomous work group program in the Rushton Coal Mine, Philipsburg, Pennsylvania, modeled after European examples, with the agreement of the United Mine Workers of America. The experiment took the form of an action-research project initiated by the private National Quality of Work Center, with the research team drawn from the University of Pennsylvania and Penn State University. A local union-management committee, known as the Steering Committee, collaborated with the research team in designing, developing, and implementing the project. Initially a 27-member work group, consisting of volunteer miners, was trained to perform a variety of jobs in a section; pay and classification differences were eliminated: and the three crew foremen were limited to planning and safety functions. The work group was given full responsibility in mining the coal. Collaboration replaced competition among the workers, interest in the work and worker satisfaction grew measurably, accidents declined, and productivity jumped. The experiment encountered many difficulties, but these were gradually overcome and the experiment was extended to the entire mine, after the plan was modified to take into account some worker objections and ideas.[11]

As noted above, the Rushton experiment was initiated by a unit originally known as the Quality of Work Program. This unit originated in the Federal Price Commission in 1972, was transferred the following year to the National Commission on Productivity and Work Quality, and in April 1974 was transformed into the private, non-profit Washington-based National Quality of Work Center in close association with the University of Michigan's Institute of Social Research. The center's goals are to develop and seek funding for demonstration projects, such as Rushton, in order to improve productivity, the quality of working life, and labor-management relations.[12]

INDEPENDENT COMPANY EXPERIMENTS[13]

In the decade or so prior to the establishment of the first commission, a number of leading companies had introduced, more or less independently, a variety of schemes designed to improve employee morale and boost productivity. Some of these schemes involved simply the redesign (enlargement, enrichment, rotation) of jobs and work practices; a few were more far-reaching, emphasizing greater participation of workers in management decision making and alteration of supervisory structures and styles. Virtually all were initiated by management, often as a result of some academician's or consultant's theories or suggestions. Most, but not all, were conducted in non-union plants or among non-union groups of employees.

Among the participative programs that received particular attention was one established in 1971 at a new Pet Food plant (General Foods Corporation) in Topeka, Kansas. All 70 of the employees were organized into relatively autonomous work groups (from 8 to 12 members) responsible for a production process. Group members were trained to perform all requisite tasks. Supervisors were replaced by team leaders, who were ultimately expected to be unnecessary. Parking lot, cafeteria, locker rooms, and other facilities were available to all on an equal basis. It was estimated that the 70 produced as much as a conventional plant of 110. But the Pet Food approach has not been widely imitated, and the General Foods Company has been cautious in extending ideas gained from this experiment to its other plants.[14]

A number of other major companies have developed self-management work groups or redesigned jobs to make them less boring, including AT&T, Polaroid, Texas Instruments, Monsanto Chemical, and Kaiser Aluminum, but these have mostly been confined to small sections or groups. No large-scale changes in company practice have

11. An enlightening account of the Rushton experiment is provided by Ted Mills, "Altering the Social Structure in Coal Mining: A Case Study," *Monthly Labor Review*, vol. 99, no. 10 (October 1976), pp. 3–10.

12. National Quality of Work Center, *The Quality of Work Program: The First Eighteen Months*, April 1974-October 1975.

13. See, in particular, Special Task Force to Secretary of Health, Education and Welfare, *Work in America* (Cambridge, Mass.: MIT Press, n.d.) ch. 4 and appendix.

14. In the case of a group program at another of its plants, the company has been charged with committing a violation of the Labor-Management Relations Act by allegedly dominating a labor organization. The case had not been decided by the National Labor Relations Board at this writing.

been reported. For the most part, it may be suggested, these job enrichment and worker participation schemes are a late twentieth-century revision of Taylorism, a new model of scientific management based on recent psychological theories about job satisfaction and communications instead of engineering concepts. Like the earlier scientific management models, they have rarely been adopted in a total system but rather have been applied in selected parts.

OTHER APPROACHES

Contemporary with the foregoing programs were scattered company experiments with other ideas about the humanization of work, the improvement of worker morale, and increases in productivity, efficiency, and profitability. One set of ideas focused on work schedules, another on financial incentives.

Experiments with unconventional work schedules reflected the belief that workers would be happier and more productive (these qualities are not necessarily correlated in practice) if they had more flexibility in coming to or leaving work or if they had a prolonged weekend.[15] The former typically provided a band of starting and finishing hours between, say, 7 and 9 A.M. and 3 and 5 P.M., maintaining the same number of hours in a work day or work week while allowing employees to avoid rush-hour traffic, carry out domestic and personal errands, or get children off to school. The latter lengthened the work day from eight to ten hours while reducing the

work week from five to four days, thereby giving employees a longer weekend and cutting down on travel time. Both schemes appeared to achieve their aims to the mutual satisfaction of some employers and employees.

In other enterprises, however, the experiments were unsuccessful either because of the nature of production or, in the extended workday case, because of opposition to a lengthening of the historic eight-hour day. Unions, in particular, objected to the latter scheme. Instead, they proposed a shortening of the work week to 36 or 35 hours and the elimination or reduction of overtime. In 1973 one of the major issues in the lengthy Chrysler strike was compulsory overtime, and the compromise settlement provided that production employees may not be required to work more than nine hours a day, six days a week, or two consecutive Saturdays except during the annual model changeover period and at key parts plants. In 1976 a central issue of the Ford strike was an increase in the number of paid days off, and the three-year settlement provided for 13 additional paid nonwork days (over the three years, not per year) beyond the existing paid vacations and holidays. But this step toward reduced work time was designed to spread work and increase job opportunities rather than to make the work situation more palatable to employees.

Since the last quarter of the nineteenth century, one of the paths to democratization of industry as well as to higher productivity advocated by some reformers was to give employees either a share in current profits or in stock ownership. In either event, it was felt that the tie of employees to the enterprise

15. See, for example, Riva Poor, ed., *4 Days, 40 Hours* (Cambridge, Mass.: Bursk and Poor, 1970); Douglas L. Fleuter, *The Workweek Revolution* (Reading, Mass.: Addison-Wesley Publishing, 1975).

would be strengthened and their productive effort would be enhanced. Neither profit sharing nor stock ownership made a great deal of headway, however, until after World War II. Changes in the tax law gave profit sharing a tremendous impetus with the result that between 1947 and 1965 the number of plans approved by the Internal Revenue Service rose from under 2,000 to nearly 43,000. Parallel tax law changes in 1974 and 1975 promised to have a comparable effect on stock ownership. A particular beneficiary was a plan developed and long advocated by lawyer Louis O. Kelso under the label ESOP (employee stock ownership plan). ESOPs have been used to enable companies to make capital investments at reduced interest and tax rates. In some cases, they have led to employee ownership of financially distressed companies. Although most of the ESOP users are comparatively small, an increasing number of major firms are exploring the feasibility and desirability of its adoption.

Whether profit sharing or stock ownership increases employee loyalty or productivity remains a debatable question.[16] There is very little hard evidence thus far that employee participation in decision making has advanced. For the most part, unions have been suspicious and antagonistic, fearing that successful schemes will weaken employee attachment to their union and unsuccessful ones will bring criticism on cooperating union leaders. Others are critical on the

grounds that whatever financial benefit accrues to companies and employees will be at the expense of taxpayers and the U.S. Treasury.

UNION ATTITUDES

Throughout the swirl of discussion and experimentation during the 1960s and 1970s in the United States and Europe, the leaders of the American labor movement have maintained a firm ideological attachment to collective bargaining as the main route to industrial democracy.

This view was clearly and succinctly expressed by Thomas R. Donahue, executive assistant to the president of the AFL-CIO, in a speech delivered at an international conference in Montreal on May 26, 1976.

We do not seek to be a partner in management—to be, most likely, the junior partner in success and the senior partner in failure.
We do not want to blur in any way the distinctions between the respective roles of management and labor in the plant.
We guard our independence fiercely—independent of government, independent of any political party and independent of management.
. . . We've watched co-determination and its offshoot experiments with interest, and will continue to do so, but it is our judgment that it offers little to American unions in the performance of their job unionism role (given our exclusive representative status and our wide-open conflict bargaining) and it could only hurt U.S. unions as they pursue their social unionism functions —seeking through legislation, political action, community involvement and a host of other approaches, to improve our members' lot by improving society generally.[17]

16. See, for example, Bertram L. Metzger, *Profit Sharing in Perspective*, 2nd ed. (Evanston, Ill.: Profit Sharing Foundation, 1966) and Work in America Institute, Inc., *World of Work Report*, vol. 1, no. 7 (September 1976), pp. 4–5, for a discussion of ESOP.

17. International Conference on Trends in Industrial Relations, "Remarks" (mimeographed), p. 5.

William W. Winpisinger, general vice-president of the International Association of Machinists and Aerospace Workers, put labor's position about job enrichment more bluntly.

I can think of no better way to sum up my opinion of job enrichment than to say that it's nothing more than good old "job evaluation" and "time and motion study" in sheep's clothing. Any time industrial engineers and management get together, the workers end up getting it in the neck.[18]

A somewhat more sanguine view has been expressed by Irving Bluestone, a top official of the United Automobile Workers Union.

. . . American unions move to meet practical problems with practical solutions. It is highly improbable that they will approach the problem of worker participation in decision making via fierce ideological struggle founded in socioeconomic theory. . . . When workers feel victimized, they combine their forces to correct the situation, case by case, problem by problem. Gradual persistent change, not revolutionary upheaval, has marked the progress of the American worker.[19]

Bluestone went on to note that decisions regarding purchasing, advertising, selling, and financing, or the selection of a board chairman, are far more remote from the immediate problems facing the worker than are job-related decisions. He foresaw, as areas of possible confrontation between union and management, decisions about plant shutdowns and relocations, sub-

contracting of work or shuffling of work among facilities in a multiplant corporation, production scheduling and standards, technological innovation, and calls for excessive overtime. Beyond the immediate job level, however, he envisaged controversy about the double standard for managers and workers with regard to hourly and salaried pay and the use of time clocks, "paneled dining rooms" versus "spartan cafeterias," privileged parking facilities, and organizing the work schedule to enable the worker to manage his personal family and home chores. Responding, in effect, to the Lordstown publicity, he stated that one of the essential tasks of the union movement is to "humanize the work place." But he also warned that humanizing the work place "must not become simply another gimmick designed essentially to 'fool' the worker by having as its primary goal or hidden agenda an increase in worker productivity."[20]

As to the sentiments of the mass of union members on the subject of industrial democracy, John Carmichael, executive secretary of the Newspaper Guild of Minneapolis and St. Paul, suggests:

. . . many trade union leaders in this country have underestimated the interests of their members in this kind of development [that is, worker participation in the decisions of the work place].

18. "The Job Satisfaction Debate— What's Relevant to Labor," remarks at Center for Labor Research and Education, Palo Alto, California, 28 September 1974 (mimeographed), p. 13.
19. "Worker Participation in Decision Making," in Roy P. Fairfield, ed., *Humanizing the Workplace* (Buffalo, N.Y.: Prometheus Books, 1974), p. 57.

20. Correspondence with the Research Department of the UAW in November 1976 revealed that following the 1973 GM agreement, 14 local participative programs had been developed within the corporation, 10 involving the UAW. Because of a commitment not to publicize the programs prematurely, the informant was not able to provide details, but he reported that in some cases discipline problems had disappeared, absenteeism had dropped dramatically, the quality of the product as well as efficiency had improved, and respect for both company and union had increased.

It may not have surfaced yet in a volatile way, but I am convinced the interest is there. You don't have to be an alienated, dissatisfied worker to be interested in worker participation. Some of the most productive, responsible workers . . . are interested in workplace decision-making and will participate.[21]

Carmichael's view is given some reinforcement by a report issued by a group of some 50 California trade unionists, members of a wide variety of unions, attending a university conference on "The Changing World of Work." The report starts out with the assertion: "This first Western Assembly of Workers calls for a major extension of democratic principles in the workplace. While our individual needs vary widely, we have the strong conviction that we as workers generally have too long been ignored in making critical decisions affecting our work life."[22] The report continues, however, with an expression of strong support for the collective bargaining system, and the belief that it is compatible with a broader worker participation role. It calls, in particular, for experiments with worker-elected supervisors, without disciplinary powers, whose primary function would be coordination.

PROSPECTS

Predicting the future course of social change is a dubious project. The history of American industrial democracy, however, suggests little

21. "Worker Participation in the U.S.: Seeds of a Quiet Revolution," paper prepared for Harvard Trade Union Program, fall 1974, p. 42.
22. "The Changing World of Work," Report of the Western Assembly of Workers, 27–29 September 1974, Palo Alto, California, sponsored by the Center for Labor Research and Education, Institute of Industrial Relations, University of California, Berkeley, and The American Assembly, Columbia University.

prospect of dramatic change in the work place during the foreseeable period ahead. Partly out of concern with domestic problems including high turnover and absenteeism, ineffective discipline, and slackening productivity growth, and partly in response to publicity about recent European industrial relations developments, American managers and unionists have displayed increasing sensitivity to methods of extending worker participation in decision making, making the work place more satisfying, and reducing job boredom. But the approaches that have been adopted in most quarters have reflected the traditional pragmatic, nonideological spirit, and collective bargaining, despite its recognized limitations and imperfections, seems certain to retain its dominant role.

Indeed, the strength of collective bargaining has been its pragmatic quality in response to changing conditions and needs. It has never been constant or static, as even a superficial review of bargaining structure and scope, contract administration, and dispute settlement procedures demonstrates. Most of the recent innovations in job redesign, employee-supervisor relations, flexible work schedules, and incentive pay schemes are compatible with collective bargaining. Joint union-management productivity and work quality committees have many forebears. Neither profit sharing nor stock ownership is novel, and recent versions, largely stimulated by tax law benefits, do not appear to promise a fundamental change in the management of most enterprises. Finally, there is little current evidence that American workers or unions desire to assume managerial responsibilities apart from the codetermination of job-related terms and conditions.

Annals, AAPSS, **431**, May 1977

Participative Management in India: Utopia or Snare?

By Subbiah Kannappan and V. N. Krishnan

ABSTRACT: In India, the appeal of worker participation has derived from the utopian premises of the Indian development model with its promise of rational planning and democratic processes. The former strengthened the directive role of the government while the latter served as the medium of interest-group mobilization and mediation. Whatever positive role one may attribute to these, in the absence of other structural changes they had, at best, negligible or uncertain consequences in terms of favoring worker participation in management. One reason for this is that the cultural and economic distances between management and labor were great, with little to take the place of weakened traditional authority structures. The government scheme for worker participation, although beset by weaknesses, failed largely because the external environment was inhospitable, and one may expect this to continue into the foreseeable future. The Indian Emergency of 1975 signaled a dramatic change, with a more explicitly top-directed scheme. If made permanent, this would move Indian practice closer to that of the Communist countries, with an integrated structure of economic and industrial authority and provision for modest but subordinate labor inputs in the decision-making process.

Subbiah Kannappan is Professor of Economics at Michigan State University. Since 1964 he has been associated with the International Labor Office, serving as visiting professor at the International Institute for Labor Studies and as a member of the ILO-United Nations Comprehensive Employment Strategy Missions to Ceylon (1971) and the Sudan (1975). He has published widely on the Indian industrial relations system and the labor problems of less developed countries, including a book (with Charles A. Myers) on Industrial Relations in India.

V. N. Krishnan is Associate Professor at Bowling Green State University. His publications include works on wages, labor markets, and problems of inflation in less developed countries and a co-authored text on modern governments.

INDIA was at the center of the development stage and the scene of much talk about democratic development and industrial democracy when, in 1956, an official tripartite committee reported favorably on the prospects for participative management.[1] Influential Indian opinion saw in worker participation an embryonic basis for broader efforts to integrate interest groups at the national level. Its appeal was no less important for those with a narrower focus, such as trade union leaders—and difficult to disregard in this discussion—for the government exercised broad and detailed regulatory power over the economy and industrial relations at national, industrial, and plant levels.

THE INDIAN ENVIRONMENT

Organized labor in India was participating in decision making in three important ways:

1. It was represented in the government's tripartite Indian Labor Conference and associated tripartite bodies at regional, industrial, and other more narrowly defined levels.
2. It was engaged in collective bargaining and related procedures and such institutions as grievance handling, complaint and suggestion systems, and works councils (which were statutorily required in registered factories over a certain size), and less explicitly in the governmental conciliation and arbitration process.
3. It was participating in joint management councils, joint consultative boards (in some of the

larger public sector undertakings), union representation on boards of directors, workers' cooperatives, and employee profit-sharing plans, all of which sought to enhance the worker's status and possibly also his stake in the system of industrial authority.

The industrial relations framework mainly affected wage-earning labor in the urban and modern sector of the economy: the factories, railways, posts and telegraphs, mines, plantations, large commercial establishments, ports and docks. Although this sector was and still is strategically well placed and total employment is substantial, it covers not more than 3 to 4 percent of the labor force.

The ingredients for successful and constructive labor-management relations generally did not exist. Except in rare instances, employers did not recognize unions. Union leaders were poorly versed in the arts of collective negotiations and more prone to resort to mass action to influence public policies.

Even when employers were legally required to recognize unions and attempts were made to structure industrial relations, as in the well-known Maharashtra (formerly Bombay state) procedures, there was no concomitant obligation for the employer to bargain in good faith. Further, in the giant textile industry —the main focus of this legislation —negotiations at the peak level in an industry characterized by many units could not readily go beyond such generalizable issues as wages and service conditions. There were also continuing disputes concerning the representative nature of the recognized union. The legal requirement was 15 percent of industrial employment, and there were no pro-

1. India: Ministry of Labor and Employment, *Report of the Study Group on Worker Participation in Management* (New Delhi: Manager of Publication, 1957).

cedures for a secret ballot to handle challenges. Even under favorable circumstances, it would have been difficult for workers to participate in decisions at such an aggregate level. Employer involvement, too, was limited to the level of the employers' associations, embracing diverse units with considerable variations in the economic and production conditions of member firms.

More generally, government action in industrial relations was aimed at the industry level, whether nationally, in major regions, or in metropolitan areas. In the public sector, decision making was centralized at the national level—for example, through the Railway Board which functioned as employer of over a million workers, or through the employing ministries, such as the one for steel which incorporated large modern plants. To be sure, there were some elements of participation and democracy in these relationships as unions had freedom to organize and employers, public or private, could challenge or otherwise seek to influence prevailing approaches by their side. Observers have also noted the growing professionalism of Indian management and, to a lesser extent, Indian unions. Nevertheless, to the extent that there was a clearly discernible national pattern, what stood out was the interplay among well-organized interest groups rather than the ingredients of effective employee participation in the managerial process. The involvement of interest groups at peak levels was at best only an exercise of shared management, with the government as the dominant figure. While the industrial and economic system led to centralized authority, the emerging political system mobilized the challenges to the system, and the

pattern of accommodation which emerged was an important lubricant.[2]

The recommendations of the 1956 tripartite committee, which ushered in an era of experimentation with joint management councils, are best seen as an effort to improve the top-heavy structure of confrontation and reconciliation. The effort was, however, a very limited and conservative one. It involved no substantive change of economic or productive relations even in the developed sectors of economic activity to which it was applied. There were no organizational changes involving union or industrial authority, or changes in the patterns of decision making. The framework of industrial relations remained unchanged. Since a good deal of the literature in and about India on this subject pertains to this particular experiment, we will briefly discuss its lessons.[3]

2. R. D. Agarwal, *Dynamics of Labour Relations in India, a Book of Readings* (Bombay: Tata-McGraw Hill Co., Ltd., 1972).

3. Important references include the following: K. C. Alexander, *Participative Management—The Indian Experience* (New Delhi: Shri Ram Centre for Industrial Relations and Human Resources, 1972); Subbiah Kannappan, "Worker Participation in Management: A Review of Indian Experience," *International Institute of Labour Studies*, Bulletin 5 (November 1968); D. P. Pandit, *Worker Participation in Management: Myth and Reality* (New Delhi: N.V. Publications, 1975); K. C. Sethi, "Worker Participation in Management," *Eastern Economist*, vol. 55 (31 July 1970), pp. 181–87; N. R. Sheth, *The Joint Management Council, Problems and Prospects* (New Delhi: Shri Ram Centre for Industrial Relations and Human Resources, 1972); Zivan Tanić, *Workers' Participation in Management: Ideal and Reality in India* (New Delhi: Shri Ram Center, 1969); C. P. Thakur and K. L. Sethi, eds., *Industrial Democracy: Some Issues and Experiences* (New Delhi: Shri Ram Centre, 1973).

THE 1956 EXPERIMENT IN WORKER PARTICIPATION IN MANAGEMENT

The 1956 recommendations drew some inspiration from the utopian aspects of practices abroad, particularly the Yugoslav experiment in self-management. Other stimuli included American attempts to identify the causes of industrial peace with a view to diffusing their influence more generally. Nevertheless, Indian conditions were regarded as so different as to warrant initially only an experimental and limited venture.

The scheme which was eventually applied envisaged the constitution of joint management councils that would: (1) be assured access to certain information about the economic and employment conditions of the firm and industry; (2) be consulted on certain issues like wages and employment conditions; and (3) be given shared authority in the administration of plant welfare and safety facilities. Overall, the executive authority of management was preserved, while the representational role and status of workers' representatives were to be enhanced.

From the very beginning, the intent was to proceed cautiously. The role of workers' representatives was to evolve in proportion to the development of their skill and training for participation. The development of appropriate attitudes was stressed, and the government was to assist the process by providing an advisory personnel management service as in the United Kingdom. The scheme was also, initially at any rate, to be introduced only in some 50 enterprises employing at least 500 persons each. All these cautions and qualifications did not,

however, obscure the more ambitious thrust, despite doubts concerning the underlying commitment. The idea was planted that workers would obtain increasing opportunities for influencing major decisions affecting the enterprise. The areas of influence would go beyond wages and bonuses and would include, at least potentially, such items as production, marketing strategies, capital expansion, technical change, and finances.

However, the Indian environment presented some features that were to frustrate these expectations. In the absence of a mandatory and well-defined procedure for collective bargaining, there was the clear possibility that the joint management councils would become bargaining rather than participative forums, although the participative scheme envisaged a clear separation of the two. Second, there were long-standing and unresolved conflicts between rival organizations over rights of representation. These conflicts extended both to the unit of representation and to the proper procedures to settle the conflicting claims. Also, the cultural and ideological climate of suspicion and distance between organized labor and management made it difficult to separate the quest for participation from potentially even more disruptive issues involving the legitimacy of (private) management and employer attitudes rooted in the traditions of authority.[4]

The scheme hoped to bypass all these problems by being both voluntary and selective. The latter criterion emphasized the need to

4. Jai B. P. Sinha, "A Case of Reversal in Participative Management," *Indian Journal of Industrial Relations* (October 1974), pp. 179–87.

choose units which had a superior record in constructive labor relations. However, the pressure for demonstrated successes led to a watering down of the selectivity criterion. Although the emphasis was on the demonstration effect of successful experiments, conflicting expectations clouded this prospect. The units which did exceptionally well by Indian standards, such as the Indian Aluminum Works at Belur, were untypical in the Indian context: they were usually capital-intensive, had a skilled labor force, and were part of the large-scale corporate structure being developed under India's import-substitution policies. The successful cases were few, and the emphasis on joint management was often counter-productive even when there was enthusiasm for consultation.[5]

There is really little to be added to the Indian literature on participative management which emphasizes the divergence between expectations and actual performance and voices the skepticism derived from contrasting official claims with observed progress. However, the experience does offer lessons of more general value, for it testifies to the enduring and intractable aspects of the Indian industrial relations scene. A brief representative sample of difficulties associated with the 1956 experiment will illustrate the point.

The record of meetings of joint councils was poor. Of 99 councils at the end of 1965, 29 had never met during the year, 25 less than once in a quarter, and of the 34 public sector units, 9 had never met.

The record of information sharing was poor, and managements, which provided the joint council chairmen, were reluctant even to supply an agenda in advance.

Joint administration of welfare measures was not observed, and there was not even an identifiable budget as a basis for shared responsibility.

Paternalistic and authoritarian attitudes were noted in managerial approaches, and in one case even the mere courtesy of providing tea or adequate seating facilities was not extended.

Worker and management representatives had conflicting emphases, the former stressing material changes and benefits, while the latter, limited in authority, were content to observe the status quo.

There was only limited consultation and follow-through, even when decisions were taken unanimously in the joint councils.

It should be emphasized, first, that the participating firms were not the "backward" segments of Indian industry but rather the modern units and, second, that they had volunteered to experiment with joint councils. The difficulties in the way of developing shared responsibility were not unique to this particular experiment and will survive well into the future. However, the scheme was not officially terminated, but allowed to fade away, a high-ranking official explaining that the former step required too much conscious purpose. Only with the declaration of an emergency in 1975 did the government announce a drastically altered course.

THE INDIAN EMERGENCY OF 1975 AND AFTER

The changes introduced in 1975 extend, of course, beyond partici-

5. N. R. Sheth, ibid., pp. 134–35.

pative management, and this fact should be noted. The dominant emphasis is on raising the level of industrial discipline and reducing work stoppages and other disruptions of work. The national tripartite machinery, including the well-known Indian Labor Conference, has been dismantled. In its place, bipartite bodies have been established at national industrial levels excluding, however, the public sector. For purposes of national consultation, the government has expressed its intention of not dealing with any labor organizations other than the three major national federations, the Indian National Trades Union Congress (INTUC), All-India Trade Union Congress (AITUC), and Hind Mazdoor Sabha (HMS). Apparently this arrangement will exclude other trade unions and groups in the country, but the scope of the exclusion is not clear as yet. Despite the revival of a plan for worker participation, there is some indication that the trade union leadership has become restive, since independent action by trade unions is now greatly restricted.[6]

On October 30, 1975, the Indian government announced a new set of guidelines for worker participation in mining and manufacturing in units employing 500 or more workers.[7] Two levels of joint councils were envisaged: a shop council at the department or shop floor level and an enterprise council. Their primary functions are to improve productivity, discipline, absenteeism, and similar shortcomings. Enterprise councils were endowed

with some appellate authority. As before, representation on the councils was equally divided between workers and managerial representatives, with one of the latter serving as chairman. Representational procedures were to be flexibly determined by individual councils.

Apart from the emphasis on productivity and discipline, it is worth noting that the new scheme was entirely government-initiated without the preliminary extensive process of tripartite consultation and consensus-building which had characterized earlier initiatives. Although the concept of worker participation and shared responsibility occupies a prominent place in the 20-point program, it would be naive to assume that the impediments noted in earlier periods will readily disappear. It is also germane to point to the increased authority of management in the new order. Issues which earlier were subject to bargaining, such as wages, bonus payments, and fringe benefits, are now to come under a centrally administered wage restraint and freeze policy. Whether the framework which will eventually emerge is, as in China and other countries, a mechanism for mass mobilization and involvement rather than participation depends on how the political system itself will evolve and what balance will ultimately be struck in the distribution of power among different groups in society, including organized labor.

LESSONS OF THE INDIAN EXPERIENCE FOR WORKER PARTICIPATION IN DEVELOPMENT

Perhaps the most important aspect of the Indian experience has been the conservative nature of the experiment. Despite lofty goals, there was hardly any change in the

6. B. M., "New Framework for Industrial Relations," *Economic and Political Weekly*, vol. 10, no. 47 (22 November 1975), p. 1789.
7. India: Ministry of Labor, *Scheme for Workers' Participation in Industry at Shop-Floor and Plant Level*, Resolution No. 561001 (4)/75-DK, I(B), 30 (October 1975).

economic and political structure, nor even in the approaches of the parties immediately affected. While some may see in this just another manifestation of a supposedly ubiquitous vacillation and softness in the Indian national character, it may really be an expression of the power structure and its disinterest in change.[8] Patterns of concentration of authority were actually reinforced by the economic policies pursued at the same time as populist pressures were encouraged in the nascent democracy. More often than not this encouraged conflict rather than cooperation. The latter remained a pious hope, while the former mushroomed into massive confrontations emphasizing the role of government as policeman rather than as reformer. While some conflicts, such as the central government employees' strike of 1960 and the railwaymen's strike of 1973, were national in scope, there were other tensions elsewhere in rural and district organization indicating similar problems with participatory expectations.

Despite the emphasis by observers on the professionalization of Indian top management and the improved caliber of trade union leadership in the more established industrial centers, one cannot be sanguine about the scope for decentralization in decision making. In spite of nearly 20 years' experience and exhortations, the situation which exists in a leading nationalized industry (that is, steel) cannot even assure managerial authority, let alone workers' participation. A

respected observer and manager, with a union background, observed in 1976:

. . . collective bargaining on really important issues remains somewhat unreal in public enterprises. Even the managers of these enterprises find it quite difficult to change the existing rules, procedures and systems. . . . Once, when I declared a very small token reward to a section of employees . . . for a particularly admirable piece of work . . . and although such reward was both well within my prescribed powers to give and in conformity with past practice, I received a pointed query from New Delhi about it. Similarly, when the revision of the national wages agreement with the union for the steel industry was being negotiated in the latter part of 1974 and the first half of 1975, neither the bargaining strategy nor the specific offers were decided in consultation with the plant managements or even the chairman or board of Hindustan Steel. . . .

In such a situation, negotiating with their own management is a frustrating and somewhat fruitless exercise for the employees and their unions. . . . The only way they feel they can fight this feeling of powerlessness and alienation is by displaying negative attitudes, indifference in work and postures of defiance. . . .

He acknowledges that there are also instances of gross indiscipline and deliberately low output, but adds revealingly that these are, by contrast, a more straightforward management task: when a problem arises, it "is often the result of management not standing—or not being allowed to stand—firm."[9] While the private sector may be free from some of these troubles, it still remains true that many items in labor-management relations are nationally

8. Van D. Kennedy, "India: Tendermindedness vs. Tough Problems," *Industrial Relations* (October 1965), pp. 1–22. Kennedy stressed the need for toughness of mind in tackling tough problems. He felt that the national leadership has not used its powers to the fullest.

9. Bagaram Tulpule, "Management and Workers in Public Sector," *Economic and Political Weekly*, vol. 11, no. 22 (29 May 1976), pp. M-49–M-58.

controlled. The emergency appears to have strengthened this framework.

It may be relevant at this stage to ask what are the sources of the pressure for participation. The 1956 experiment was introduced from above, although there was an accompanying chorus of demands from national trade union federations. The revived interest in worker participation in 1975, in the context of the Indian emergency, is an innovation directed from the top which has dispensed with the formality of prior consultations with affected groups. What is not clear is the extent to which Indian workers, even before the emergency, were interested in the promise of participatory management and in expanding the scope of their interests to cover issues other than wages, bonuses, and job security. A top-directed scheme, without a corresponding worker demand or enthusiasm for participation is likely to remain a pious hope.[10] Alternatively, it might develop into an instrument of national mobilization but hardly of participation. Under optimistic assumptions, one could envisage the new system as being more efficient and equitable in solving problems of production and work-place relations. A more realistic possibility, however, is that it will minimize the divergent pulls inherent to the earlier system of industrial and economic authority and patterns of political mobilization and articulation.

Whether workers accept or reject the new order will depend fundamentally on their anticipations. Lest

one forget, when in 1968 Charles de Gaulle spoke of the need for participation, the radical students of Nanterre chanted:

Je participe
Tu participes
Il participe
Nous participons
Vous participez
Ils exploitent

This reaction is potentially applicable to India, China, or any other country where participation is seen as a panacea. A similar inclination toward unrealistic expectations was noted by the senior author in Sri Lanka in 1971 in the context of a national emergency. Both national and visiting experts seemed ready to latch on to the promise of worker participation as a vehicle for developing a national purpose.

This brings us to another aspect of the Indian experience. A great deal of effort has been devoted to separating conflict issues, such as bonus and wages, from participatory issues such as production, discipline, and other day-to-day concerns. The effort is well intentioned and, within certain limits, sound. At the same time, it is clear that these issues are interdependent, and it would be futile to keep them artificially separate in the face of festering discontent, no matter how skillful the procedural compartments. More generally, this point also applies to the scope of worker participation as a contribution to the national purpose. Both conflict and cooperation are part of the participatory processes, and the utility of participation depends on how well it can handle both. Attempts to separate them, except as a device for orderly progress in both respects, or attempts to smother one while encouraging the other are likely to fail or at best to yield illusory progress which convinces no one but the faithful.

10. A post-emergency observation by a distinguished Indian economist is pertinent: "There has been much talk of workers' participation in industrial management. But it provides, at best, some window-dressing." V. M. Dandekar, *Illustrated Weekly of India*, 17–23 October 1976, p. 11.

ANNALS, AAPSS, **431,** May 1977

The Industrial Community in Peru

By WILLIAM FOOTE WHYTE AND GIORGIO ALBERTI

ABSTRACT: The Industrial Community is a government-imposed reform program for private industry in Peru. Created in 1970, the Industrial Community was designed to improve relations between labor and management, to increase productivity, to redistribute income and enhance social justice, and to accelerate economic progress. The record shows that the Industrial Community has fallen far short of the expectations of government leaders on all of these points. Reasons for the generally negative outcomes are examined.

William Foote Whyte received his Ph.D. in sociology from the University of Chicago in 1943. He has been Professor of Industrial and Labor Relations at Cornell University since 1948. From 1961 to 1975, Whyte's research was concentrated on problems of agricultural and industrial development in Peru.

Giorgio Alberti received his Ph.D. in industrial and labor relations from Cornell University in 1967. He teaches sociology at the University of Bologna, Italy. From 1967 through 1975, Alberti served as research coordinator for Cornell in a joint program with the Instituto de Estudios Peruanos (IEP) in Lima.

In 1976 Whyte and Alberti published Power, Politics and Progress: Social Change in Rural Peru, the major report in English of this Cornell-IEP program.

THE Peruvian Industrial Community (IC) was brought into existence by government decree through the General Industrial Law of July 1970. The terms and conditions were specified in more detail in the Industrial Community Law announced in September of that year.[1]

The IC was envisaged as an important part of a broad program of the revolutionary military government, designed to restructure all of Peruvian society. According to government spokesmen, this reform of private industry had the following objectives:

1. to improve relations between labor and management;
2. to increase productivity;
3. to redistribute income and enhance social justice;
4. to accelerate economic progress.

There may have been one further objective, which, though never expressed by government spokesmen, was often reported by those who claimed to be close to the government: the IC in the long run would give workers sufficient power and economic stake in their firms to eliminate the necessity of unions. After coming to power in October 1968, government leaders had repeatedly argued that the existing political parties had served the interests of party leaders at the expense of the population. Unions, being closely linked with political parties, were similarly distrusted by the new leaders of Peru.

1. The present report is part of a larger study being published in book form in Peru. We base our conclusions on close examination of 44 firms and extensive documentary records and interviews with management, union, and IC leaders by the Instituto de Estudios Peruanos.

THE LEGISLATIVE FRAMEWORK

The application of the law on the Industrial Community was initially limited to private manufacturing industry, but in succeeding months the government decreed similar legislation to cover mining, energy, and fishing. The original law decreed the establishment of an Industrial Community in every manufacturing firm with six or more employees or with a volume of sales amounting to more than 1 million soles per year (about $24,000). With the exception of individuals holding stock in the firm, the IC was all-inclusive in its membership, making no distinction between blue- and white-collar workers or between workers and members of management. The law required each firm to turn over annually to the Industrial Community 15 percent of profits before taxes in the form of stock. If the firm reinvested enough profits to make up this 15 percent, the payment could be made in newly issued stock. Otherwise, management was required to turn over the required percentage by drawing on the holdings of the existing private stockholders. The distribution process was to go on until the IC had accumulated 50 percent of stock ownership. From that point on, the 15 percent payments would be made in cash.

The General Industrial Law also required each company to make an annual cash distribution of 10 percent of its profits before taxes to all employees. While this clause was not an integral part of the section establishing the Industrial Community, there was nevertheless a general tendency among workers to credit their gain to the IC since it came into being at the same time.

In each firm, a so-called general

assembly of all members of the IC elected a council of five to nine members, depending on the size of the firm. The council elected a chairman and also a representative to the board of directors of the company. While the IC was entitled to have a representative on the board even before it had come into possession of any stock, the law also provided that in the future IC representation on the board of directors would increase proportionately with the stockholdings of the community.

The law imposed an important shift in power relations between management and the workers. The government decreed that IC representatives on the board of directors should have the same rights as representatives of the private stockholders. Implementing regulations issued several months after the passage of the law decreed that IC representatives on the board were to have access to the company's books and also had the right to hire outside accountants, lawyers, or other specialists to help them interpret these documents. Furthermore, to prevent management from retaining control through a divide-and-conquer strategy as the IC holdings approached 50 percent, the law specified that the IC representatives on the board must vote in a bloc. Finally, so as to separate the IC from unions—and perhaps also to weaken the unions—the law provided that individuals holding union office could not be elected to the IC council.

THE CONTEXT OF GOVERNMENT INTERVENTION

The ability of the government to impose such drastic changes upon private industry can only be understood in terms of the weakness of the private manufacturing sector in Peru. Peru's industrialization came late and progressed slowly. The census of 1940 found only 17.2 percent of the economically active population employed in manufacturing and construction. Particularly during and following World War II, manufacturing appeared to be expanding rapidly, and yet the 1961 census counted only 16.8 percent of the economically active population employed in manufacturing and construction.[2] The expansion of jobs in this sector had not even kept pace with the expansion of the economically active population.

Most of the important firms in manufacturing, mining, and banking were foreign owned. Furthermore, Peruvian-owned manufacturing enterprises had been founded mostly by immigrants or sons of immigrants whose foreign origins retarded their movement into positions of economic and political power. Members of the economic and social elite were divided by rivalries between those whose primary interests were in agriculture and mining and those devoted to manufacturing. There was also a small but vigorous group of manufacturers who were seeking government support for their growing exports.

Organized labor was weak and divided. The labor federation CTP (*Confederación de Trabajadores Peruanos*) had been founded by members of the APRA party (*Alianza Popular Revolucionaria Americana*) of Haya de la Torre, and APRA had had a long history of conflict with the military and particularly with previous military

2. Magali Sarfatti Larson and Arlene Eisen Bergman, *Social Stratification in Peru* (Berkeley: University of California Institute of International Studies, 1969), pp. 319-20.

governments. The present military government granted official recognition to a rival organization, the Communist-led CGTP (*Confederación General de Trabajadores Peruanos*). The move was regarded by some of the government's critics as evidence that the military leaders were Communist sympathizers, but the decision can be more plausibly explained in terms of a divide-and-conquer strategy.

While Peru previously had many military governments, the junta that came to power in 1968 was the first one committed to a program of restructuring society. This new direction can be accounted for by changes which had taken place in the structure and education within the military establishment. In the 1950s, Peru established for the first time a joint chiefs of staff organization which set the stage for what are now called institutional coups. Instead of some individual strongman seizing power, the joint chiefs simply make a collective decision to move from the barracks into the presidential palace, with the head of the joint chiefs becoming president. Such a collective move is more likely to be based on prior discussion of program and policy than in the case of an individual leader who seizes power on the basis of his popularity and personal influence within the officer corps.

The 1950s in Peru were also marked by the establishment of CAEM, the Center for Higher Military Studies, which developed a 10-month educational program for senior officers in the army, air force, and navy. The CAEM program gave relatively little attention to strictly military matters and concentrated on the social, economic, and political problems of Peru, reflecting the philosophy of its founder that "to

have a strong national defense, the first requirement is to have a country that is worth defending."[3]

The CAEM program was the capstone of an ambitious military educational system. Luigi Einaudi[4] has pointed out that promotions in the Peruvian military establishment have long been based primarily upon educational achievements.

The CAEM program developed along ideological lines congruent with the changes taking place in Peruvian intellectual circles, that is, basically from laissez-faire economics to the structural emphasis of dependency theorists.[5] The program focused upon Peru's needs for structural change, for gaining control over its own vital resources, and for controlling its destiny through economic planning.

While the intellectual roots of the IC have not been fully documented, the basic conception seems to derive from three sources: the social doctrine of the Catholic church, an examination of certain European experiences, and the urge of government leaders to create an original Peruvian model. The church supplied a vision of society in which class conflict would give way to a harmonious order with greater social justice for working people. Peruvians had been greatly attracted to self-management, but they recognized that the system in Yugoslavia had arisen out of a set of wartime and postwar develop-

3. Personal conversation with General José del Carmen Marín, founder of CAEM.
4. Luigi Einaudi, *The Peruvian Military: A Summary Political Analysis* (Los Angeles: The Rand Corporation, 1969).
5. Joseph A. Kahl, *Modernization, Exploitation and Dependency in Latin America: Germani, Gonzalez Casanova and Cardoso* (New Brunswick, N.J.: Transaction Books, Inc., 1976).

ments which had largely eliminated private ownership of industrial plants so the way was cleared for the government to establish a new set of relations between workers and management. Peruvians were also interested in West German code-termination but did not think it went far enough in changing relations between workers and management. Finally, government spokesmen repeatedly proclaimed that their regime was "neither capitalist nor communist" but was building a distinctively Peruvian model of society. They took pride in the fact that nothing like the Industrial Community had ever existed anywhere before.

THE IMPACT OF THE IC

The announcement of the IC was greeted with shocked surprise by leaders of private industry. While they objected to the double-barreled 15 percent and 10 percent distributions of profits to the IC and employees, their main concern was the threat to the control of their companies. Their anxieties were increased by government measures affecting other parts of the economy. The government had expropriated the International Petroleum Company in the first days of the regime and had followed up with expropriations of some foreign-owned banks and mining companies. A drastic agrarian reform program was decreed in 1969. Furthermore, within a few months after the decree establishing the IC, public discussion turned to the creation of an even more "advanced" form of industrial organization: social property, a worker-managed set of enterprises to be financed largely by government. Government spokesmen repeatedly proclaimed that social

property was destined to become the predominant form of industrial enterprise in Peru. Since such a development could not be achieved with the limited resources the government had to invest in social property, private industry leaders naturally feared that the government would respond to worker and union pressures to accelerate the structural changes by transforming the industrial community into fully worker-managed enterprises.

As soon as the Industrial Community Law was decreed, private industry leaders began to study it in hopes of finding ways by which they could retain control of their companies. If they did not reinvest profits and had to provide the 15 percent stock distribution annually from holdings of existing shareholders, clearly they would accelerate the loss of control. If, on the other hand, they did follow a policy of reinvesting each year at least 15 percent they found that, as the law was being interpreted, such a policy would only postpone for a few years the eventual acquisition of 50 percent by the IC. While management critics of the law at first concentrated their fire on the impracticality of having a 50-50 division of power between the IC and private shareholders, they gradually came to realize that the "tipping point" at which control could shift to the employees might come well before the 50 percent level had been reached. As the IC approached a 50 percent holding, many private stockholders would anticipate that, on gaining control of the company, the IC would raise wages to take 100 percent of potential profits for employees instead of dividing the returns equally. Such an expectation could lead to panic selling on the part of individual shareholders, thus allowing the IC to gain an absolute majority through purchases of stocks thrown on the market.

There seemed to be only three ways by which managers representing the private shareholders could retain control:

1. ensure such poor economic performance that there would be few or no profits to share with the IC;
2. raise executive salaries at the expense of profits in those cases where members of management held large blocks of stock;
3. expand the capital base of the company through reinvesting more than the 15 percent slice taken by the IC and bringing in additional capital.

None of these options offered a satisfactory solution to private management. The first course would have meant retaining control of a firm constantly on the edge of bankruptcy. The second course, while apparently followed in some firms, naturally provoked conflict with the industrial community which now had full access to the company's books and could challenge exorbitant executive salary raises in the press and before the Ministry of Industry and Tourism responsible for administering the law. A substantial increase in the capital base was simply not practical in a climate characterized by lack of investor confidence.

Union leaders in the CTP were as surprised as management by the creation of the Industrial Community, but their reactions were quite different. While some of them expressed concern that the IC might weaken unions, they welcomed both profit sharing and participation in managerial decision making. At the same time, they tended to regard the IC as a hybrid that could not be expected to have a long life. Therefore, when the discussion on social property began, radical union leaders and a number of intellectual leftists argued that the IC should only be a transitional form, eventually giving way to social property.

Marxists were divided in their stance toward the IC. Some viewed it as a dangerous move toward class conciliation, while others argued that the IC deserved support because it gave more power to the unions and the working class.

CONFLICT OR COOPERATION?

As a measure to promote industrial peace, the IC has been a disappointment to its sponsors. In the five years preceding its establishment, the official statistics record 1,889 strikes. In the five years following the IC creation, there were 2,993 strikes, an increase of almost 60 percent. There were 372 strikes in 1969, the last year before the IC. The 1975 total was 794, second only to the peak year of 1973 when 824 strikes were registered.[6] In the early months of 1976, as industrial conflict mounted, the government found it necessary to outlaw strikes. While it would be an oversimplification to blame all of the increase on the IC, clearly the record lends no support to the government's predictions that the new institution would create harmony between workers and managers.

An examination of specific cases shows that the IC's impact has varied according to the characteristics of the parties. In general, the larger the firm, the greater the rise in levels of conflict. Firms located in the political and economic center of the country, the Lima metropolitan area,

6. *Industria Peruna* (January 1976).

where about 70 percent of manufacturing is concentrated, have been more involved in conflicts than firms in the provinces. In firms where union leaders had ties to a leftist political party, there tended to be more conflicts with the IC than in firms where union leaders were not so heavily politicized. Of course, these variables often go together, since most of the large firms are in the Lima metropolitan area and the political commitments of union leaders in the capital are likely to be stronger than in the provinces.

The relationship between conflict and profits was rather complicated. High conflict situations existed among both highly profitable and highly unprofitable firms, but all of the firms where the IC and management and union leaders considered relations to be harmonious had above average profits.

Although some well-known cases of union-management cooperation in the United States have arisen during economic crises where the firm was facing bankruptcy, there do not seem to be any counterparts in Peru. The failure of the parties to close ranks and seek cooperation when the firm is facing bankruptcy is probably due to the quite different social, political, and economic setting. IC leaders seemed less inclined to cooperate with management and instead preferred to give an additional push toward the precipice in the hopes that the government would step in following bankruptcy and reorganize the firm on a social property basis.

We were unable to find a single case where the creation of the Industrial Community had changed a conflict situation to one of labor-management cooperation. On the contrary, we were impressed by the continuities in labor relations before and after the establishment of the new institution. Where union and management had a history of conflict and mistrust, the IC became, as several executives called it, "just a second front in the war." Where relations between union and management had previously been reasonably harmonious, the introduction of the IC was accomplished without any serious disturbances, but there was no evidence that the IC itself had improved the already existing good relations.

Instead of fading away with the development of the IC, at least at the local level, as the government had anticipated, the unions appeared to be gaining strength. In fact, in some cases formation of the IC actually precipitated the organization of unions where none existed before.

Whereas government spokesmen envisioned the IC as strictly separate from the union, the record shows that these expectations have been illusory. Since all union members also belong to the IC of their firm, the aim to keep the two organizations separate has turned out to be clearly unrealistic. In general, where the union has been well organized and strong, its leaders have controlled the nomination and election of IC council members. Close relations between the two organizations can be an important aid to militant union leaders, especially since the IC enables union leaders to obtain information from the company's books on financial and other previously confidential matters.

A general atmosphere of conflict does not necessarily preclude instances of cooperation. Occasionally, when bargaining between union and management has broken down, IC leaders have assumed a mediating role. There are also cases where the IC and management have worked together to protect mutual interests. For example, they may jointly urge government to grant a price increase for their product, to make available the foreign exchange necessary to import raw materials needed by the firm, or to block the establishment of a competing firm in the same industry.

Initially, government leaders did not plan to have a national organization of industrial communities, but as IC leaders from various firms went through common orientation and training programs, their association naturally suggested the desirability of a national organization. When the government finally permitted a national meeting of Industrial Communities, it quickly got out of control. While government leaders emphasized the distinction between the ICs and unions and denied that the ICs were simply a way-station to social property, the delegates overwhelmingly passed a set of militant resolutions, urging the government to push the IC toward social property and defining the IC as primarily an instrument to strengthen unions so as to advance the interests of the working class.

Being unable first to prevent and then to control the national organization CONACI (*Confederación Nacional de Comunidades Industriales*), government officials sought to divide it by sponsoring and financing a dissident group representing the smaller firms with less highly politicized IC members. While this schism persisted for several months, the two groups eventually proceeded to negotiate their differences and form a more or less unified national organization.

PRODUCTIVITY

Management often acknowledges that the IC has stimulated technological change, at least in profitable firms. While private investors have been reluctant to put up new capital, there has been a general tendency of firms to reinvest 15 percent of their profits, not only to improve output but also to save private investors from having to transfer some of their shares to the Industrial Community. The IC also has apparently lowered worker and union resistance to the introduction of new machinery. This is not to say that unions have ceased resistance to layoffs due to technological change, but they have put less pressure on management to replace workers who quit or retire. Management is thus able to reduce the workforce through attrition.

Since the IC is made up of blue-collar and white-collar workers, as well as accountants, supervisors, and engineers, there is at least a theoretical possibility that the IC might develop into an internal consulting organization capable of suggesting improvements in efficiency. We found no case where this possibility had even been attempted. Management has been highly sensitive to even the appearance of infringements on managerial prerogatives. IC criticisms and suggestions regarding managerial efficiency have not resulted from systematic study but have been couched in the form of attacks on management extravagance. For example, IC council leaders tend to question executive salaries and bonuses, consultation fees, expense accounts, the private use of company cars, and similar vulnerable areas.

In the early months following enactment of the IC law, some management and IC leaders commented on improvements in worker motivation. However, as time went on such comments became less frequent. There is reason to believe that the dramatic announcement of the Industrial Community generated expectations of a new era in labor relations. As the old frictions and conflicts broke out again, attitudes on both sides seemed to revert to the old pattern. However, there may have been one lasting change: a greatly increased worker interest in training programs both for job skills and for an understanding of management.

Utilization of the knowledge and ideas of rank and file workers depends upon a structural innovation that Peruvian management has been most reluctant to carry out. The law requires worker participation only at the top level, in the board of directors. Except in a very small firm, this is a most inappropriate place for serious discussions of productivity because the management representatives are far removed from the shop situation and the worker representatives can know intimately only small parts of the total operation. If workers are to contribute valuable productivity information and ideas, they must be involved in the decision-making process at the level of the shop or section where they work. While there have been occasional statements from government officials to the effect that it would be a good idea to extend worker participation in decision making down to the shop level, leading spokesmen of private industry have vigorously rejected such suggestions as involving further encroachment on the prerogatives of management.

DEVELOPMENT AND SOCIAL JUSTICE

Government rhetoric has emphasized the redistribution of income for the benefit of low income groups. In these terms, the IC can hardly be considered successful. The incomes of Peruvian blue-collar workers in the more modern sectors of industry put them within the top 25 percent of the population. Thus, the distribution of profits from private industry through the IC amounts to taking money from the top 1 percent and distributing it within the top quartile of the income-earning population. And since the better paid workers are generally employed in the more profitable firms, profit sharing tends to benefit workers who already hold a favored position.

As we saw above, the IC has stimulated reinvestment of profits, but this policy is less likely to create jobs than to substitute capital for labor—in a country of growing urban unemployment.

Since the creation of the IC there has been a sharp reduction in new capital investment in Peruvian manufacturing enterprises. Executives in foreign controlled firms have been told by their home offices that they may reinvest local profits but they cannot expect to import capital, no matter what the potential demand for their product. Peruvian investors have also been reluctant to risk their money on a new enterprise in which they may eventually lose control to the Industrial Community. It is not only the existence of the IC that puts a damper on investment, but also the opening up of other investment opportunities that promise greater returns with less risk. For example, investors in high tax brackets can escape taxation entirely on money invested in enterprises designed to stimulate tourism. They can also invest in tax-free government securities with a guaranteed return of 10–12 percent, without any risks except those affecting the economy as a whole.

THE FUTURE OF THE INDUSTRIAL COMMUNITY

As Peru was sinking into a severe economic crisis, with an increasing rate of inflation and enormous foreign debt, many government officials became convinced that the IC must be drastically modified in order to stimulate foreign and domestic investment. But abandonment of the IC would be regarded by militant critics on the left as capitulation to the imperialists and the local capitalists.

After many months of debate within government, President Francisco Morales Bermudez finally announced a decision which, in effect, ended the threat of worker control. Shares held collectively by the Industrial Community will be distributed to individual workers, who from now on will receive divi-dends as well as retaining their 10 percent individual profit sharing.

In its early years, the revolutionary military government of Peru attracted favorable attention around the world as a new type of military government: an authoritarian regime which nevertheless ruled in a relatively non-repressive manner and which showed an extraordinary commitment to structural reform designed to improve the position of the working class. As economic and political difficulties have pushed the regime toward increasing reliance on physical force, this goal is fading, so that it is now unlikely that outsiders will look to Peru as a new model for restructuring society. On the other hand, the disappointing results in Peru must be examined partly in terms of Peruvian culture, the evolution of industrial relations, the social structure, and the distribution of power that prevailed in society in the past. Another country where social class lines are not drawn as sharply, where organized labor has been more fully involved in cooperative projects, might be able to avoid the negative results of the Peruvian model by applying it in some modified form. Nevertheless the record of the IC certainly lends no support to those who would wish to apply the same general development strategy elsewhere.

Worker Participation in Israel: Experience and Lessons

By ELIEZER ROSENSTEIN

ABSTRACT: This article examines the record of experience with a succession of worker participation programs in Israel over the past 50 years. Collective bargaining has been the universal form of industrial democracy, but it has been accompanied and supplemented at various times by joint productivity councils, plant councils, and joint management boards. The latter have been limited so far to enterprises owned by the General Federation of Labor in Israel, the Histadrut. Profit sharing as a form of participation is presently in the process of being instituted in that sector of the economy known as the Labor Economy. Self-management and self-government have always constituted the basic principles of Kibbutz and Moshav movements as well as the cooperative enterprises. However, the introduction of industrial enterprises into the once purely agricultural Kibbutz settlements has brought with it a substantial amount of hired labor, and consequently the integration of hired labor into the self-management structure has raised substantial difficulties. Evaluation of Israeli experience must pay special attention to the problems of integrating representative participation with direct shop-floor participation.

Eliezer Rosenstein is senior lecturer and head of the Behavioral Sciences and Management Program of the Faculty of Industrial and Management Engineering at Technion—the Israel Institute of Technology—in Haifa. He received his M.A. from the Hebrew University, Jerusalem, and his Ph.D. in sociology from the University of California, Berkeley. His research has covered workers' participation in management, maritime manpower, promotion practices in industrial plants, plant-level trade union representation in Israel, and labor relations in Israeli shipping. He has also served as a United Nations consultant in Ceylon. In 1976 he was Visiting Associate Professor in the School of Management, State University of New York at Binghamton.

THE idea that workers should participate in managerial decision making has deep roots in the social ethos of the large labor sector of Israeli society. Several innovative social institutions have emerged from that sector. Best known are probably the Kibbutz and the Moshav which developed in agriculture and are based on communal principles. Less well known abroad are the consumer and producer cooperative enterprises of the labor movement in the so-called Labor Economy. All these economic activities are an integral part of the Labor Federation of Israel—the Histadrut—which was founded in 1920. It is a unique organization in its combination of purposes and its structure and functions.[1]

The Histadrut has always been guided by four interrelated aims: a nation-building program of pioneering and development; the formation and development of a laboring class; the creation of a just society; and the development of a high standard of living. Unique to Histadrut is the co-existence of a powerful and virtually all-embracing trade union wing and an extensive set of economic activities, organized in the Hevrat Ovdim (community of workers).[2] These two principal units are combined with a broad network of cultural and educational activities, extensive welfare services, and consumers' and producers' cooperatives.

Membership in Histadrut is direct. Upon joining, the member is entitled to all the services, including trade union protection and social welfare. He also becomes a member of Hevrat Ovdim and automatically a co-owner of its properties. Over the years, the Histadrut has grown into a mass organization.[3] Its economic sector now accounts for about 23 percent of national employment, 19 percent of the net national product, and 19 percent of total exports.

We shall examine, first, the most universal aspect of workers participation in Israel, namely collective bargaining. We shall then examine the participatory mechanisms in Histadrut enterprises and also in the self-managed economy, that is, the cooperatives, the Moshavim, and the Kibbutzim.

PARTICIPATION THROUGH COLLECTIVE BARGAINING

Labor relations in Israel are based on a system of collective agreements

1. In spite of its unique characteristics, relatively little has been published about the Histadrut in foreign languages. The most comprehensive bibliography is Mordechai Mironi and John J. Flager, *The Histadrut* (Minneapolis: University of Minnesota, Industrial Relations Center, 1975). See, also, United States Department of Labor, Bureau of Labor Statistics, *Labor Law and Practice in Israel*, BLS Report No. 315 (Washington, D.C.: Government Printing Office); Nadav Halevi, "The Israeli Labor Movement," THE ANNALS, vol. 310 (March 1957), pp. 172–82; Yehuda Slutzki, "The Histadrut —Its History, Structure and Principles," in *Labor and Society in Israel*, ed., Isiah Avrech and Dan Giladi (Tel-Aviv: Tel-Aviv University, Department of Labor Studies, 1973), pp. 6–23. For a most interesting historical-sociological examination of the Histadrut in its early stage (1920–1948), see Israel Kolat, "The Concept of the Histadrut," in *Labor and Society in Israel*, pp. 204–27.

2. Hevrat Ovdim is presently made up of five components. In descending scale of their contributions to the net product of the economy, they are: (1) cooperative settlements—Kibbutzim and Moshavim; (2) wholly and partially owned enterprises; (3) manufacturing, transportation, and service cooperatives; (4) marketing and consumer associations; (5) Histadrut nonprofit organizations.

3. Presently, 75 percent of Israel's labor force holds direct membership in the Histadrut. The members now total 1,100,000, or approximately 60 percent of Israeli citizens above the age of 18.

concluded between an employer or employers' association and the trade union side of Histadrut.[4] Usually the top-level organizations conclude "skeleton" agreements which are then adapted to conditions in each industry by means of subsidiary agreements negotiated between an individual trade union or a local labor council and the corresponding section of the employers' organization. In general, the skeleton agreements are renegotiated every two years by the Histadrut in its capacity as a trade union organization and the Israeli Manufacturers' Association. They lay down conditions of work, including wages, social benefits, working hours, shift work, rules of conduct and discipline, hiring, employment termination, negotiating procedures, settlement of disputes, and the rights and obligations of the parties.

At national level, the Trade Union Department of the Histadrut speaks for more than 80 percent of wage and salary earners in the country. Its policies are heavily influenced by the country's economic problems and tend to reflect a compromise between worker expectations and national economic interests.

At local level, the labor councils represent Histadrut in most of its multifarious activities, including its trade union activities. Together with plant level bodies—the workers' committees—the labor councils represent the workers vis-à-vis plant management.

As a rule, plant-level labor relations are the joint responsibility of local management (plant manager and personnel director) and the workers' committee. The labor council intervenes only in the event of a dispute when no agreement is reached between the two sides.[5] A workers' committee, consisting usually of three to seven persons, represents the workforce in all matters related to the collective agreement. It negotiates supplemental agreements and takes up with management any question concerning working conditions or discipline that may arise from the administration of the agreement. Members of the workers' committees are elected by the workforce at least every two years. In view of their broad frame of reference and the direct election of their members, they have accumulated great power and influence in the labor relations system.[6]

To the extent that a strong union side in collective bargaining represents a form of worker participation in management, Israel may serve as a model. Through their

5. For analyses of plant labor relations in English, see Milton Derber, "Plant Labor Relations in Israel," *Industrial and Labor Relations Review*, vol. 17, no. 1 (October 1963), pp. 39–59; Eliezer Rosenstein, "Histadrut's Search for a Participation Program," *Industrial Relations*, vol. 9, no. 2 (February 1970), pp. 170–86; Arie Shirom, "Workers' Committees in the Israeli Labor Relations System: An Appraisal," *Industrial Relations Journal*, vol. 2, no. 1 (Spring 1971), pp. 66–74.

6. Accumulation of power in the hands of shop stewards is not unique to Israel, although the extent to which workers' committees have ignored or objected to Histadrut policies has grown considerably in Israel in recent years. One suggested explanation for the contradictory approaches of the trade unions (national or local) and the plant level workers' committees in Israel is that the first behave as political organizations whereas the second act as economic ones. See A. Friedman, "Workers' Committee and Trade Union—Partners in Rivalries," in *Structural Changes in Labor Unions*, ed., A. Friedman (Tel-Aviv: Industrial Relations Research Association of Israel, 1972), pp. 22–40.

4. These agreements may be special, applying to a particular enterprise or employer, or general, applying to the whole or part of the country or to a specific type of work. The system of collective agreements is recognized in the Collective Agreements Law (1957).

representatives, employees at all levels have a strong voice in the determination of their terms of employment, and Milton Derber recently characterized union participation in setting wages, hours, and working conditions as substantial. However, at least in the private sector, participation is still extremely limited or nonexistent in such important areas as product choice, production and engineering methods, plant location, selection of managerial personnel, marketing, and accounting. On the other hand, workers' committees often have considerable influence in the personnel management area, including individual upgrading and wage increases, fringe benefits, redundancy, transfer, discipline, and sometimes even selection of first-line supervisors.

REPRESENTATIVE PARTICIPATION IN THE LABOR ECONOMY

During the last 30 years or so, several attempts have been made to introduce in Israeli organizations participatory schemes beyond collective bargaining. These schemes were usually initiated by the leadership of the Histadrut and introduced in enterprises which belong to the Labor Economy. One of these—the Joint Productivity Council—was adopted by the private and state sectors and now constitutes an integral part of the Israeli system of industrial management. Since all new experiments started in the Labor Economy, we shall begin there.

The participation programs to be examined were originally designed mainly for Histadrut industrial enterprises known as the administrative or institutional plants. The terms refer to the industrial enterprises which are directly owned by

Hevrat Ovdim and its holding companies. The biggest holding company is Koor, which is the industrial arm of Hevrat Ovdim and Israel's largest industrial complex. It comprises more than 60 major plants in almost every industry and 30 commercial companies.[7]

The background for the introduction of the participative experimentation in Histadrut-owned enterprises is the nature of the labor-management relationship which has developed in them. Histadrut-owned industrial plants have grown substantially in number, size, and employment since the early 1940s, and gradually the pioneering and intensely idealistic workforce of the early days has been replaced by newcomers for whom a Histadrut-owned plant has been just another work place. At the same time, the growing complexity of the production process compelled abandonment of the idea that professional management could be dispensed with. The introduction of technical experts, bureaucratic procedures, and related processes produced a growing similarity between the Histadrut-owned enterprises and the private enterprises, at least in terms of worker perception. To counteract these trends, the top

7. Koor was launched in 1944 as a subdivision of Solel Boneh (another holding company of the Histadrut), became independent in 1958, and today operates some of the largest manufacturing facilities in the Middle East. Of its 90 major plants and companies, 40 are wholly owned by Hevrat Ovdim through Koor, while Koor maintains a 50 percent interest or more in the others. Private business firms from Israel and abroad, including major international corporations, are associated with Koor in many jointly owned companies. Koor's impact on the national economy is reflected in the fact that the concern produces 9.3 percent of the total output of Israeli industry and accounts for 10 percent of its industrial exports.

Histadrut leadership introduced participation programs, the aim being to reconcile the exigencies of production with the original ideology of the Labor Economy. In other words, economic development was to remain a key component of nation building, and strong cooperative and harmonious relationships were to prevail between managers and managed.

THE JOINT PRODUCTIVITY COUNCILS

Joint productivity councils (JPC) were first developed in several Histadrut enterprises during the mid-1940s. They were intended both to raise output and to provide a mechanism for participation of employees in management. Soon after the establishment of the state of Israel in 1948, the Histadrut adopted the JPCs as a long-term instrument to raise national productivity.

The councils, of which there are now about 400 in all sectors of the economy, consist of equal numbers of workers' representatives and management appointees. Their role is an advisory one to plant management, and they operate under rules agreed to between the Histadrut and the association of (private) employers.

All the efforts of the JPCs have concentrated on increasing productivity through incentive payment systems. That has been a source of strength, but also a major limitation. Strength has flowed from opportunities for increased income for employees and decreased costs for employers. But the focus on incentive payments has led to the neglect of other aspects of decision making related to productivity, such as planning, equipment selection, and training. Nevertheless, most stu-

dents of labor relations in Israel consider the JPC program to have been a limited success in promoting participation over a narrow but important area of management decisions.

THE PLANT COUNCILS

Unlike collective bargaining and the JPC program, plant councils (and joint management boards) were always confined to enterprises owned by the Histadrut. The experiment began in 1956, covered about 30 plants, and for all practical purposes ended in 1961. The motivation for the program was ideological. The top leaders of the Histadrut became convinced in the early 1950s that Histadrut-owned plants were undergoing a "social and moral deterioration" by neglecting their social purpose of creating a sense of fraternity and community in industrial plants on the model of the Kibbutz.[8] The solution was to be the formation of joint councils, consisting of five to ten elected representatives of workers and two to five appointees of management, which were to meet monthly to discuss and decide all matters pertaining to the enterprise except wages and working conditions, for these were to remain under the jurisdiction of the workers' committees. From the very beginning the councils ran into difficulties, and by 1961 it was clear that they had failed. There was more than one reason for the failure, but the major one was probably the widespread feeling among both managements and workers that the

8. Histadrut leaders in those years took the communal life of the Kibbutz as a model and inspiration for the industrial plants owned by Koor. Koor managers objected to the analogy, claiming that all over the world workers worked as hired labor and were by and large content.

councils were of little relevance to their needs and interests. Basically, workers remained indifferent and managers more or less opposed the whole idea in principle.

THE JOINT MANAGEMENT BOARDS

The current participation program of the Histadrut is based on joint management boards. For the time being, they have been introduced only in some units of the Labor Economy. The rationale for the program does not differ basically from that of the previous participation programs.

Joint management boards were conceived in the late 1950s as a higher level of participation, to be introduced when warranted by future conditions. In the early 1960s, after it became clear that the plant council plan had failed, the Histadrut leadership was faced with a dilemma: whether or not to proceed to the higher stage when the lower one had not succeeded. The decision was eventually made to take the step but to proceed with great care.

Both social and economic factors played a role in the decision. Top leaders of the Histadrut firmly believed that the Labor Economy would not be able to fulfill its historic mission of developing the country and its social mission of building a free workers' community as long as managers viewed workers as hired labor and workers viewed management as the owners.[9] A new program of participation also offered the possibility of introducing a qualitative difference betwen Histadrut and non-Histadrut enterprises.

In 1964 the Histadrut Council endorsed in principle a joint management program, but it was several years before the rules of the program were worked out. The most interesting thing about this process was the compromise concluded between the management groups of the Labor Economy and the ideologues-politicians designated by the Histadrut to administer the new program.

The program envisages participation at two levels: the company (central) level and the plant level. Very little research exists on the first level which includes both the board of directors and the central management board of the large Histadrut enterprises.[10] Some Histadrut top executives believe that participation at that level is most effective and fruitful, but we shall not be able to expand here on participation at this level.

The plant level program provides for the establishment in each plant of a joint management board consisting of the directors of the plant and an equal number of worker representatives and appointees of management.[11] The board is responsible

10. In 1975 workers' representatives were included in the boards of directors in at least 12 of Histadrut's companies.

11. A 1975 survey of 94 members of joint management boards in 23 plants provides some socio-demographic comparisons of workers and managers on these boards. All members are males between the ages of 45 and 50. Most of them were not born in Israel but had lived there on average for 25 years. The average number of years of formal education of the managers (13) is only two years above the average of the workers' representatives (11). Differences between the two groups exist mainly with regard to ethnic origin and occupation. Management appointees are mostly of Western origin (76 percent), whereas workers' representatives are of Middle Eastern (45 percent) and Israeli (17 percent) origin. A. Bar-Haim, "Innovative Managerial Patterns in Israeli Enterprises," first draft (Hebrew University of Jerusalem, Work and Welfare Research Institute, 1976), in Hebrew.

9. Aharon Becker, *Bahistadrut*, July 1963, p. 7. Becker was then the general secretary of the Histadrut, the highest executive officer.

for the operation of the enterprise. It decides all issues except working conditions and wages, which continue to be negotiated between the workers' committee and the general manager or his personnel manager.

Information on some of the 30 plants in which the program has been introduced reveals considerable variation in implementation.[12] Three problem areas stand out: (1) Some boards are active and deal with important issues, while others merely have formal meetings and deal with marginal questions. (2) In some cases the workers' committees and the workers' representatives on the boards coordinate their work, while in others a rivalry between the two has emerged which endangers the continuation of the program. There is evidence that the rivalry has considerably abated in the last few years. (3) Lack of communication between the workers' representatives on the joint boards and the rank and file is a common weakness.

The most revolutionary element in the new plan is the encouragement of profit sharing. The issue had been discussed in Histadrut for many years but had been rejected by the managers of Histadrut enterprises for economic reasons and by the politicians for ideological reasons. A breakthrough occurred in the late 1960s when the new joint management plan was being developed. The clinching argument was that profits resulting from participation in management should be shared with the workers. In practice, however, profit sharing, at least in Koor enterprises, has become dissociated

from the existence of joint management, and there are now strong indications that it will spread to many enterprises in the Labor Economy.[13] This is so because of widespread belief among managements that profit sharing promotes job satisfaction and employee identification with the plant and the economy.

The most recent development is the declared intention of the government to put employee representatives by law on the boards of directors of the large state-owned enterprises, excluding banks.[14] The Histadrut was most instrumental in the formulation of this proposal. The scheme calls for two elected representatives of the employees to serve as part-time members of the board of directors of each enterprise.[15] These directors, who are not to occupy other elective union offices, are to be elected for a three-year period once renewable. Their income is to be the same as before their election, and they will continue to perform their regular work,

12. See the study of "Phoenicia" (Israel Glass Works) in Jay Y. Tabb and Amira Goldfarb, *Workers' Participation in Management: Expectation and Experience* (London: Pergamon Press, 1970), pp. 201–45.

13. Profit sharing is not unique to the Labor Economy. There has also been a trend in the private sector to introduce profit sharing schemes of various kinds.

14. Such representation exists in a dozen Histadrut companies as well as in the Israeli Electrical Corporation. However, it has not been part of the management system of the state-owned enterprises.

15. In 1975 a joint committee of representatives of the Histadrut and the Ministry of Labor as well as social scientists from the universities was established to explore the needs and forms of worker participation in the Israeli economy. It also reviewed measures taken in other countries for the implementation of participation. The major recommendation of the committee was to adopt the representative model at the board of directors level and to implement it through formal regulations. It is doubtful, however, that the Finance Committee of the Knesset (Israeli parliament) will approve the draft regulation in view of recent political developments.

although they are to be given adequate time to perform their duties as members of the board. Top management personnel will not be eligible for election to board membership by the employees. Basically, these are the same conditions under which worker-directors in some Histadrut companies have already been functioning for some time.

PARTICIPATION IN THE SELF-MANAGED ECONOMY

Collective principles in economic life have been part of the Israeli ethos since the first pioneering waves of immigration arrived in the old-new land in the latter part of the past century. These principles have found special expression in the development of the self-managed economy: the cooperatives in the urban areas and the Moshavim and the Kibbutzim in the agricultural areas. Most of them are an integral part of Histadrut's Labor Economy.

More than 90 industrial cooperatives flourish in textiles, printing, glass making, building, and the food industry. The largest cooperatives are Egged and Dan, the two bus transportation services. Both the industrial and service cooperatives are affiliated with Hevrat Ovdim, the economic arm of the Histadrut.[16] Members of cooperatives participate in management through the election of all official bodies, including the management boards. Major problems remain, however, in relation to the existence of hired labor and its integration into the management system. For years the Histadrut has been putting pressure on the cooperatives to accept their hired workers as full members, but this has turned out to be a long and tedious process.

The Moshavim—organized settlements based on family farms—have grown considerably since their beginning in 1921.[17] There are, at present, about 350 with nearly 30,000 farms—6.2 percent of the Jewish population.[18] Each Moshav is organized as a cooperative society for agricultural settlement and constitutes a unit of local government administered by the management of the society. Annually, each Moshav elects its management which comprises a managing committee, a control board, and committees for economic, social, educational, and cultural activities. The major threat to the principle of self-management is the existence of hired labor, especially in the labor-intensive Moshavim which need seasonal help and often utilize unskilled Arab labor from the West Bank.

The Kibbutz is the best known and purest self-managed community and Israel's most original contribution to communal life. There are, at present, nearly 250 Kibbutzim with a population of over 90,000—about 4 percent of the Jewish population. Their impact on the country has always been very profound.[19]

16. For an examination of the ideological basis of the cooperative movement, see Abraham Daniel, "Ideology and Reality in the Cooperative Movement," in Avrech and Giladi, eds., *Labor and Society in Israel*, pp. 120–36.

17. For an examination of the Moshav form, see Dan Giladi, "The Moshav—Changes and Prospects," in ibid., pp. 137–54.

18. The settlers are apportioned land by the National Fund and it remains formally the property of the fund. It can neither be sold nor redivided. When a family leaves the Moshav, the property is purchased by the cooperative and another family is settled in its place.

19. It is impossible to examine here all the characteristics of the Kibbutz community

Self-government and self-management are major institutions of Kibbutz life. The basis of Kibbutz administration is a weekly general meeting of the membership which formulates policy, elects officers, and supervises the working of the community. Affairs of the Kibbutz are conducted by elected committees. At any given time, no less than 50 percent of the adult membership of the Kibbutz serves on the various committees. Through rotation, almost every adult member is drawn into the management process. Not so, however, the many temporary residents (especially young volunteer workers) and the hired laborers and specialists.

A relatively recent development in Kibbutz life has been a kind of industrial revolution. Until several years ago, farming was by far the main source of income. Recently, however, most Kibbutzim have established industries, and their number has grown at a relatively high rate. There are now more than 200 industrial plants employing more than 10,000 persons, and estimates are that each Kibbutz will soon own at least one plant.[20] Of those engaged in "productive" work in the Kibbutz population, about 30 percent work in an industrial plant. In some Kibbutzim, industrial workers already constitute more than 50 percent of the working force, and in many more cases this figure is between 30 and 50 percent. The contribution of industry to the Kibbutz gross income has passed 50 percent.[21]

Behind the industrialization of the Kibbutz is the need to provide older persons and women with suitable jobs; a labor surplus in agriculture due to intensive mechanization, profit considerations, and the aim to raise living standards; and the technological orientation of many second generation Kibbutz members.

Ideally, the functioning of a Kibbutz plant would be based on the same democratic principles governing the operation of the Kibbutz as a whole. The selection of the general manager and major policies would then be made by the general assembly of the Kibbutz, and the internal affairs of the plant would be regulated by the general assembly of workers and elected committees. A recent study of 10 Kibbutz plants indicated, however, that practices varied considerably and that the actual decision-making process conformed to the ideal in only one plant.

As in the other self-managed institutions—the cooperatives and Moshavim—the Achilles heel of the participative structure in many Kibbutz plants is their hired labor. Although the percentage of hired labor varies considerably, it amounts to more than 50 percent in the aggregate. Except for a small group of experts, hired labor is usually unskilled and uneducated. Hired workers are excluded from at least part of the self-management process since they do not participate in the Kibbutz general assembly which has an important decision-making

and its impact on society. The reader is referred to Haim Darin, *The Other Society* (London: Victor Golancz, 1962); D. Leon, *The Kibbutz: A New Way of Life* (Oxford: Pergamon Press, 1969); and Joseph E. Shatil, "The Kibbutz and Israeli Society," in Avrech and Giladi, eds., *Labor and Society in Israel*, pp. 155–71.

20. Kibbutz plants are usually small. In 1971, 75 percent of them employed fewer than 50 persons and only 15 percent employed more than 100.

21. J. Buber-Agassi, "The Israeli Experience in the Democratization of Work Life," in *Sociology of Work and Occupations*, vol. 1, no. 1 (February 1974), p. 69.

role in relation to the operation of the plant.[22]

CONCLUSIONS

Although Israel is a young state, it has a relatively long tradition of worker participation in management as an expression of industrial democracy. The development of the social structure of Israel, which preceded the establishment of the state, was based to a great extent on innovative economic institutions characterized by cooperative principles. The strong trade union movement, the Kibbutz, the Moshav, the

22. The Kibbutz movement does not at all encourage employment of hired labor. In early 1977 the Kibbutz movement exerted strong pressure on one of the Kibbutzim to sell its industrial plant in which 200 out of the 220 workers were hired labor.

cooperatives, and the Labor Economy are all representative of these principles.

It is a major lesson of the Israeli experience that neither formal ownership nor the adoption of formal programs can determine the outcome of participative schemes. The long and varied experience with worker participation in Histadrut enterprises shows that for a participation program to function effectively a considerable degree of integration between labor and management at the plant level is required. The success of such programs, thus, seems to depend heavily on local conditions, and these are only beginning to be carefully examined. The paucity of empirical knowledge as compared with the abundance of ideological beliefs is not unique to the Israeli situation.

The Soviet Model of Industrial Democracy

By J. L. PORKET

ABSTRACT: Soviet-type Communist systems are organized hierarchically and are highly formalized and bureaucratized. So are their industrial relations systems and schemes of worker participation in management. Between 1953 and 1975, the Soviet Union and the Soviet-controlled countries of Eastern Europe underwent a certain measure of modernization. Nevertheless, their basic nature remained intact. The trade unions continued to be subordinate to the ruling parties, and the main forms of participation by the working people in management continued to be production conferences and socialist emulation. During the same period, the Soviet model of industrial democracy was severely challenged in Poland (1956), Hungary (1956), and Czechoslovakia (1968). In addition, Yugoslavia launched a rival model as early as 1950. While spontaneous strikes occurred only occasionally, certain apolitical or non-ideological forms of deviance remained permanent features of the Soviet-type system, ranging from lateness for work and indifferent performance through evasion and violation of formal norms to absenteeism, labor turnover, and pilferage. Although in the mid-1970s the prospect of any far-reaching reforms was bleak, the contradictions inherent to the systems had not disappeared. Consequently, they were by no means free of potential conflict.

J. L. Porket is consultant to the East European History Project at St. Antony's College, Oxford University. He holds Ph.D. degrees from Prague University (1968) and the London School of Economics (1973). Before emigration, he was engaged in research work at the Prague School of Economics. In 1969–70 he was lecturer in sociology at Brunel University, England. He is a member of the Royal Institute of International Affairs, and his publications have appeared in Czech and English.

WITHIN a few years of the end of the Second World War, Communist parties took over power in eight East European countries and began to transform the existing political, economic, social, and cultural systems according to the Soviet model. The transformation was characterized by the formalization and bureaucratization of institutions and relations, and hence by a decline in the significance of historically (organically) developed institutions and relations.

As a result of this transformation, the differences between these societies diminished and the similarities increased. However, in 1950 Yugoslavia launched a rival model, and in 1956, at the twentieth Congress of the Communist party of the Soviet Union, institutional diversity received an ideological justification, albeit merely a conditional one. Subsequently, greater diversity along national lines did assert itself. Yet, as of 1976 the systems established in the Soviet Union and in Soviet-dominated Eastern Europe (since 1961 without Albania) continued to disclose significant similarities. They were variants of a single type. Of course, that observation applies also to the autonomy, structure, and functions of the industrial relations systems.

THE POLITICAL SYSTEM

From the point of view of participation in and competition for political power, the Soviet-type Communist political system is an authoritarian system controlled and directed by the party. The party itself is controlled and directed from the top by a small group, the Presidium or Politburo. This group constitutes the party elite, has the actual monopoly of political decision making, is neither controlled by nor responsible to the people—including the party members—nor is it restrained by the law.

From the point of view of the scope of political power, this system is totalist. That is to say, the party elite is determined to control and direct all spheres of nonpolitical behavior and opinion as well. Consequently, the political and nonpolitical spheres are not separate, and the distinction between political and nonpolitical behavior and opinion tends to be blurred.

In the early 1970s, as throughout the preceding two decades, power in these countries continued to be ultimately centralized and concentrated in the hands of the respective party elites. Yet, compared with 1953, there existed three major differences.

First, the extent, scope, intensity, and brutality of coercion diminished. The system of coercion became less arbitrary and, thus, less unpredictable, and more regularized and, thus, more predictable. And its principal function shifted from initiation to deterrence and punishment. Simultaneously, greater reliance was placed on material rewards as a basis for obedience, although constant efforts to strengthen obedience based on identification with the party and regime and internalization of official values and norms persevered.

Second, political control and direction of nonpolitical behavior and opinion decreased. More contextual controls were substituted for highly prescriptive ones and, as a result, personal freedoms widened. Nevertheless, despite liberalization, the regimes were still far more totalist than liberal.

Third, pure authoritarianism was superseded by consultative authoritarianism. By invitation from the party elite, selected individuals, groups, and social categories were given the opportunity to participate in a consultative capacity in political decision making. Even broader political opportunities, amounting to a species of quasi-pluralistic authoritarianism, opened up in Hungary and to a lesser degree in Poland.

ECONOMIC MANAGEMENT

Because of its totalist orientation, the party elite in Soviet-type Communist systems rejects private ownership of the means of production and a pluralistic economy and instead prescribes social ownership of the means of production. Its basic forms are state ownership and co-operative ownership, together with central planning and management of the national economy.

Economic management by directive, relying on binding administrative orders, was introduced in the Soviet Union in the early 1930s and copied in Eastern Europe after the Second World War. On account of its demonstrated drawbacks, attempts were made in the second half of the 1950s and especially during the 1960s to modify or reform it either toward a more indirect form of directive economic management, relying on state-parametric information, or toward non-directive economic management, relying on market-parametric information. In the early 1970s, non-directive economic management went generally out of favor, and its advocacy was banned since it seemed to spell the end of the party elite's control over the economy. It was believed that the application of advanced mathematical methods and computers would modernize central planning and management, enable a

more rational allocation and utilization of scarce resources, and stimulate economic growth.

The only exception in the early 1970s was Hungary, where an indirect form of directive economic management with some elements of non-directive economic management was formally launched in January 1968. Nevertheless, the state retained the right to issue administrative orders and did intervene directly in the micro-economic sphere. Moreover, Hungary's New Economic Mechanism (NEM) produced its domestic critics, supported by powerful voices in other Communist countries, and already in 1972 a partial recentralization of economic management took place. In March 1975, the Hungarian party Congress emphasized the need to reassert state and party control in all spheres of life.

As one would expect, central planning and management are organized hierarchically. In the early 1970s, the hierarchy of central planning and management in the various countries consisted of the following levels: the party elite, the government, the State Planning Commission, economic ministries, associations, and individual enterprises. The party elite determined the main lines of economic development. The government and the State Planning Commission transformed these political decisions into statewide economic plans. Economic ministries ensured execution of their portions of the plans by subordinate units. Associations and enterprises executed assigned tasks.

Throughout, the principle of democratic centralism continued to be applied to the economic sphere. This meant that central planning and management were combined with a grant of adequate executive rights to lower organs and with participation by lower organs in the preparation of decisions made by higher organs. But participation was required to be in accord with entrusted rights and responsibilities and to respect the interests of society as a whole, as defined by the party elite.

The principle of one-man management also remained in force. It meant that one individual, the enterprise director, was in full charge of the day-to-day running of the enterprise, being responsible for it to the superior organ which had appointed him. The only exception was Romania where, in 1968, collective management was adopted.

Just as the party elite does not relinquish control over the economy, so it retains control over the industrial relations system. This system, too, is organized hierarchically. At the macro level, the main actors are the party elite, the government, the trade union leadership, and the working masses. At the enterprise level, the main actors are the enterprise director, the enterprise party committee, the enterprise trade union committee, and the workforce. The operating rules are made unilaterally by the party elite.

MAIN FEATURES OF TRADE UNIONS

In Soviet-type Communist systems, trade unions are a unified mass organization with a nominally voluntary membership, authorized by law to represent both members and non-members.[1] Theoretically, they are independent, that is, neither party nor state organizations. Nevertheless, in their constitutions they acknowledge the leading role of the party, and in practice their autonomy is low or, at best, moderate.

Because trade unions are regarded as a unified mass organization, their members are not allowed to split off from existing unions and form new ones, either within or outside the official trade unions. Any other policy would endanger the unity of the official trade unions and eventually even the principle of "one plant—one trade union organization." And in time it would increase the articulation of group interests, conflicts of interest, and popular pressure on enterprise management as well as the regime.

Traditionally, the two main functions assigned to trade unions in Soviet-type Communist systems have been promotion of production and political indoctrination. Another but limited function is the defense of workers' interests. Additional functions include participation in management, supervision of management's observance of labor legislation and health and safety regulations, industrial training, cultural activities, physical training, and the administration of social insurance.

To perform their manifold functions, the trade unions are endowed with extensive rights. First, they have the right to make suggestions. Second, they have the right of prior consultation, without their viewpoints being binding on the competent decision makers. This means, inter alia, the right to participate in the drafting of economic plans at all levels. Third, they have the right of codecision in the sense that certain decisions may come into force only with their consent. At the enterprise level, this applies to the introduction or change of the wage system and of output norms, the setting of the total size of the labor

1. In the Soviet Union in 1973, 97.6 percent of blue-collar and white-collar workers were trade union members. E. A. Ivanov, *Profsoyuzy v politicheskoi sisteme sotsializma* (Moscow: Profizdat, 1974), p. 40.

force, and so on. Fourth, they have the right of supervision over the observance of labor legislation and of health and safety regulations. Fifth, they have a right of decision, but this is confined nearly exclusively to internal trade union matters such as the distribution of enterprise funds allotted for social and cultural purposes. Sixth, they have the right to conclude collective agreements. However, these agreements are not, and under directive economic management cannot be, a result of collective bargaining in the proper sense; both the conclusion and content of agreements are regulated by legal norms and directives laid down by superior organs.

In sum, although in the early 1970s trade unions enjoyed theoretically extensive formal rights, their meaningful assertion was severely circumscribed by the nature of the environment in which they operated. Yet, compared with 1953, some differences did exist. At the societal level, trade unions were given the opportunity to participate in a consultative capacity in political decision making. Greater emphasis was put on their welfare functions. And at the enterprise level, trade unions were allowed to protect the workers, albeit within strictly defined limits.

PARTICIPATION IN MANAGEMENT[2]

Verbally, the party elite is an ardent advocate of mass participation, and every citizen has both a right and a duty to participate in the daily business of society. In the economic sphere, declares the official ideology, the application of the

principle of democratic centralism means that central planning and management are combined with participation by the working people in management. Moreover, the objective need to consolidate and incessantly improve central planning and management is coupled with incessant deepening of participation by the working people in management. On the other hand, the party repeatedly warns that industrial democracy cannot be opposed to state guidance.

In practice, the party elite strictly regulates participation in management, as it does participation generally. It requires active and responsible participation but permits only participation organized and controlled from above and rejects spontaneous and uncontrolled participation. Expressed differently, no one is allowed to participate in management without a license, without official sponsorship.

Participation by the working people in management is both indirect (through functionaries and committees of the primary party organization, the trade union organization, the youth organization, and the like) and direct.

INDIRECT PARTICIPATION

As a rule, a primary party organization embraces only a minority of the personnel. Yet, it is conceived as the leading force in the enterprise ensuring the consistent assertion of the party line. Over the years, the officially defined scope of the rights of the primary party organizations and the officially required intensity of their activities have varied. Sometimes they were criticized for laxity and at other times for excessive activism.

In the early seventies, the necessity of enhancing the influence of

2. J. L. Porket, "Participation in Management in Communist Systems in the 1970s," *British Journal of Industrial Relations*, vol. 13, no. 3 (November 1975), pp. 371–87.

the primary party organizations was emphasized in the several countries. But the tasks assigned to them were contradictory. While they were expected to supervise enterprise management without substituting for it, simultaneously they were generally required to assist enterprise directors and managers in fulfilling their economic duties.

Although the primary party organizations were to refrain from interfering in the work of enterprise management, in practice they often did interfere. The actual role played by the primary party organization in the enterprise raises, of course, the perennial problem of one-man management versus collective management. The more a primary party organization interferes in management and substitutes for managers, the less the principle of one-man management is implemented in practice.

The same problem inheres to relations between the enterprise management and the enterprise trade union committee. As mentioned above, the latter has the right to receive information, to protest decisions, to make suggestions, to be consulted, to supervise, and to codecide. On top of that, it may even have the right of veto.

Yet, in practice, participation by these committees in management is restricted by the nature of directive economic management, by the content of legal norms, and by their position as an element of a hierarchical structure controlled and directed by the party. All in all, their participation in management actually amounts to participation in administration, not in policy making.

DIRECT PARTICIPATION

The main forms of direct participation are production conferences and socialist emulation. Both are organized and guided by the trade unions.

Production conferences are usually confined to the workshop and departmental levels in order to enlist active involvement of the greatest possible number of workers. At the plant and enterprise levels, general meetings and conferences of the personnel may be convened from time to time. In such cases, however, the agenda tends to consist only of reports prepared in advance, and discussion is either limited or excluded entirely.

Besides production conferences, so-called permanent production conferences can also be found. They were set up in the Soviet Union in 1958 and in the German Democratic Republic (GDR) in 1959 as elected trade union organs operating at different levels within the enterprise. Permanent production conferences are to deal with matters concerning technology, production, and labor productivity. According to the GDR Labour Code of 1961, for instance, they were to cooperate in the preparation, fulfillment, and supervision of the enterprise plan; to examine critically the organization of production; to draw attention to shortcomings and help in eliminating them; and to submit proposals with a view to achieving the best possible results at work.

In the past, their performance was often considered unsatisfactory, and they were repeatedly accused of formalism. On the other hand, many an enterprise director saw their main function to be the strengthening of work discipline.

The number of permanent production conferences in the Soviet Union rose from 104,000 in 1959 to 162,000 in 1971, when over 6 million workers served on them.[3] In the GDR, the number of workers serving on them reached 434,000 by the early seventies.[4]

Socialist emulation assumes various forms, including the movement of socialist work brigades and the movement of innovators (rationalizers, inventors). Although moral as well as material incentives are to be applied in its development, the primary emphasis is on the former, on the mobilization of the workers for increasing labor productivity.

At first sight, socialist emulation seems impressive. Over 80 million Soviet workers took part in it in 1974,[5] and in Czechoslovakian plants more than 80 percent of the personnel in the early 1970s.[6] In the GDR, in 1973, precisely 3,412,291 workers competed for the title of "Collective of Socialist Work," and 26.4 percent of all persons employed in state enterprises were involved in the innovators' movement.[7] Yet, as frequent official complaints of formalism in socialist emulation suggest, its results are less satisfactory.

OTHER FORMS OF PARTICIPATION

Other forms of participation by the working people in management may also exist. For example, in connection with the economic reforms of the 1960s, several countries set up production committees at enterprise level and sometimes at higher levels. Their role was purely advisory and supervisory. In their composition, appointed and ex officio members predominated, while elected representatives of the personnel were in a minority. In the GDR, where they were introduced in 1963 and abolished in 1971, there were 160 of them in the larger enterprises in the mid-1960s, and 3,500 persons served on them.[8]

Collective agreements have already been mentioned. They must be recalled again, though, because they are also regarded as one of the forms of participation.

Whichever forms of participation in management are allowed, the party elite unwaveringly disowns the idea of workers' councils elected by and responsible to all persons employed in the enterprise. In the early 1970s, they were found only in Poland. There they were incorporated in the so-called workers' self-management conferences (composed of the members of the workers' council, the enterprise trade union committee, the enterprise party committee, and committees of some other organizations), their rights were limited, and their activities were often purely formal.

The party elite rejects workers' councils for two reasons. First, being legitimized from below, they would be independent bodies, not elements of a hierarchical structure. Consequently, even under directive economic management they could exert greater pressure on superior organs than the enterprise director, the primary party organization, and the trade union organization are able

3. L. Khitrov, "The Role of Management and Workers in Raising the Efficiency of Soviet Industry," *International Labour Review*, vol. 111, no. 6 (June 1975), pp. 521.

4. *Introducing the GDR*, 2d rev. ed. (Dresden: Verlag Zeit im Bild, 1971), p. 61.

5. *KPSS o profsoyuzakh* (Moscow: Profizdat, 1974), p. xvii.

6. That included over one million workers taking part in the movement of socialist work brigades. Lubomír Procházka, *Strana a společenské organizace*, Nová mysl, vol. 28, no. 2 (1974), pp. 195–206.

7. *Statistisches Jahrbuch der Deutschen Demokratischen Republik 1975*, pp. 66–7.

8. *Introducing the GDR*, p. 61.

to do and, thus, defend more effectively the economic interests of the enterprise. Second, if they were introduced, a significant difference between the Soviet and Yugoslav models of enterprise management and industrial relations would be obliterated.

To conclude, in Soviet-type Communist systems, the theory and practice of participation diverge. In theory, participation is hailed as a significant contribution to socialist democracy, and it is said to be growing incessantly. On the other hand, in practice it is restricted by the nature of directive economic management and the industrial relations system and by the content of legal norms. In some cases, it actually amounts to participation in the implementation of the decisions made, not participation in decision making itself. Expressed differently, it is both highly formalized (that is, regulated by formal norms), and, hence, bureaucratized, and affected by the unpredictable interference of superior organs in the day-to-day running of enterprises.

For the rank and file, participation in management is both direct and indirect. Insofar as it is direct, it mostly means to receive selected information, to protest decisions, to make suggestions, to be consulted, and possibly to supervise, and tends to be confined to operational matters, technical issues, trivia, and routine decisions. Yet, despite its limitations, it may be of importance to the individual worker if through it he can influence his tasks and working conditions in the way he desires.

From the point of view of the distribution and exertion of power within the enterprise, indirect worker participation is of greater significance—that is, through func-

tionaries and committees of the primary party organization, the trade union organization, the youth organization, and the like. However, such participation is not sufficiently responsive to and representative of the rank and file.

DEVIANCE, PROTEST, CONFLICT

Available evidence suggests that not all workers in Soviet-type Communist systems are satisfied with existing industrial relations, working conditions, and material rewards. Their behavior shows it. Responsibility is at least partly attributable to the failure of trade unions to defend and assert the interests of their members; to their display of excessive submissiveness to enterprise management, the state, and the party; and to the absence of internal union democracy.

Given the relatively tight controls on overt protest, working people express discontent by lateness for work, prolonged breaks, indifferent performance, drinking during working hours, working-to-rule, evasion and violation of formal norms, quitting early, malingering, absenteeism, thefts of tools and materials, passivity and non-attendance at obligatory meetings and production conferences, and a high rate of labor turnover.

They do occasionally engage in spontaneous strikes, though these are usually of short duration and confined to sub-units of an enterprise. On at least four occasions, however—Czechoslovakia, 1953; the GDR, 1953; Poland, 1970 and 1976 —they expressed themselves through rebellions. And on three occasions— Poland, 1956; Hungary, 1956; Czechoslovakia, 1968—they responded by attempting to modify or transform the existing system.

Thus, tensions do exist and conflicts do occur within enterprises. Yet, because the conflicts take place in an environment created and maintained by the party elite, in most cases their objects are merely particular matters, not general ones, and their resolution has to be in conformity with the law and, ultimately, with the party elite's will.

CONCLUSION

Between 1953 and 1975, the Communist systems in Eastern Europe underwent a process of modernization. Nevertheless, they continued to be organized hierarchically and to be highly formalized and bureaucratized.

In contrast to the mid-1960s, the prospect in the mid-1970s of any far-reaching economic and political reforms was bleak. In each of the countries, power continued to be exercised by forces with vested interests in the maintenance of the system. On top of that, any kind of major change depended upon the consent of the Soviet Union.

On the surface, the systems were stable and their regimes and ruling party elites secure, particularly in the case of the Soviet Union. But they were characterized by four major contradictions inherent to Soviet-type Communist systems.

One contradiction is between authoritarianism and political pluralism. While the regime is authoritarian and bars factionalism and groupism within the party and political opposition outside it, the formal political culture contains both bureaucratic-elitist and democratic-egalitarian values. In addition, the actual political culture includes political subcultures favoring substantive participation in political decision making and, at least in some of the countries discussed, also political countercultures.

A second contradiction is between centralization and decentralization of the national economy, that is, between central planning and management and the autonomy of enterprises. Although economic efficiency requires the latter, the party elite has obstinately stuck to the former because it is unwilling to lose control over the economy.

Still another contradiction is between professional management and worker participation in management at the enterprise level. In a way, this is evidenced by relations among the enterprise director, the primary party organization, and the trade union organization. But it does not stop there. A number of factors tend to substantiate professional management. On the other hand, many workers desire a kind of participation in management that would be capable of defending and asserting their interests.

The fourth contradiction is between the long-term interests of the national economy and the short-term interests of the workers. The party elite gives priority to investment and social consumption. In contrast, quite a few workers are concerned mainly with their immediate incomes. The material rewards often do not meet their rising expectations even though, paradoxically, the party elite itself has contributed to that very rise in expectations.

At the time of writing (end of 1976), the party elites were able to contain the contradictions so they could not really come into the open. However, more than ever before, consumerism is at present widespread among the population. The average individual concentrates on his material comfort and personal interests and conforms predominantly on the bases of utilitarianism (in order to attain certain specific material rewards) and coercion. Mass loyalties are gained largely through the regime's ability to guarantee job security, to provide stable and growing incomes, and to deliver desired goods and services, as well as through the extent of its non-interference with personal conduct. Consequently, if the party elite were to reduce the population's capabilities abruptly and drastically, for example by lowering the standard of living, while expectations remained the same, the resulting dissatisfaction could potentially lead to an explosive situation, as almost happened in Poland in mid-1976.

Yet, protest that is voiced mainly in a spontaneous and unorganized way would most probably result not in changes of the system but, at best, in a temporary retraction of the unpopular decisions, as shown by the reaction of the Polish leadership. Such actions are not likely to bring about and assure permanent liberalization and democratization of Soviet-type Communist systems.

Self-Management in Yugoslavia

By MARIUS J. BROEKMEYER

ABSTRACT: Yugoslav self-management is a complicated and far-reaching system of industrial relations and social organization that began some 25 years ago in a society that was initially still of the Soviet-type. It endeavors to eliminate any domination of nonproducers in the economy and society (the liberation of labor) through a decision-making structure that is neither a compromise nor a mixture of Western-type and Soviet-type industrial relations. The system has been steadily extended to encompass the individual worker, who in the process has ostensibly been acquiring ever more rights. However, in reality the power position of the individual worker has not changed all that much. The political party structures were, and still are, of paramount importance. On behalf of self-management it may be said that it has certainly alleviated the ills usually inherent to industrialization, that it has facilitated the transformation of a predominantly agrarian to an industrial society, and that it has encouraged a certain measure of political democratization. But it has not resolved basic economic differences between the several republics of Yugoslavia, nor has it diminished large-scale unemployment. It is difficult to conclude whether the achievements and shortcomings are attributable to general human failings or whether they are due to specific Yugoslav conditions.

Marius J. Broekmeyer is a staff member of the East Europe Institute of the University of Amsterdam. He studied Slavic languages and law at the Universities of Groningen, Amsterdam, and Zagreb, Yugoslavia, and wrote his doctoral dissertation on "Workers Councils in Yugoslavia, 1950–1965." In January 1970 he organized an international symposium on Yugoslav self-management attended by Yugoslav and Western specialists. The proceedings were published under the title Yugoslav Workers' Self-Management *(1970). He is also coauthor (with J. J. Ramondt) of a case study on self-management in the Yugoslav Natron works at Maglaj.*

IN MOST countries the industrial relations system reflects more or less faithfully the state of prevailing political and economic conditions. This truism operates in reverse, as it were, in the case of Yugoslavia where the overall political and social set-up is modeled on the principles of the system of self-management that is supposed to govern relations in industry. Indeed, Yugoslav industrial relations form the very heart of the country's system of government and society.[1]

It is extremely difficult to discuss properly Yugoslav industrial relations in their own right, because to do it well one should take into account other spheres of Yugoslav public and private life as well. That, however, is precluded here for reasons of space. There is also a second difficulty. Because the principles and assumptions underlying the organization of Yugoslav industrial relations—the self-management system—are so closely interwoven with, and have to such a large degree permeated, the total political and social make-up of the country, any criticism of industrial relations is almost automatically interpreted as a criticism of the very foundations of Yugoslav society. On the other hand, certain groups in Western countries are so keenly on the lookout for more humane and ideologically more acceptable patterns of industrial relations that, given their hostility to the existing order in the

West and their disillusionment with Soviet-style methods, they tend to accept unconditionally every facet of the Yugoslav system. We shall try to guard against both excessive enthusiasm and unwarranted criticism.

Yugoslavia's philosophy of industrial relations is based on the assumption that neither the state, as in Soviet-type societies, nor the private owners, as in capitalist societies, shall decide how industry is to be run and how production relations are to be arranged, but instead the workers shall manage their own affairs.[2] Included in "their own affairs" are all decisions concerning the way enterprises are to be managed and production is to be organized. With some restrictions and modifications that are due to the specific nature of the services performed, the same holds true for relations in the operation of other institutions, such as the social security, educational, and health care systems.

To achieve this, from an ethical point of view, lofty goal, all personnel employed in enterprises (blue- and white-collar employees alike) elect from their midst a workers council. The council acts as a kind of enterprise parliament, deciding on general policies, appointing specialists to key posts, and supervising the work of the executive organs of the

1. Without being able to go into details here, it should be noted that the development and maturing of self-management occurred in a society characterized by (1) large economically underdeveloped areas; (2) the presence of several different and to some extent competitive nationalities and cultures; (3) a moderate form of one-party dictatorship; (4) a commitment in principle to the operation of a free market, with competition between individual enterprises.

2. There was a sharp discussion some years ago on the question of who is a worker and how should one define the term "working class." Official Yugoslav self-management theoreticians switched at that time to the term "working people." They explained that the term had to be broad enough for the bureaucracy and the politicians to be included in it. Of course, the change was very convenient: attacks on bureaucrats can now be regarded as attacks on the system itself, in the same category as attacks on the workers.

enterprise. A management board and director complete the administrative structure of the enterprise, or at least did so during the earliest phase of Yugoslav industrial relations, the phase of representative democracy.

THE MAIN DIRECTIONS

The Yugoslav system has now been in operation for some 25 years, a span sufficiently long to enable one to draw certain conclusions. In the course of these 25 years, the system developed in three directions, interconnected but distinguishable one from another. First, ever more people in industry became involved in some sort of decision making. Because the workers council was physically unable to oversee all details of administration in the enterprise, many auxiliary commissions and committees were set up to prepare decisions for the workers council. These committees were also at times given executive powers.

Second, the self-management organs assumed more powers by gradually eliminating influences coming from outside the enterprise, for example from government or the ruling party. The acquisition of enterprise autonomy developed parallel with the gradual development of a market economy and fostered the individuality and independence of enterprises.

Third, the system gradually extended to the smaller and smallest enterprise units. In the beginning, certain self-management rights had been given to only two or three of the largest departments in the enterprise, with ultimate power remaining vested in the workers council constituted for the enterprise as a whole. Subsequently, however, self-management rights were also bestowed on what were called economic units, and most recently they have been given to the smallest units for which separate financial accounts are kept and whose production performance can be measured. These subenterprise units are called Basic Organizations of Associated Labor (BOAL). Thus, self-management is henceforth to be performed at the lowest feasible level, and only the powers that cannot be exercised at that level may be wielded at the next higher level. In other words, the enterprise is no longer to be regarded as divided from above into a number of units; instead it is the units at the base— the BOALs—which decide to form an enterprise. This conspicuous development in extending self-managing rights as far downward as possible is in accordance with the philosophy that professes as its goal that every man shall decide, for himself and with his fellow citizens and workers, what is to be his part in industrial and public affairs.

In 1959–1960 the present writer happened to be present in a modern Yugoslav enterprise when the decentralizing movement first got underway. Making due allowance for possible preconceived opinions and for possible windowdressing, he continues to this day to be impressed by the creative forces set free at that time in a process that gave wide decision-making powers to ordinary workers.

RECENT TRENDS

Around 1970, however, when the self-managed enterprise was about to acquire an even more substantial amount of independence and it seemed that the ruling Communist party would limit even further its supervisory role in favor of the correspondingly increased autonomy of self-managed organizations, the authorities became concerned over the continually growing social and economic differences between different regions, between branches of industry, and between the several enterprises in the same branch. They also expressed worry over the growing influence of so-called technocratic tendencies exhibited by enterprise directors and managers. In support of such concerns, it was pointed out that the percentage of manual workers represented in self-management bodies had been declining precipitously in workers councils, management boards, party committees, and the assemblies of communal, republican, and federal bodies.[3] At about the same time when nationalist forces, especially in Croatia but not only in that republic, gained momentum and popular support after initially having been encouraged by the highest party organs in the country to come to the fore, the Central Committee of the League of Communists suddenly realized that events might take a course contrary to the interests and will of the party. Marshall Tito said at the time that the party had allowed the reins of power to slip from its hands and it needed to restore its influence by first of all reassuming control over personnel policy, that is, the appointment of persons to important posts. Although many Yugoslav and foreign observers had earlier assumed that the power of the party would gradually wither away while

self-management bodies would take over, the resulting purge in effect restored the old order. In the process, many politicians, judges, teachers, professors, journalists, enterprise directors, and editors lost their jobs.

In the years immediately after these events, which became years of tightened controls, hardened party policy, restored party powers, and vanishing public criticism, a campaign was launched with a direct bearing on industrial relations. Its slogans were: "The working class must have the decisive voice everywhere" and "A workers' majority in all decision-making bodies." Yet, in fact, the purpose of the campaign was to bring self-management again under the direction of the party. The campaign culminated in the adoption, in November 1976, of a mammoth act (95 pages of small print, containing 671 articles) called the Law on Associated Labor.

Until the adoption of the 1976 act, the self-management rights of Yugoslav workers were restricted to enterprise affairs. They did not extend, for example, to such areas as the financing of education, medical care, and social security. These services were financed centrally by the state out of taxes, although the employees and the users of these service institutions participated in their administration. Yugoslav theoreticians on self-management had long maintained that as long as the financing of social services remained separated from individual workers, the latter were deprived of influence over an important part of their income. The new law stipulates that each enterprise (or part of an enterprise) will negotiate the amount and cost of the services to be provided with the corresponding

---

3. Left-wing philosophers, sociologists, and students have for years sharply criticized not only the emerging nationalism in the different regions, but also tendencies indicating the increasing influence of the middle class.

self-management bodies of the social service institutions. This arrangement is called the free exchange of labor between the self-management organs of different branches of social activity. Thus, the norm-setting activity of the state and the regulatory influence of state organs are to be replaced in these spheres by self-managing agreements and self-managing compacts resulting from negotiations between self-managing bodies. The way in which enterprise income is formed and distributed, as well as the allocation of personal incomes (wages), will also be determined through such agreements and compacts. Specific prices must also be determined in this way.

It is clear that the new system will require an enormous amount of negotiating, that it will be a very time-consuming process, and that it will necessitate the establishment of numerous committees, commissions, and boards. When we add that each enterprise is legally obliged to draw up an enterprise statute; that each Basic Organization of Associated Labor must draft its own written regulations; that the BOALs are supposed to enter into business relations with other BOALs; and that trade unions, local authorities, and chambers of commerce will also be engaged in the drawing up of social compacts, it is clear that the running of a self-managed society is likely to be a somewhat strenuous affair.

RECRUITMENT

It is, in any event, obvious that such a system requires people willing to serve on all sorts of representative boards and bodies. The length of their term of service is limited by law to one or two years. This limita-

tion is necessary, so it is argued, lest the representatives become too accustomed to the perquisites of their posts and to the powers they exercise. A healthy development of self-management is believed dependent on continuous rotation. This view, of course, presupposes the existence of an adequate number of qualified people, a rather doubtful assumption.

As far as top level posts are concerned, capable representatives to fill them are very scarce. At lower levels, the levels of rank and file workers and employees, people tend to look on their posts in self-management bodies as a burden they must perform, at least after the initial period when the first enthusiasm of sitting on a decision-making board has subsided. (One should not forget that self-management in Yugoslavia was imposed from above.) In any event, it has become a problem to induce people each year or two to accept membership in one of the numerous bodies of self-management. Despite or perhaps because of the rapid turnover, there is also a hard core of committee members who rotate from one self-managing body to another, from party committee to workers council, and from enterprise executive board to trade union committee. It may well be impossible to staff the necessary bodies without these professional self-managers, but their constant presence adds to the feeling of ordinary members that they are not actually making the decisions.

REWARDS

Willingness to participate depends partly on the rewards, but they are few indeed. The sense of cooperating with others in an effort to reach an agreed goal may be one. An unintended but very real reward is the chance to be promoted because of work performed on some board. But there are also negative rewards. Self-management duties are generally performed after ordinary working hours. The work is not paid. While others may leave for their homes, board members must sit and listen to tedious procedures and monologues that sometimes extend for hours. When unpopular measures must be taken, fellow workers become resentful. Moreover, as the Belgrade newspaper *Politika* wrote on January 7, 1977, of the 4.7 million working people in the country about 3 million hold a second job. People with a second job are not very prone to participate in self-management. Besides, a physical presence at council and board meetings is only one aspect of self-management. Another is the time required to read the materials, to prepare reports, to form opinions. These, too, can be exceedingly time-consuming activities.

EXPERTISE

The making of important decisions in the workers councils and other self-management bodies raises new problems. During the meetings, the specialists, who may be nonmembers of the council, are present. If necessary they are called on to explain the proposals submitted by management. To be sure, the proposals may already have been debated in specialized subcommittees of the workers council, but there, too, the specialists have a very important say. Occasionally a workers council member asks a question. The specialist's answer may be long and not always easily understandable. The evident inequality of the participants in the decision-making process is often a source of frustration, for both sides to be sure: for workers because they must pronounce themselves on problems without always being able to see possible implications, results, or alternatives; for specialists because of the need to explain the same issues over and over again to new self-managers. The frustration of self-managers will, of course, become even greater when a proposal adopted with their support turns out to have been detrimental to the enterprise. The specialists will then seek to shift the responsibility to the workers council by emphasizing that their proposal was officially endorsed.

Some observers of the Yugoslav system maintain that there is an unbridgeable gap between expertise and democracy because the specialists are almost always in a minority when decisions are made by vote. This is especially true in cases where people resist arguments and where diverging interests exist between various work groups, with the result that not every group strives for the same goals.

This point leads to another phenomenon—industrial conflicts and strikes in self-managed enterprises. In the beginning of self-management, it was the official view that strikes could not occur. After some time, however, strikes became more or less accepted as a reality, though an undesirable one. When a strike occurs, it is often directed against the management of the enterprise, including of course the top levels of self-management bodies and possibly also trade union and party leaders. Most strikes last only several hours or a few days. As a rule, the authorities are quick to give in to demands, for a strike hurts the image of self-management as the dominant institution in society. It also tends to undermine the fiction that the enterprise director has a united workforce behind him.

Self-management notwithstanding, it seems that the actual power structure in Yugoslav enterprises has not changed very much. Time and again Yugoslav and foreign researchers have found that workers still perceive the existing power structure as a descending line which runs from the director through the workers council down to the worker.

Is Yugoslav self-management, then, a fascinating innovation but a serious mistake? That would be jumping to the wrong conclusion, although there are good reasons to believe that the more far-reaching intentions and pretensions of self-management have not been met in practice. In fact, the disjunction between reality and professed goals may even be growing. Nevertheless, self-management should be judged by what it has achieved, and some of its achievements are quite impressive.

In the first place, self-management seemingly responds to some fundamental human needs. At least nowadays, people do want to be informed at an early stage of changes that are likely to affect them, and they do want to be informed on how decisions of vital importance to them are implemented. They are interested in how their "superiors" are chosen, and they want to be asked their opinion about important enterprise matters. One Yugoslav sociologist has put it this way: participation diminishes the meaninglessness of work, although it does not diminish the powerlessness of the worker. Second, self-management has provided a new mechanism for upward social mobility, a very important element in a developing society. Third, self-management has taught many workers at least some rudimentary notions about the structure of the enterprise, the economy, and society as a whole. Fourth, during the period of self-managed industrial relations, considerable parts of Yugoslavia have been industrialized. This transition from an agricultural to a semi-industrial modern society has occurred without severe convulsions. There have been no famines, no bloody clashes between workers and the police, as for example in Poland, and no widespread misery as in so many other countries. On the contrary, Yugoslavia has managed a smoother transition to industrialization than either Western or Eastern Europe experienced. Moreover, the transition took place more rapidly than elsewhere. Finally, the self-management structures have constituted a serviceable instrument for the still unfinished task of democratization. In the past, there was even reason to believe that the economic democracy of self-management would eventually lead to political democracy. But on this point various observers, myself included, went wrong, as the events of the last few years have demonstrated.

There are, of course, also negative sides. Self-management has not been able to prevent the exodus of more than a million Yugoslav workers to look for work in Western Europe, while at home considerable unemployment continues to persist. Nor could industrial relations under self-management prevent the growth of social differentiation, as shown for example by several sociological investigations on housing conditions which point to the existence of social segregation. There are now separate residential quarters for workers and the enterprise elite. Belgrade's elite quarter, Dedinje, has its counterpart in many other Yugoslav towns. Some observers have even argued that self-management, which ties the interests of the worker to his enterprise, tends to break the unity of the working class (if there is such a unity and if it can be broken). The trade unions, generally not held in high esteem by the workers, are either unable or unwilling to compensate for that loss.

It is very difficult to know exactly to what extent self-managed industrial relations are responsible for the positive and negative outcomes. It would certainly be wrong to ascribe only the positive developments to self-management and to attribute the negative ones to isolated instances where self-management did not work. It is equally difficult to determine whether self-management has been impeded by the economic, social, and educational differences among the several Yugoslav republics or whether, on the contrary, these differences actually require a sort of self-management. Even more crucial is the question of whether self-management has been hindered by the existence of a Communist party which, notwithstanding continuous reorganization in its own make-up, maintains an authoritarian line of command. Or is it the very presence of such a party that has enabled self-management to work at all?

One certain lesson may be drawn: it is very dangerous to draw a lesson from the Yugoslav experience, fascinating though the experiment is to observe.

PUBLICATIONS FROM UNITED NATIONS

NEW SOURCES OF ENERGY
Proceedings of the United Nations Conference on the New Sources of Energy. Reprinted in 1974 and 1976. Each volume is fully illustrated with charts, tables and photographs.

Volume 1	General Sessions	Order No.E/F.63.I.2	$12.00
Volume 2	Geothermal Energy I	Order No.E/F.63.I.36	$18.00
Volume 3	Geothermal Energy II	Order No.E/F.63.I.37	$20.00
Volume 4	Solar Energy I	Order No.E/F.63.I.38	$20.00
Volume 5	Solar Energy II	Order No.E/F.63.I.39	$16.00
Volume 6	Solar Energy III	Order No.E/F.63.I.40	$16.00
Volume 7	Windpower	Order No.E/F.63.I.41	$16.00

ENERGY CRISIS AND THE FUTURE
Order No.E.75.XV.RR/21 $ 4.00

PETROLEUM IN THE 1970s: REPORT OF AD HOC PANEL OF EXPERTS ON PROJECTIONS OF DEMAND AND SUPPLY OF CRUDE PETROLEUM AND PRODUCTS
Order No.E.74.II.A.1 $ 8.00

MINERAL RESOURCES OF LOWER MEKONG BASIN AND ADJACENT AREAS OF KHMER REPUBLIC, LAOS, THAILAND AND REPUBLIC OF VIETNAM
Order No.E.72.II.F.12 $ 3.50

PROCEEDINGS OF THE FOURTH SYMPOSIUM ON DEVELOPMENT OF PETROLEUM RESOURCES OF ASIA AND THE FAR EAST (MINERAL RESOURCES DEVELOPMENT SERIES NO. 41)

VOLUME I: REPORT OF THE SYMPOSIUM; DOCUMENTS ON REVIEW OF PROGRESS IN THE PETROLEUM INDUSTRY AND IN PETROLEUM GEOLOGY
Order No.E.73.II.F.14 $16.00

VOLUME 2: DOCUMENTS ON PETROLEUM EXPORTATION AND EXPLOITATION METHODS AND TECHNIQUES, AND TRANSPORTATION AND UTILIZATION OF OIL AND NATURAL GAS
Order No.E.73.II.F.14 $10.00

VOLUME 3: ECONOMICS, TECHNICAL TRAINING; UNITED NATIONS ASSISTANCE, PETROLEUM LEGISLATION, POLLUTION BY PETROLEUM PRODUCTS
Order No.E.73.II.F.14 $ 7.00

REPORT OF THE UNITED NATIONS CONFERENCE ON THE HUMAN ENVIRONMENT
Order No.E.73.II.A.14 $ 4.00

WORLD ENERGY SUPPLIES 1950-1974
Order No.E.76.XVII.5 $38.00

OIL AND NATURAL GAS MAP OF ASIA AND THE FAR EAST
Order No.E.74.I.3 $27.50

PROCEEDINGS OF THE SEMINAR ON PETROLEUM LEGISLATION WITH PARTICULAR REFERENCE TO OFFSHORE OPERATIONS
Order No.E.73.II.F.13 $ 4.00

ELECTRICITY COSTS AND TARIFFS: A GENERAL STUDY
Order No.E.72.II.A.5 $ 5.00

LEGAL AND ADMINISTRATIVE FRAMEWORKS FOR ELECTRICITY ENTERPRISES
Order No.E.73.II.A.1 $ 3.00

PROBLEMS OF MEETING PEAK ELECTRICITY DEMANDS: A GENERAL STUDY
Order No.E.73.II.A.8 $ 6.00

INCREASED ENERGY ECONOMY AND EFFICIENCY IN THE ECE REGION
Order No.E.75.II.E.2 $ 6.00

PROCEEDINGS OF THE INTERGOVERNMENTAL MEETING ON IMPACT OF THE CURRENT ENERGY CRISIS ON ECONOMY OF THE ESCAP REGION
Order No.E.75.II.F.7 $10.00

United Nations Publications
Room LX-2300
New York, N.Y. 10017

or

United Nations Publications
Palais des Nations
1211 Geneva 10, Switzerland

Book Department

INTERNATIONAL RELATIONS

ARTHUR MACY COX. *The Dynamics of Detente: How to End the Arms Race.* Pp. 256. New York: W. W. Norton & Co., 1976. $8.95.

Arthur Cox argues that detente is worthwhile and achievable—despite opposition on both sides. He believes that the arms race is dangerous and wasteful. (Cox estimates that each side can save up to $25 billion per year [p. 96].) According to him ultimate control over the situation lies in Washington: "The arms race will end when the U.S. decides to end it" (p. 202).

Cox admits that persuading the Soviets to cease threatening U.S. security through covert support of revolution will not be easy (p. 217). But he concludes that "the majority opinion of the Moscow leadership favors detente" (p. 224), and that "though the hawks may insist that the ideology calls for continuing support of wars of liberation, they [also] will *probably* conclude in time that the success of the Soviet economy, and perhaps their own political survival, take precedence over adventures in far off lands" (p. 219). [Emphasis added.] He dismisses the possibility of a Soviet military attack on either Western Europe or the United States, arguing that even significantly reduced Western military strength will be a sufficient deterrent for the foreseeable future (p. 213).

To curtail Soviet support for revolution Cox suggests the use of "block trading" by the West. If the Soviets did not cooperate we would refuse to provide them with the technology they badly need (p. 141). The political feasibility of this suggestion on the Western side unfortunately is not really discussed. In addition, he recommends U.S. restraint in developing and deploying new weapon systems, which he believes will generate momentum toward disarmament (pp. 230–31).

Cox presents a thought-provoking but not entirely persuasive argument. He acknowledges that the Soviets see detente differently from the West (p. 222). For one thing, they argue that it promotes wars of national-liberation by restraining American intervention. While Cox's conclusion is that the Soviets can be persuaded to change their behavior if not their rhetoric, there are several factors which might prevent this from happening. For example, the alliance of ideological conservatives, the military, heavy industry and the KGB against detente may prove to be more formidable than Cox assumes. For one thing, any negative influence of these "groupings" cannot be openly criticized in the Soviet Union. In addition, this alliance could be further strengthened in at least three ways not discussed by Cox. First, even extensive trade with the West may not save the Soviet economy, thus encouraging the Kremlin to believe that only expanding Soviet influence can protect the Soviet system. (Lenin's imperialism turned into socialist imperialism!—to borrow the Chinese phrase.) Refusal to trade with the Soviets, on the other hand, can be expected to promote the argument that the "West cannot be trusted" and that therefore Soviet security requires promoting revolution. Finally, as the Soviet Union approaches strategic parity with the U.S. and as Washington is "restrained from intervening against the national-liberation movement," the Soviet leadership may be tempted to take advantage of the "favorable shift in the correlation of forces" to actively support the flow of history—as they did after the first sputnik in 1957. It should be remembered in this connection that Moscow has not been in such a seemingly favorable position before and that Soviet leaders have "theoretical" reasons for believing that they will be more successful in using their new strength than the capitalist U.S. at the height of its power.

While Cox may believe that "the Soviet wave of the future is dead" (p. 214), the current Soviet leadership probably does not. If this is the case, then only a major change in leadership is likely to result in the type of detente and subsequent arms reduction that Cox desires. In the meantime unilateral U.S. action of the type recommended by the author could encourage Soviet leaders to take actions, such as in Angola, that might lead to disaster for both sides—as nearly happened during the 1962 Cuban missile crisis. At the very least, increased tensions could bring on a new Cold War.

One final point. Cox asserts that "those Americans who know the most about Soviet affairs are also strong supporters of detente." In this group he includes George Kennan, W. Averell Harriman and Marshal Shulman (pp. 168–69). He does not mention Zbigniew Brzezinski, Richard Pipes or Foy Kohler. All three of these men—and others—qualify as knowledgeable, and each of them would disagree with Cox on major points.

RONALD R. POPE
Illinois State University
Normal

JOHN GIMBEL. *The Origins of the Marshall Plan.* Pp. viii, 344. Stanford, Calif.: Stanford University Press, 1976. $15.00.

Since the end of World War II the subject of United States-Soviet relations has ignited an impressive accumulation of monographs and as additional records become available it is certain the historical profession will have still further studies served up to it. Among the efforts of several scholars has been the desire to examine and clarify certain mileposts in the United States as a contributing factor to the polarization of Soviet-United States relations to this most recent effort by Professor John Gimbel of Humboldt State University which explores the role of France in the onset of the armed truce which has so dominated the lives of the generation of the 1950s.

Professor Gimbel is no newcomer to this aspect of historical investigation. *The Origins of the Marshall Plan* follows his *Marburg, 1945–1952: A German Community Under American Occupation* and also his *The American Occupation of Germany: Politics and the Military, 1945–1949.* It is on the foundation of these two earlier studies that Professor Gimbel has drawn supporting evidence to correlate with fresh material in this most unique, and neo-revisionist, explanation of the conceptualization of the basic Western weaponry of the "Cold War"—the Marshall Plan.

It is the author's contention that the accepted versions of the onset of the freeze in Russian-American relations, on both sides of the debate, need reassessment. He maintains that neither Russia nor the United States deserves the indictment for the collapse of four-power occupation of Germany but rather the truculence of France brought on perhaps by anxiety. And while this stands as a departure in itself, no less is the author's contention that the Marshall Plan, while successful in most ways, began as a scratch pad scheme that mushroomed in scope as well as administration with multiple causative forces contributing to it. It most definitely, so says the author, "was not a plan conceived by long-range planners as a response to the Soviet Union or as an element in the cold war." It was, so the author's investigation would support, an attempt to intertwine the singular economic resurrection of Germany into a broader scheme for the economic recovery of the Continent, in particular the Western powers. But it was never the sophisticated, comprehensive design for a rejuvenated and possible united Europe as its mystique would suggest. It was, as Professor Gimbel satisfactorily illustrates, "a series of pragmatic bureaucratic decisions, maneuvers, compromises, and actions," replete with social, political, economic and strategic ingredients. It became more in the minds of those who supported it, or contributed to it, than existed in the germ of the idea at the start, and therein rests the value of this work apart from the originality of the author's thesis: ". . . Myths and Realities" as the author states, need reworking and reflection. All too often what lingers is the assumption rather than the fact and a book of this type can have the worth of a historical alarm clock—it alerts and arouses.

CALVIN W. HINES
Stephen F. Austin State
  University
Nacogdoches
Texas

LEON GORDENKER. *International Aid and National Decisions: Development Programs in Malawi, Tanzania, and Zambia.* Pp. 190. Princeton, N.J.: Princeton University Press, 1976. $13.00.

While the UN General Assembly, ECOSOC, and associated UN agencies increasingly generate "programmatic declarations" on UN Development Decades, World Food Plans, and New International Economic Orders to equalize economic opportunity, Leon Gordenker assesses the end results of three projects. Working from interviews done in 1966–68, he analyzes negotiations in the countries, and with New York (UNDP) and Rome (FAO) headquarters on a Zambia game park, and on Tanza-

nian and Malawi river development projects. Central to his assessment of UN influence is the role of the UNDP Resident Representative as the senior UN official in each country, and as presumably the UN coordinator. Painting a largely negative picture of the influence of UN "doctrine" and of the UNDP Country "Rep" specifically, he attributes the shortcomings to factors such as: lack of external financial leverage; lack of the UNDP Country Rep's individual status as an economist; multiplicity of donors and advisors (UN agencies, IBRD with its formidable finances, ECA, Ford, for example). As a result, he says that the UNDP Representative was limited largely to administrative management and response to requests. He knew little about UN global doctrine; and his country counterparts were not interested.

Since 1966–68, Western GNP, "trickle-down" development models have been downgraded. A new generation of African planners is planning for Africans; is beginning to plan from the "bottom up," on the expressed needs of the "poor majority"; is balancing human needs with production economics. Gordenker cites a very early, and major, example of independence in this new direction of development: Tanzania's rejection of the UN/IBRD "investment pay-off" doctrine in favor of its own Arusha doctrine in its valley development program. Yet in this logical move toward "states' rights," so to speak, global issues of population, environment, and the like, still need to be reconciled with country development programs.

Among the entrees to "marry" international and national doctrines are:

1. *Aid in Building the Political Base for "Doctrinal Change"*—The UN and other bodies can offer *welcome* cooperation to countries in areas such as the orientation of decision-makers, and the education of the public, in building the political base for the country's own and the global issues.

2. *International Years and Conferences*—Gordenker cites participation in international conferences as a bridge

between national and international leaders—and philosophies. The UN Years, and associated and unassociated country, regional, and international conferences on population, technology, and other subjects, offer an increasingly important potential in blending national and international development philosophy.

3. *Incentives*—It seems safe to assume future international revenue generation—and grants, shared revenue, and loans to countries—will be linked with global issues; but, hopefully, with latitude for the "Tanzanias" to develop their individual models.

4. *Organizational Development*— Gordenker proposes "organizational behavior theory" as another tool to facilitate UN/country, and in-country, adoption of development "doctrine." The National Training Laboratories for Applied Behavioral Science offer useful experience in that direction.

As for the UNDP Country "rep," or any other coordinator, the personality, background, and influence of the individual will always be a factor. But more important than his eminence as an economist will be his abilities, his resources, in the role of catalyst and facilitator, and his knowledge of "organizational development" and of the processes of "change." As the UNDP moves to recover from four years of a catastrophically abortive "management reform," as it operates under the fresh competition and independence among UN agencies and world regions, these qualifications will become increasingly critical.

Somewhat "dated" though it is, Gordenker's analysis still offers a useful "Gray's Anatomy" of the international-national development bureaucracy—and its pathology.

DANA D. REYNOLDS
International Center for Dynamics
of Development
Arlington
Virginia

BARUCH A. HAZEN. *Soviet Propaganda: A Case Study of the Middle East Conflict.* Pp. iii, 293. New Brunswick, N.J.: Transaction Books, 1976. $12.95.

For a work designated as a case study this book takes a long time to get to the case. It is only in the fifth of seven chapters (page 144 of 282 pages of text) that the author turns to Soviet propaganda on the Middle East conflict. The first half of the book takes up two other subjects: propaganda in general and the whole Soviet propaganda operation in particular. The volume, then, is really three longish essays on separate but related topics, and it will be treated as such in this review. Chapters 1 and 2 amount to an abstract and theoretical examination of propaganda as a process. The analysis literally teems with jargon, for example, "inputs," "absorption screen," personality screen" and the like, and the exhaustive attempt of the author to define the term propaganda seems to this reviewer unnecessary.

Chapters 3 and 4 examine the whole Soviet propaganda effort, including both the regular propaganda apparatus as well as "impregnational propaganda," which appears to mean Soviet films, exhibits, sports teams, performing arts and the like, which "concentrate on building up a positive image of the Soviet Union." The author describes this as "drilling pro-Soviet holes in the audience's absorption screen or, more probably . . . turning that screen pro-Soviet." As these quotations suggest, the analysis in part two is still freighted with jargon and unnecessary theoretical discussion. This section of the book contains much interesting information about Soviet propaganda organs such as TASS, Novosti, radio and television. In many ways, however, these chapters resemble parts of a reference work rather than a monograph. Chapter 3 is full of tables and other listings of Soviet publications having foreign propaganda purposes, foreign language radio broadcast schedules, and like material. Very few readers will be willing or able to absorb this material, while the interested specialist is likely to want to go back to the original sources.

Part 3 is the case study of "Soviet operational propaganda and the Middle East conflict." This is the best part of the book. Although the author does not hide his biases (he is a professor at Bar-Ilan University in Israel), he demonstrates enormous knowledge of the subject as well as a good grasp of the subtleties of Soviet propaganda. He details the early (1948) Soviet sympathy with the new Israeli state and the development of improved Soviet-Arab relations in the context of discussing various issues in the Middle East conflict. Even here, however, the author sometimes loses sight of his main focus as, for example, in a section on Jewish life in the USSR. This is an interesting topic to be sure, but hardly of great relevance to the Middle East conflict.

Professor Hazen concludes by questioning the general effectiveness of Soviet propaganda. He believes that it suffers from serious shortcomings. His reasons for this conclusion seem sensible, but for a variety of reasons his book did not develop the foundation for such statements nearly as well as it might have.

DONALD D. BARRY
Lehigh University
Bethlehem
Pennsylvania

EVAN LUARD. *Types of International Society.* Pp. viii, 389. New York: The Free Press, 1976. $14.95.

The central thesis of this book is that "international relations are best examined within the framework of a study of international societies" (p. 375). This "sociological approach," it is claimed, "corresponds more closely than most other approaches to the *reality* of international relationships" (p. 362), is more comprehensive than other approaches, provides greater scope for "intangible factors," and helps "to apply the *comparative* method in a specific way to the study of international relations" (p. 363). The approach is in fact as much historical as sociological. Certain "key factors in international society" are described within seven "international societies," which flourished at time periods ranging from 771 B.C. to 1974.

Within this framework the treatment is rather conventional and quite repetitive. The "key factors in international society" that are selected for special examination are ideology, elites, motives, means, stratification, structure, roles, norms, and institutions. A separate chapter is devoted to each of these factors. The seven "international societies" are analyzed in each chapter with reference to each factor. The societies are the Chinese multistate system (771–221 B.C.), the Greek city-states (600–338 B.C.), the age of dynasties (1300–1559), the age of religions (1550–1648), the age of sovereignty (1648–1789), the age of nationalism (1789–1914), and the age of ideology (1914–1974).

In the next to last chapter Professor Luard considers five so-called "future international societies," which he labels "the transnational society," "the international society," "the sphere of influence society," "a world of regions," and "the rich-poor society." The treatment is very general and imprecise, and has little value, even for students of "futurology." The final chapter, on "The Nature of International Society," is even more general. It therefore seems to be anticlimactic after a chapter on "Future International Societies."

Professor Luard is a competent scholar, whose *Conflict and Peace in the Modern International System* (Boston: Little, Brown, 1968) is well known to students of international relations. Apparently he felt impelled to write this more general and much less rigorous book to provide a reminder of the continuing relevance of historical and sociological approaches as needed supplements to more quantitative and less comprehensive a-historical studies. In this postbehavioral era one wonders whether such a reminder is any longer needed. If so, this lengthy and repetitive extended essay should provide a useful antidote to less humanistic and less comprehensive approaches.

NORMAN D. PALMER
University of Pennsylvania
Philadelphia

GIOVANNI SARTORI. *Parties and Party Systems: A Framework for Analysis.* Vol. I. Pp. xiii, 370. New York: Cambridge University Press, 1976. $32.50. Paperbound, $10.95.

Sartori, formerly of the University of Florence and now Professor of Political Science at Stanford, has set a standard by which years of comparative research on political parties are likely to be measured. *Parties and Party Systems* is an effort to bring order to a rapidly growing, global body of information about parties and elections and to lay the groundwork for a comprehensive theory of politics.

The book is in two parts, the first on the origin and rationale of parties, the second and larger on party systems. Another more theoretical volume is promised on party types, organization, and functions, and on the social and cultural contexts of parties and the influence of electoral systems. Sartori's broad purpose is to identify different kinds of parties and party systems and to explain the forces at work in and around them.

He builds slowly, in early chapters defining his units of analysis—including the party as "any political group identified by an official label that presents at elections, and is capable of placing through elections (free or nonfree), candidates for public office." Next he develops a classification of party systems: one party, hegemonic party, predominant party, two party, limited pluralism, extreme pluralism, and atomized. The reader who follows the gradual unfolding of cast and clues with patience will be rewarded in the final chapters with the coalescence of the threads of argument.

The literature is reviewed thoroughly and critically. Maurice Duverger, who worked on a theory of parties a quarter of a century ago, in the absence of abundant data, is felt in some degree to have raised impediments to the study of parties. Similarly, V. O. Key and others are faulted for having regarded the Solid South as a one-party rather than a predominant-party area, and more generally for failing to respect the discontinuity between competitive and noncompetitive systems.

Sartori is also critical of students of multi-party systems who neglect the distinction between limited and extreme pluralism—the one with centripetal competition among governing-oriented parties, the other with antisystem parties, polarization, and a tendency to break down. Ultimately he extends the Hotelling-Downs model of centripetal party competition to illuminate this distinction, settling both empirically and logically on about five "relevant" parties as the line dividing stable and unstable multi-party systems.

Parties and Party Systems sparkles with ideas. It should be read by all serious students of political parties.

ROBERT J. SICKELS
University of New Mexico
Albuquerque

RICHARD VEATCH. *Canada and the League of Nations.* Pp. xi, 224. Toronto: University of Toronto Press, 1975. $15.00.

This long over-due survey of Canada's participation in the deliberations of the League of Nations will be welcomed by all informed observers of Canadian affairs—and most especially by those of us who will no longer have to piece together, for ourselves and our students, the record from several partial accounts. If Professor Veatch's meticulous mining of several hitherto unused or unavailable primary sources has added little of substance to what the specialist has known for some time, his great service has been to draw the record together in a very readable form and to remove, in a convincing manner, some of the nagging doubts which persisted from having access only to non-classified materials. At the cost of some repetition, he has provided the less informed observer with a very useful summary of the functioning and problems of the domestic political system during the period in which his major story unfolds.

Canada sought full membership in the League not because of a sense of commitment to the Wilsonian ideal of collective security but rather because she saw rightly that the prestige of League membership, together with the legal implications associated with it, would strengthen her efforts to win a degree of independence from Britain. It would be false to suggest that Canada wanted to pursue an entirely independent foreign policy—unless "independence" is used in a narrowly legalistic sense. What she wanted was to be free from any semblance of being automatically bound by British imperial decisions. On the other hand, she did not want to substitute a League commitment for a British commitment or to deny herself the opportunity to influence and benefit from British policy. So even as she secured from the Big Three at Paris approval for League membership, she began her fight against being bound by the automatic sanctions (as she saw them) in the proposed League Covenant. Wilson's "heart" of the Covenant, Article 10, was an anathema for Canada—she fought unsuccessfully for its deletion at Paris and for its deletion or amendment through three Assemblies and under two governments. Even though the letter of the Article was not changed, the spirit of collective security was much weakened by Canada's efforts, which are so well documented by Professor Veatch. Yet it would be an exaggeration to conclude that Canada was responsible in any major way for the eventual failure of collective security—without universality of membership and most especially with the American rejection of Wilson's League, collective security was dead from the very beginning.

Thus it is not surprising, as Professor Veatch confirms, that no serious consideration was given by the League to collective sanctions against Japan in 1931. What is surprising, however, is the implication in his otherwise excellent account of Canada's role in the League charade during Italy's rape of Ethiopia that collective sanctions could have worked. While he is careful to avoid exaggerating the negative influence of the "Riddell incident," his omission of any reference to the first Hoare-Laval "agreement" of September 1935 (which we have known about since 1936) tends to imply that Britain and France might have been more effective had Canada under Mackenzie King not backed away from initiatives taken by Riddell without prior authorization from Ottawa. Britain and France had no intention of either applying total economic sanctions or of backing them with the threat of military sanctions. Canada's role was perhaps indefensible, but certainly not influential.

Canada did attempt to make some positive contributions to the work of the League on such matters as disarmament, the protection of minorities and the development of international conciliation. Nevertheless, Professor Veatch's conclusion that her impact was primarily negative is not unfair. What would be a distortion of history would be to see Canada's negative impact in isolation from the forces which rendered the League ineffective almost from the beginning.

GRANT R. DAVY
The University of Alberta
Canada

WILLIAM WALLACE. *The Foreign Policy Process in Britain.* Pp. vii, 320. Atlantic Highlands, N.J.: Humanities Press, 1976. $22.50.

Quite different from the long-standing preoccupation of American scholars with the formal and informal institutions and with the process of foreign policymaking, there has been a noticeable void of similar undertakings in Britain. Only within the last decade has there been a change in this situation marked by the publication of a few interesting studies dealing with British foreign policy. David Vital's *The Making of British Foreign Policy* is probably the outstanding example.

However, the first comprehensive treatment of this subject matter, both in terms of the policy-making process and the administrative apparatus, is the work of William Wallace, a Research Fellow at the Royal Institute of International Affairs and lecturer in government at the University of Manchester.

The two primary objectives pursued by the author are:

The first is to uncover and describe the process through which foreign policy is made. It will be argued that foreign policy-making is as deeply affected by the domestic political environment as by international constraints, and that an understanding of this political environment is necessary to any full understanding of the evolution of British foreign policy. The second is to explore the extent to which the traditional boundaries between foreign and domestic policy have been undermined by the increasing interdependence of the developed countries of the North Atlantic area—to ask whether it is still possible to distinguish any separate and discrete field of policy which we can label 'foreign', or whether it would now be more accurate to talk about an international dimension which touches most important areas of domestic policy (p. vii).

There is no doubt in this reviewer's mind that the author fully accomplishes the tasks he had set for himself. His reference to the fact that he does not claim to present an exhaustive study especially with his treatment of British involvement in world affairs certainly does not apply to his primary objectives. He deals with them competently as he does with selected problem areas in the form of case studies.

In order to obtain the material for his analysis and evaluation of the "Whitehall Machinery," concentrating on the structure and process of foreign policy-making during the period from 1969 to 1972, the author made extensive use of available government publications, House of Commons reports, memoirs, and newspaper coverage. He also interviewed several hundred people including officials in almost every Department in Whitehall and in several overseas missions, Members of Parliament, former ministers, and representatives of interest groups. Interestingly enough, Mr. Wallace pointed at the great difficulties he encountered as a result of "the secrecy which pervades the whole machinery of government" (p. viii).

His findings include the recognition that the lower and middle levels of the administrative machinery which deal primarily with routine matters of varying significance, the Whitehall machinery operates well. The great shortcomings are at the higher level where the "questioning of the assumptions underlying foreign policy has successfully been suppressed" (p. 274) and where alternative policies have been denied and decisions once taken rarely ever have been reexamined. He also regrets the lack of clear public presentations of foreign policy alternatives which could serve to educate public opinion and ensure a wider debate of the issues at hand especially in recognition of the diminishing boundaries between foreign and domestic policies.

In his conclusion the author quotes David Vital who considers one of the main problems of the British situation:

That by and large there is nothing in the British political system, unlike that of the United States, for example, which imposes upon a British Government the need to take into serious account views and information which have not emerged from within the formal machinery established for the administration of foreign affairs and subject, ultimately, to its control (p. 276).

Mr. Wallace's study greatly contributes to a better understanding of the foreign policy process in Britain and it might even encourage leaders of political parties not only to espouse needed changes while in opposition but also when in possession of political power.

ERIC WALDMAN
University of Calgary
Alberta
Canada

ASIA, AFRICA AND LATIN AMERICA

DELIA DAVIN. Woman-Work: Women and the Party in Revolutionary China. Pp. x, 244. New York: Oxford University Press, 1976. $10.95.

The main value of this meticulous study of Women-Work in China lies in two areas: it is probably the most detailed description of any type of social change that has occurred in "mysterious" China in the 1930 to 1950 period. Some data are given for the 1960s al-

148d

The Military and Politics in Modern Times

On Professionals, Praetorians, and Revolutionary Soldiers

Amos Perlmutter

A major contribution to our understanding of the role of the military in politics that offers an historical, comparative, and theoretical analysis covering close to fifty modern states on four continents over a time span of 200 years.

"A major work of interpretation and synthesis. It should constitute a scholarly landmark in the development of the literature in civil-military relations."
—Samuel P. Huntington $15.00

Antonio Gramsci and the Revolution That Failed

Martin Clark

A study of Gramsci's political activity during the years after the First World War when he led the movement to set up Factory Councils in Turin and edited the *Ordine Nuovo*. Clark examines the origins of the Italian Communist Party and the subsequent rise of Italian fascism as well as the continuing impact of Gramsci's intellectual legacy on leftist parties throughout the world.
$15.00

Preparing for the Next War

American Plans for Postwar Defense, 1941–45

Michael S. Sherry

"Michael Sherry has done an excellent job of showing the planning which the armed forces performed, 1941–45, in preparation for postwar organization and policies. It is undoubtedly original work of a high order. I consider the work highly important to an understanding of the postwar services."
—Forrest C. Pogue $12.50

Between Center and Periphery

Grassroots Politicians in Italy and France

Sidney Tarrow

A study of politics on the French and Italian periphery—the remote agricultural villages as well as the cities and towns known collectively as "the provinces."

"Will certainly be indispensable to anyone working on France and Italy, on comparative local government, on center-periphery relations, and on comparative public administration."—Peter Gourevitch $15.00

The Rise and Fall of the Cyprus Republic

Kyriacos C. Markides

Much has been written on the international politics affecting the island of Cyprus, but this is the first serious study of the internal dynamics of the Greek community that made foreign intervention in 1974 possible and successful.

"A historical, sociological analysis of the major community in a country which, though smaller in area than Connecticut and containing only slightly over half a million people, tragically occupies a crucial position in the geography and power politics of the Eastern Mediterranean."—Leonard Doob
$12.50

Yale

Yale University Press
New Haven and London

though less information was apparently available in that decade. It enables an important second step—that of making a rigorous comparative study of the effect of induced as compared to normal or less regimented change in women's position in rapidly changing traditional societies. For much the same problems have been faced by women in other industrializing countries with long historical traditions, such as India, which, when it acquired its independence, attempted to handle them in a more democratic, persuasive way.

The author defines Woman-Work as being equivalent to the Chinese term "funü gongzuo" which "covers all sorts of activities among women, including mobilizing them for revolutionary struggle, production, literacy and hygiene campaigns, social reform, and so on." The book is divided into an Introduction which describes the position of Chinese women in early times followed by chapters on Women's Organizations, Marriage and the Family, Women in the Countryside, Women in the Towns and an impressive Bibliography of some 147 books and pamphlets in Chinese, 47 articles in Chinese-language periodicals, 125 books on the Chinese and other families in Western languages, and 18 articles in Western-language periodicals.

In view of the three-week-tour journalistic accounts that provide most of our scant knowledge of China the author's qualifications for writing this study are impressive. She taught for two years in a Peking college and in 1975 returned for a year to work as translator at the Foreign Language Press. In between she lectured in economics and social history and did research in Leeds, Tokyo, Hong-kong and Paris.

Non-communists are apt to regard communist governments as well-oiled machines marching steadily towards clearly defined goals. The author dispels this view in her description of the Chinese government's contradictory policies over time towards women. To the young intellectual leaders the emancipation of women was an important goal of the revolution and their views were supported by the practical need for women's labor in areas which would assist the war efforts. For the book covers the period of the Jiangxi Soviet and the anti-Japanese and Civil wars. And so the women were induced to work in the textile and industrial factories, on the railways and become teachers, doctors, health workers and so on. But after many women had painfully accommodated to their new roles over the years, often against bitter opposition from the men, they found that the tide had turned and they were faced with just as strong government pressures to return to their homes. Thus the position of women fluctuated from time to time, much as it has done in other countries under less authoritarian governments.

As usual in studies about women, the Chinese men are rather left out of the picture. But we can imagine the depth of their feelings when we are told, for example, that their traditional authority was sometimes reversed to such an extent that the powerful women's associations could even arrange beatings for husbands who ill-treated their wives. It would seem possible that the men suffered more in accommodating to the new patterns than the women, as it is easier to go "up" in the power hierarchy than "down."

The book tells a great deal about the various women's associations and the important role of the Women's Federation—a government sponsored organization which grew to be the binding national women's organization and managed to be effective in promoting and easing change at the grass-root as well as the national levels.

This is undoubtedly a very important study, even though sociologists may feel that it cries out for a theoretical framework which would make these momentous changes in women's position more meaningful especially, as has been said, in view of similar problems of change in other countries. Now, however, with the assistance of this competent study, someone can begin this second task.

AILEEN D. ROSS
McGill University
Montreal
Canada

WARREN DEAN. *Rio Claro: A Brazilian Plantation System, 1820–1920.* Pp. xv, 234. Stanford, Calif.: Stanford University Press, 1976. $11.50.

Between 1850 and 1930, in the heydey of free trade, Brazil discovered its aptitude for coffee production and proceeded to exploit it, to the limit of its resources and possibly beyond. Coffee was the catalyst that hastened the transformation of Brazil from an archipelago of autonomous, export enclaves into an integrating, economic system. But while coffee's reign is the watershed dividing colonial from modern Brazil, the coffee boom has remained an historiographic wasteland, poor in both monographic studies and interpretive works.

Dean's book is first of all a well-researched and skillfully written revisionist account of the evolution of the relations between masters, slaves, and farm laborers during the expansion of coffee planting in São Paulo. It begins with the expulsion of the aboriginal population, which left their numbers "decimated" and their culture "shattered." All too briefly thereafter, Rio Claro was a frontier Arcadia which attracted "people who sought a refuge from the oppressiveness of colonial rule." But despite its suitability for European farming techniques and its temporary freedom from the restraints of settled society, smallholding did not develop. Colonial authorities strengthened planter hegemony by distributing large land grants to affluent planters, their poor relations, and the rising young men who married their daughters.

Just as the colonial authorities preferred planters to smallholders, planters preferred slave to free labor. Economic consideration as well as racial attitudes weighed heavily in their choice. "Their plantations were less attractive to the rural propertyless population than the alternative of squatting on still unclaimed land, because the plantations were no more productive than swidden farming. . . ." Unwilling to offer additional incentives to the free *caboclo*, they chose instead to form a slave labor force. The non-economic elements of their decision are documented in a definitive account of Senator Vergueiro's famed, but ill-fated trial of free, immigrant labor. Dean concludes that although free labor was economically viable, the immigrant's rejection of fixed-wage, indenture contracts and semi-servile status proved its undoing. Rather than meet the laborer's demands for better wages and decent treatment, planters persisted in their use of "higher-cost slave labor."

Several tenets of Brazilian historical mythology come under Dean's critical scrutiny. It is widely believed, for example, that under the weight of its moral, political, and practical liabilities, slavery fell to a non-violent wave of national revulsion. But whatever influence the abolition movement and anti-slavery sentiment had on the national scene—and Dean seems strangely reticent on those subjects—"the slave population, not the planters . . . brought ruin to the system of forced labor by refusing to participate in it."

Without doubt, Dean's book will have a major impact upon Brazilian studies. It contributes to a relatively uncrowded area, maintains high intellectual and literary standards, and is original, challenging, and skillfully constructed and sedulously researched. To this favorable judgement, one must, in fairness, add that flaws in the logic of some of its hypotheses and inadequacies in its documentation, greatly reduce its persuasiveness. Some assertions seem downright dubious. The "luxuriant," semi-deciduous forest may have appeared mild and temperate in comparison to its surroundings; from a European standpoint it was among the best agricultural resources of tropical South America. But direct translation of contemporary European, mixed, peasant smallholding, to the São Paulo plateau would have been far more difficult than Dean suggests. To explain the failure of free labor to develop midway through the nineteenth century, Dean alleges that swidden farming was as productive as coffee planting. This was most unlikely, if for no other reason than that plantations occupied the best land and the most convenient locations.

Other arguments seem incomplete

and tendentious. Different accounts of Brazilian abolition differ in the role that they accord to various forces and groups. But none, that I know of, entirely discounts the role of the abolition movement and of anti-slavery sentiment. Likewise, what Dean cites as strong evidence that the Brazilian economy, per capita, did not grow before abolition, is merely a model of the relation between money supply and national income that was employed just one other time, and then in the United States. Overall, it is not analytic virtuosity but Dean's close and subtle reading and telling citation of primary sources, and strong, mordantly ironic and often witty narrative style that provide the principal support for the study's hypotheses.

Dean's study draws much of its strength from its distinction between economic growth and improvements of the general welfare. It is with the rigorous application of this principle to the economic history of coffee that many will disagree. Dean forcefully states his case when he writes that "Rio Claro exhibits the futility of confusing private profitability with the advancement of a society." Others, who are more impressed or more distressed with the rarity of sustained economic growth and with the burdens that stagnation imposes upon *every* member of society, are less discriminating. Just division of the costs and the benefits of economic growth, and far-sighted, unselfish elite concern with the general welfare are, to put it mildly, scarce qualities in *any* country's history. Perhaps, it is only the achievement of a minimum standard of affluence that permits the search for the good life to successfully compete with the obsessive pursuit of material goods.

PAUL I. MANDELL
Barnard College
Columbia University
New York

WILLIAM J. DUIKER. *The Rise of Nationalism in Vietnam, 1900–1941.* Pp. 313. Ithaca, N.Y.: Cornell University Press, 1976. $15.00.

Drawing on French archival materials recently opened to scholars, Duiker

elaborates the historical record of Vietnam early this century. In lucid prose he integrates with his narrative not only political biographies of Phan Boi Chau, Phan Chu Trinh, and Ho Chi Minh, but also analyses of why two earlier phases of nationalism failed and the third succeeded. The resulting book is attractive and persuasive.

Particularly useful is Duiker's account of the endemic disunity among nationalists of various persuasions, a disability which repeatedly proved fatal until overcome by the Viet Minh at a relatively late date. Prior to that time protonationalism led by scholar-gentry was characterized by learned debate and schismatic intrigue and gallant but futile armed uprisings against French rule. The urban nationalists who succeeded them were divided among Francophiles, reformers, radicals, and Marxists, with little common ground between them.

The non-Communist nationalists did not prevail not only because of disunity but also because the religio-cultural symbols that linked elites with peasants in Burma, Thailand, and Indonesia were absent in Vietnam after the erosion of Confucianism by French education and culture, the author argues enticingly but with insufficient elaboration.

The gap was bridged organizationally by the Indochina Communist Party. It was the ability of the Party leaders to learn from past disasters such as the Nghe-Tinh Soviets, to transcend their bourgeois origins, and to subordinate their Communist doctrines pragmatically to those of nationalism that allowed the Viet Minh to emerge predominant in 1945.

Even so, it took the Japanese occupation to create the necessary conditions for eventual Communist victory, as Chalmers Johnson has shown for China, a point Duiker passes over rather too lightly.

Finally the author offers the thesis that the Communists were authentic Vietnamese nationalists who used Marxist and Leninist doctrines and Comintern and Kuomintang support as means to pursue their ends. They were not an alien element but rather heirs of the scholar-gentry proto-nationalists both by family line and by patriotic conviction. The policies of the present generation of leaders seem to bear out Duiker's judgement.

J. STEPHEN HOADLEY
The University of Auckland
New Zealand

J. P. JAIN. *After Mao What?* Pp. xiv, 276. Boulder, Colo.: Westview Press, 1976. $13.75.

The future of Chinese leadership after the death of Mao Tse-tung is presently a subject of lively interest and speculation among China specialists. Dr. Jagdish Prasad Jain's *After Mao What?* attempts to answer this question by identifying various group rivalries which might play significant roles in the coming Chinese leadership.

The publication of such an undertaking could not have been more timely. On the other hand, Dr. Jain is especially unfortunate to have had his principal candidates for leadership at least temporarily excluded from consideration. Yeh Chien-ying at the age of 78 is already semi-retired and cannot be a serious contender for the vital leadership China will need. The other two principals are Teng Hsiao-ping and Chang Chun-chiao. Teng, after being named senior-most Vice-Premier and Chief of Staff of the People's Liberation Army has been purged from leadership ranks. More recently Chang Chun-chiao, second-ranking Vice-Premier and Director of the Army's General Political Department has been arrested for plotting usurpation of power. These men were leaders of the most important rival political factions in China: Chang Chun-chiao in the Chiang Ching (Mao's widow) radical faction; and Teng Hsiao-ping, a leader of the moderates.

Dr. Jain has written a very short book (144 pages of text) to which has been added 105 pages of appendices, tables and charts. Although most of the book is taken up with discussion relating to the Army, Jain concludes that the Army is not "an independent entity or a clearly distinguishable . . . group struggling for power and/or top leadership positions . . ." (p. 120). He goes on to say that the Army has not developed an institutional position, and thus is not a contender for leadership. Other prospects deemed unlikely in *After Mao What?* are: (1) establishment of military dictatorship, (2) dictatorship of the Party apparatus, or (3) resurgence of warlordism or regionalism. Dr. Jain also discounts the likelihood of a de-Maoism movement reminiscent of deStalinization, or a period of anarchism such as seen during the Cultural Revolution.

The eventual conclusion of the book is that: "the moderates and radicals . . . would try to avoid serious conflicts and adopt decisions by consensus and compromise" (p. 132). At the present writing such a conclusion would appear rather hopeless, but perhaps in the long run Dr. Jain may be vindicated.

JAMES D. JORDAN
The American University
Washington, D.C.

WAYNE S. KIYOSAKI. *North Korea's Foreign Relations: The Politics of Accommodation, 1945–1975.* Pp. v, 133. New York: Praeger Publishers, 1976. $16.50.

Dr. Kiyosaki, presently with the Foreign Broadcast Information Service, has written a compact analysis of North Korea's attempt to chart its own course in foreign affairs. Although the book does pay some attention to the role played by the United States and Japan, the author's principal concern is North Korea's relationship with the Soviet Union and the People's Republic of China.

The story is a familiar one. President Kim Il-song, ushered into power by Stalin in 1945, consolidates power in North Korea and asserts independence. When the Sino-Soviet dispute intensifies, he attempts to restore bloc solidarity, but soon is compelled to side with the Chinese. After Khrushchev's fall, Kim moves to the middle and incurs the wrath of the Chinese. Then the North Korean leader takes the radical path until the Soviet-American and Sino-American detente leads him to follow a more moderate course. All these events are described and analyzed in a brisk manner. Dr.

Kiyosaki writes succinctly and at times eloquently.

Those familiar with the literature in the field will find very little in this work that is new. Occasionally, one may also find his assertions unconvincing. But even the specialists will find some of his conclusions refreshing. For example, the author concludes that excessive bellicosity on the part of North Korea "alarmed the Socialist countries as much as many of the other countries" (p. 112) and that the North Korean actions "helped to accelerate the trend toward detente among the great powers" (p. 113).

General readers, on the other hand, will find the short volume informative. But they may wish that the discussion was not as compressed and that some of the incidents and terms were better explained.

CHONG-SIK LEE
University of Pennsylvania
Philadelphia

MARTIN LOWENKOPF. *Politics in Liberia: The Conservative Road to Development.* Pp. 237. Stanford, Calif.: Hoover Institution Press, 1976. $9.95.

Martin Lowenkopf, formerly a research analyst in the Department of State and thereafter an academic political scientist, has written an important book. The volume is important because of the debates and study of the last decade concerning Liberia's unique modernization process; and it is important because of the high competence of this particular blend of sociology, economics, and history.

Lowenkopf argues that in a conservative pattern of modernization, economic development may precede and require the evolution of modern political values and institutions, rather than vice versa. Thus Liberia's modernization has been a process of political adaptation to social changes both incident and consequent to economic development brought by foreign investment. Under the benign authoritarianism of President William V. S. Tubman, who held office from 1944 to 1972 (and who retained power of signature over every government check for

more than $100), Liberia welcomed foreign capital in its own "Open Door" policy, experienced real growth though with maldistribution of income, and advanced toward nationalism, all without the revolutionary instability which has accompanied such development elsewhere in Africa and the former colonial world. The great question: Can Liberia be a model for third world states seeking some alternative to socialist or democratic patterns of nationalist, modernizing development? Despite Lowenkopf's competent and interesting treatment of Liberian development, his suggestion that Liberia could be such a model is less than convincing. This observation, one must hasten to add, is an assessment, not a condemnation; for comparative development studies pose extraordinary challenge and provoke wide dissensus. Regrettably, the book is difficult to read because of over-elevated diction, really prosy excesses, as when the author wrote "retrospective determinism" and meant a variety of hindsight (p. 45), and "parastatal" for semi-official (p. 75).

One element of Liberia's experience seems clearly relevant to today's international economic context: Liberia welcomed foreign investment, and did so without forfeiting its sovereign competence. With the West afflicted by an as yet incurable economic malaise, it may be dangerous for the capital-poor, would-be developing nations to threaten or harass potential sources of development capital. It will be some time yet before internationally-administered development agencies supersede the function of private foreign investors, and that time may be critical to the economic well-being of all concerned in such transactions.

THOMAS H. ETZOLD
United States Naval War College
Newport
Rhode Island

E. K. LUMLEY. *Forgotten Mandate: A British District Officer in Tanganyika.* Pp. vii, 178. Hamden, Conn.: Archon Books, 1976. $12.00.

This is not a scholarly study but a testimonial. Apart from three short chapters on the role of the District Officer, Indirect Rule and an evaluation of the role and the success of British Administration in Tanganyika, the contents tell us of the experiences of the author from 1923 to 1944. He served successively in Tanga, Kibondo, Bugufi, Lindi, Turundu, Korogwe, Mbulu, Lindi, Ulanga and Bukoba never staying in a single post for more than two and a half years. These are not full memoirs but selections intended to remind many people how colonialism actually functioned (p. 9). The materials derive from the author's diary.

Studies of Tanganyika or parts of the colony exist for this period and this study has no genuine revelations to report, although the author met some well known figures of the period such as chief Towegale of the Bena or Francis Luamgira at Bukoba. The specialist for one or the other area where Lumley was stationed will perhaps find some unknown or little known facts but the value of the book does not lie there. The absence of an index is therefore not as irritating as it might seem. More vexing are misprints such as Batinda for Bahinda and others.

This is the story of a career and a somewhat average career at that, since it suffered two setbacks as a result of a confrontation with a Provincial Commissioner and with "the Government," the central administration in Dar es Salaam. The value of this work is the District Officer's point of view and vignettes about his career. We see him organizing famine relief, building roads and ferries, raising taxes, trying court cases, dealing with Native Authorities and in one way or another trying to promote economic development for the sake of the people and for the sake of the Treasury, moving from one post to another, from one set of problems to a fresh set. We see the man going home forfeiting three weeks off-duty pay to see the Oval test match; we see him returning, never knowing where he will be posted nor in which capacity. After he had just married he found out that he was posted at Kiberege (Ulanga) which had the reputation of a "penal settlement" for D.C.'s. The cricket match is a purely insular trait but most of the others were shared by colonial officers everywhere, down to the conviction that there were "penal settlements" for Officers who were not to be promoted but should serve out their time.

Moreover, working from his diaries, Lumley has preserved the opinions current in the administration during this period. The condensed version about Indirect Rule (chapter two) repeats most of the stereotypes and it will set many a tooth on edge. We meet the African "not far removed from the savage background of his forbears" (p. 19) and the usual prejudices about careless and irresponsible people and leaders. The D.C.'s knew that their advice to the Native Authorities "was tantamount to an order" (p. 18), but still saw a great difference between their indirect rule and the German rule, as they were told about it, where *akida* were appointed to administer.

But the concerns for local welfare also come through as does the fact that often the District Officer was the scapegoat if policies from above were not successfully carried out. It is a revealing comment that the D.C. took a heavy rap and more than once suffered loss of promotion—an all important consideration in this career—as a result of the dishonesty of a Native Authority for which he was responsible. The mixture of altruism or the sense of mission and the claims of a career to be made is striking in this account.

Yes, this is a very useful book. It focuses on the execution of colonial policy by a class of administrators which has not been studied yet. And in its way it leaves us with vivid images of a period unknown to most Tanzanians and the younger scholars. As it is a typical career in many ways, with a typical officer doing typical things, believing typical prejudices (including the one about the sterner methods in the colony next door) and with typical aspirations it is a welcome addition to the reading lists of students.

JAN VANSINA

University of Wisconsin
Madison

MASASHI NISHIHARA. *The Japanese and Sukarno's Indonesia: Tokyo-Jakarta Relations, 1951–1966.* Monograph of the Center for Southeast Asian Studies, Kyoto University. Pp. v, 244. Honolulu: University Press of Hawaii, 1976. $12.00. Paperbound, $7.50.

RAUL S. MANGLAPUS. *Japan in Southeast Asia: Collision Course.* Pp. v, 151. New York: Carnegie Endowment for International Peace, 1976. $3.75.

Both of these publications give us an account of Japan's phenomenal rise to economic power with its political consequences. Relying on primary documentation and extensive interviews, these volumes provide a Japanese and a Southeast Asian perspective of Japan's role in Southeast Asia.

Nishihara focuses on the relationship between Japan and Indonesia from the San Francisco Peace Treaty in 1951 to the rise of Soeharto in 1965–66, dealing first with the protracted war reparations negotiations (1951–57). Japan, at first, did not take these seriously, which is not surprising given the initial Indonesian claim for $17.5 billion. As negotiations proceeded, Japan began to give a flexible interpretation to the Peace Treaty's concept of reparations to be paid in "services" by including payment in capital goods. The December 1957 agreement contained, in effect, a $400 million grant and an additional $400 million in loans and investments. Reparation payments stimulated Japanese domestic production and increased Japanese exports to Indonesia (p. 88).

Nishihara intertwines the main theme with a recording of informal, non-governmental efforts. Spokesmen for the "Peace Lobby" (those interested in normalizing Japanese-Indonesian relations) were Japanese with wartime experience in Indonesia, those Indonesians with whom they had developed "comradely friendships," and Japanese industrialists aware of Japanese opportunities in Indonesia—referred to by some as a "sort of second Manchuria" (pp. 211–12). The subsequent "Reparation Lobbies" developed these contacts to assure a piece of the pie for themselves. This generated "an informal decision-making system in which those with political authority or influence had dominance over the selection of reparation projects and distribution of the funds" (p. 121), including lucrative contracts for the Japanese businessman who introduced Soekarno to the cabaret girl who became Dewi Sri Soekarno.

Nishihara's conclusion that Japan's increasing dominance over the Indonesian economy, might well aggravate Indonesia's "subordinate nation-complex" (p. 217), leads conveniently into the Manglapus publication. Manglapus, former Philippines Under-Secretary and Secretary of Foreign Affairs and a Senator from 1961 to 1967, is fascinated and worried by Japan's incredible economic growth. This leads him into a discussion of Japanese social organization, its "constructive tribalism," the importance of the "household group" in all Japanese activities (pp. 25–34), and the *oyabun* ("parent")—*kobun* ("child") relationship, all of which causes a "vertical division of labor" and, when applied to Southeast Asia, places it in the *kobun* position.

Two metaphors Manglapus uses frequently are: "bicycle overinvestment" (Japanese capital must keep pushing in order not to fall) and "The Tokyo Express," a monorail locomotive on a collision course. Neither of the metaphors is particularly helpful, although Manglapus ties them in with his notions of "performance pressure," "relentless dynamism," and "a growth-oriented development strategy which commits Southeast Asia to an ever-increasing and more irrevocable dependence" (p. 114). The Tokyo Express ran into two collisions in 1973–74: the vicious riots accompanying Prime Minister Tanaka's visit to Bangkok and Jakarta.

In surveying the problem, Manglapus lays out various options, discarding most as impractical or unlikely: a "change from within" Japan, either by a change of government or the legalization of the "Guidelines for Investment in Developing Countries" drafted in mid-1973; and Southeast Asian "countervailing power" either by the one oil "giant," Pertamina, or by ASEAN. He also discusses Japan's possible reactions to a (unlikely) radical shift in Southeast Asian development strategy.

Readers may not agree with all of Manglapus' facts and assertions, but it seems hard to deny that "Japan's dynamism and vulnerability" constitute "a rare and explosive combination." Or that continued Japanese penetration and investment will create increasing dependency, which is bound to lead to increased resentment. Finally, Nishihara has given us enough information on informal, non-governmental activities to make Manglapus' point of "eagerness to pay" and his expectation of "intensified corruption" another explosive issue.

PAUL W. VAN DER VEUR
Ohio University
Athens

LOUIS A. PÉREZ, JR. *Army Politics in Cuba, 1898–1958.* Pp. xvi, 240. Pittsburgh, Pa.: University of Pittsburgh Press, 1976. $9.95.

The disintegration of the Cuban army prior to and immediately after the flight of Batista on January 1, 1959 removed what might have been a powerful obstacle to the implementation of revolutionary policies by Fidel Castro. Why in the Cuban case was the fall of a government accompanied by the disbandment of the armed forces when in other Latin American countries governments have come and gone while the armed forces have remained intact? *Army Politics in Cuba, 1898–1958* by Louis A. Pérez, Jr., Associate Professor of History at the University of Southern Florida, does not provide the definitive answer to the question. It does, however, offer several good insights into the problem. Like other Latin American militaries, the Cuban armed forces became highly politicized as a result of the efforts of Cuban politicians to offset their lack of popular support through the creation of an army personally loyal to them. Professional standards for promotion were replaced by political criteria, producing a serious lack of continuity within the military establishment. Despite their increasing weakness as an institution, however, the armed forces were strong relative to the fragmented political parties, and beginning in the 1930s, they began playing an ever more overt role in Cuban politics.

Up to this point Cuba looks like many of its Latin American neighbors. What distinguishes the Cuban situation is the role of the United States. The Cuban military early recognized that its power in Cuba depended upon its ability to preserve a facade of political stability within the country. Once it became apparent that the armed forces were primarily responding to the interests of a foreign power, the little legitimacy they had within Cuba evaporated. The Castro-led insurgency ultimately convinced the United States that the Cuban military could not keep order. The ensuing withdrawal of United States' support, combined with the absence of popular backing for the army within Cuba, caused the armed forces to disintegrate.

Pérez's book, which is mainly descriptive and chronologically organized, does not draw comparisons with other Latin American countries. Nor does the author spend more than a page or two examining the Cuban experience in the light of the considerable literature that exists on civil-military relations in Latin America and the Third World. Nevertheless, *Army Politics in Cuba*, which draws heavily upon collections of personal papers and memoirs, public documents and State Department records, constitutes a valuable contribution to the literature. It is the first full-length scholarly study in English of the development of the Cuban military and merits reading by those persons seeking to understand the complexity of the process that led to the Cuban Revolution.

SUSAN KAUFMAN PURCELL
Woodrow Wilson International Center
    for Scholars
Washington, D.C.

EUROPE

ABRAHAM ASHKENASI. *Modern German Nationalism.* Pp. v, 222. New York: Halsted Press, 1976. $12.50.

Professor Ashkenasi's monograph is a concise analysis of nationalism's past and prospects in twentieth century Germany. Nationalism's virulent and destructive past in Germany, most especially during the twelve year National Socialist period, gives great significance to the question of its future prospects for Germany and the world. Ashkenasi's book discusses the complex origins, development, crisis period, and contemporary nature of the nationalist ideology in Germany. The book's excellent first chapter on nationalism in world history in the modern period places the German example in its proper historical, conceptual, and social settings. Although the book's emphasis is on the period after World War II, one chapter out of the total of seven chapters analyzes the historical development of nationalism in nineteenth and twentieth century Germany.

The core of the book concentrates on German nationalism after 1945, with special emphasis on bulwarks of contemporary German nationalism such as organized nationalist groupings, the Christian Social Union, the *Bundeswehr*, and conservative German newspapers. Ashkenasi places a great deal of emphasis on the role of public opinion and public political attitudes. Accordingly, he has made extensive use of public opinion polls, statistics, electoral results, and newspapers and periodicals. He concludes that a movement like National Socialism can't materialize in contemporary Germany. It is fairly certain that neither social conflict nor regalvanization of extremist conservative social groups could fan the flames of extremist nationalism in modern Germany. However, severe international or economic crisis could inflame passions which existing political parties and powerful conservative social groups could exploit. Germany's past

and her central economic and political role in Europe give Ashkenasi reason to be cautious about his rather optimistic general assessment of Germany's future.

JOHN S. WOZNIAK

Fredonia
New York

ROY DOUGLAS. *Land, People & Politics: A History of the Land Question in the United Kingdom, 1878–1952.* Pp. 239. New York: St. Martin's Press, 1976. $14.95.

The vexatious land problem in Ireland during the Parnell era is a well known and widely studied historical phenomenon, but, as this useful study demonstrates, the problem had much broader geographical and chronological ramifications. Douglas, a lecturer at the University of Surrey who previously authored the well-accepted *History of the Liberal Party, 1895–1970*, draws on a truly impressive array of manuscript and printed sources in presenting his thesis.

Essentially, he argues the land problem was a continuous and central thread woven through the fabric of British social, economic, and political life in the period he covers. Particularly revealing are his excursions into the social manifestations of land as a peculiar kind of property. A great deal of social turmoil grew out of rack rents, differences over fixity of tenure, urbanization, land redistribution, and the like. These disturbances in turn gave rise to recurrent legislative efforts aimed at land reform and the alleviation of human distress associated with land usage. Another consideration implicit throughout the book, although the author surprisingly ignores its timeliness, is the manner in which land use affects society at large. With today's ever-growing environmental consciousness, it would seem to this reviewer that more comparison might have been made between the evolution of the land problem in Britain and those which confront much of the world today.

However, this is essentially criticism

of what the author might have said, and when one considers the book itself, it can only be accorded an overall favorable evaluation. This is a solid work which ties many apparently disparate elements into a skillful narrative. Douglas has a shrewd appreciation of the manner in which economic realities and political necessities mesh, and he convincingly demonstrates that, at least as far as land is concerned, the end result is of great social importance. All students of modern Britain will find material of interest in this work, and not the least of its merits is the manner in which it challenges traditional interpretations and approaches to the land problem. The debate this work will stimulate will certainly, in the end, result in a fuller understanding of all facets of the land problem.

JAMES A. CASADA

Winthrop College
Rock Hill, S.C.

LEONARD D. GERSON. *The Secret Police in Lenin's Russia.* Pp. 347. Philadelphia, Pa.: Temple University Press, 1976. $15.00.

Lord Acton's observation that power corrupts has become a cliche and is accepted as conventional wisdom, but Professor Gerson's recent addition to the already substantial literature on the Soviet secret police forces one to reconsider the proposition. One can ask whether the Cheka was corrupt when it ruthlessly and without pity executed and imprisoned untold numbers of "enemies of the people," or was it faithfully fulfilling its role as the sword of the revolution. While Professor Gerson does not address this question explicitly, he does provide us with about all the information currently available in the public domain concerning the secret police. The author writes with vigor but has not organized his work well, and consequently it loses some of the impact a more sharply focused treatment would have had. The work is neither wholly chronological nor topical in its organization, but falls somewhere between the two, placing considerable burden upon the reader. Yet one cannot read this book without feeling the power of the subject. The preservation of Bolshevik power was the prime task of the Cheka, and the implication of Professor Gerson's work is that it did its job well, whether the cost in human lives was as few as 12,000 or as many as half a million. In the process, an instrument for future state control was perfected, and with the death of Lenin it gravitated to Stalin, materially assisting his drive for power.

If one accepts the logic of terror and if one notes that the enemies of the regime were many and real, the conduct of the Cheka in its defense of the new Soviet state becomes consistent and comprehensible. Felix Dzerzhinsky, the creator of the Cheka and its chief during its first nine years is portrayed by the author as a selfless, ascetic revolutionary, whose values and practices accorded closely with those of Lenin, although the Cheka clearly was an embarrassment to other highranking Bolshevik leaders. While Professor Gerson notes that Chekists at the provincial level were occasionally abnormally attached to the more sordid aspects of their duties, the impression of high-mindedness lingers.

The Cheka possessed almost no check upon its powers, being subject only to the will of the Politburo. It successfully avoided interference from the courts and from all guarantees of law and judicial procedure. Its police powers down to 1923 (when it became the GPU or political police) were comprehensive, and sentences were both administrative and summary. The raw power of the Cheka may not have been corruptive in the sense of Lord Acton's observation, but it certainly raises questions about the limits of police powers, even when those who exercise them are convinced that their cause is of overriding importance. One can only wish that Professor Gerson had reflected more upon the implications of his exposition and had made explicit some of these implications.

FORRESTT A. MILLER

Vanderbilt University
Nashville
Tennessee

EDWARD L. MORSE. *Foreign Policy and Interdependence in Gaullist France.* Pp. xiv, 336. Princeton, N.J.: Princeton University Press, 1973. $14.50.

In this provocative study the author has taken a novel approach to French foreign policy under the Fifth Republic. Instead of focusing on the unique elements of Gaullist foreign policy, notably its anachronistic and even quixotic nationalism, he has chosen the French example as a model to exemplify a generalized condition of foreign policy in the contemporary world. The contradiction between self-assertive independence and the exigencies of interdependence is singled out as characteristic of all highly modernized states, not only of France. Modernization itself, he notes, has paradoxically brought about increasing interdependence among nations and a simultaneous reinforcement of nationalism, with no transnational political organization available as a substitute for the nation-state.

The study presents itself in two parts. The first is a theoretical examination of the conduct of foreign policy in modernized societies, the second a detailed case analysis of France from 1958 to 1969 during the eleven years of Charles de Gaulle's presidency. Among other matters, Morse examines de Gaulle's efforts to overcome the tension between foreign and domestic affairs, the obstacles provided by foreign economic policy ("low policy") which compelled de Gaulle to climb down from some of his loftier ambitious heights, and the use of crisis management and crisis manipulation, especially in the Common Market, as an integral part of his foreign policy. He analyzes the constant pull between welfare and warfare, the tension between the quest for defense autonomy and the dilemma of insufficient resources, the unsuccessful campaign to reform the international monetary system, and such manifestations of crisis diplomacy as French pressures in the Common Market. At the same time, mindful of his larger theme, he presses the thesis that the interplay between nationalistic objectives and the constraints imposed by international interdependence was not characteristic of France alone, the trenchant nationalistic rhetoric of de Gaulle merely crystallizing the more general problem of such constraints elsewhere. Despite the extraordinary efforts of de Gaulle, interdependence served to thwart national autonomy. The central focus of the General's reshaping of politics was the effort to seek independence from the electorate as a prerequisite for maneuverability abroad, to recapture an independence from domestic politics somewhat in the "monarchic tradition" so that one could be free to take surprise initiatives. Like other political leaders, he discovered the domestic limitations on his external goals. In the end, the demands for welfare and social services, dramatized in the events of May–June 1968, undermined his efforts; and currency crises, including the devaluation precipitated by the events of May–June 1968, frustrated his position on monetary reform as well as his program for an independent nuclear force. To provide a political apparatus that would guarantee permanence and continuity in foreign policy was de Gaulle's goal, and indeed his chief legacy to his successors in the Fifth Republic, yet even he could not overcome the interrelatedness of foreign and domestic affairs in modern society. The central feature of international politics remained for de Gaulle as for others the "dual reality of transnational interdependence and national sovereignty."

Whether or not the theoretical framework of this volume will satisfy everyone, or whether or not the Gaullist experience in coping with interdependence is the most appropriate case study for the tensions facing modernized societies, the study illuminates many aspects of the Fifth Republic—its economic planning, its military programs, its activities in the EEC. Some readers may resist the author's conclusions out of the conviction that de Gaulle was a unique political phenomenon, transcending ordinary political leaders in his national self-assertiveness. Some readers will wonder, too, whether the interdependence of the modern world is as new as the author deems it to be, and whether de Gaulle's "monarchic" tradition may not have been "Jacobin" as well. In any event, this interesting and astute study will be read with profit at both the theoretical and historical level.

JOEL COLTON

The Rockefeller Foundation
New York

H. GORDON SKILLING. *Czechoslovakia's Interrupted Revolution.* Pp. xvi, 924. Princeton, N.J.: Princeton University Press, 1976. $45.00. Paperbound, $15.00.

The Prague Spring of 1968 was the high season of Czechoslovakia's brief history. Not only was the non-communist world admiring of the brave attempt "to give socialism a human face" but so too were party members inside and outside the East bloc as well as the communist governments of Rumania and Yugoslavia. The invasion of the five 'brother nations' that put an end to the Prague reforms was as shocking to Czechoslovakia as it was to the West but as a move of sheer power it seemed wholly successful. The reformers were thrown out to be replaced by orthodox, Moscow party-liners who have remained in control. The author however, as is evident in his title more than in his guarded text, seems inclined to take an optimistic view of the Czechoslovakian revolution and its possible future. The title suggests that the Prague Spring may well, one day, be renewed, that the invasion and subsequent repressions consumed the harvest not the roots. The text (page 851) says questions on its future both in Czechoslovakia and the Communist imperium defy an answer.

The past however, and how and why Czechoslovakian communism took the course it did is thoroughly documented in this exhaustive account of the personalities and political forces at work. Mr. Skilling has examined all the records available to him through interviews, party files, memoirs, newspaper accounts—everything that has

been written about the period—and he has as well a long, first-hand knowledge of the country and its divided people. And the latter, as the polls he cites indicate, wanted what the leaders were talking about, a liberated socialism which a large portion of the electorate thought should be led by the Communist party although a considerable majority rejected both a one-party system and a return to a pre-1948 polity.

The book is obviously the product of formidable industry but its structure produces a certain stagnation in the flow of events. For example the circumstances of Secretary Novotný's removal from office are described in pages 161–179, on page 201 a meeting calls for his resignation and then, hundreds of pages later (pages 453 and 571) we are back again, in other contexts, in the time of his ouster. Since a book of this scope and detail is not in any event likely to be read as narrative history, these are doubtless minor defects; the materials are certainly all there—almost every page has its quotations—and the events are described with accuracy and good sense to provide the reader with everything he might need to make his own judgments.

EUGENE DAVIDSON

Conference on European Problems
Chicago
Illinois

FRANK B. TIPTON, JR. *Regional Variations in the Economic Development of Germany during the Nineteenth Century.* Pp. xiii, 270. Middletown, Conn.: Wesleyan University Press, 1976. $22.00.

Economic history has increasingly demanded attention alongside the more traditional political, diplomatic and military genres. A major focus—especially in the history of western societies during the last two centuries—is the problem of industrialization or modernization. It is tempting to perceive this process as a generally uniform phenomenon, if not for western civilization as a whole, then at least for individual nations. Such an approach is both convenient in providing accepted units and conforms very roughly to economic realities. Since it can, however, mislead in implying homogeneity within national aggregates, a regional approach supplies a necessary corrective. All too frequently such regional studies suffer from myopia and do not relate local characteristics to national developments. In offering a synthetic and comparative treatment of German regional development during the late nineteenth century, Tipton not only alleviates this deficiency in the German case but also provides a model for studies of other developing economies.

The book is well conceived, exhaustively researched, clearly organized, and straight-forwardly written. It manages the rare feat of acknowledging the historian's concern for the particular and unfamiliarity with economic theory while satisfying the economist's demand for theoretical framework and quantification. Concentrating the massive data base very largely in tables, statistical appendix and notes, Tipton keeps the text admirably brief (less than half the book). Within a chronological arrangement, the study is organized topically and specific details of individual regions are related to other cases and the national aggregate.

The most striking features of German modernization are regional disparities and differing rates of development. Measured by a specialization index indicating divergence from the national aggregate, industrial development caused increased differences among regions as the 19th century progressed. As a result there emerged the now familiar patterns of emigration from rural to urban areas and differentiation between developed and backward economies. These developments occur at different rates: East Prussia and Saxony emerge by mid-century as the prototypical agricultural and industrial societies (respectively), followed in the next half century by the Ruhr.

While possibilities for development are limited by material factors, the idiosyncracies of regional development are profoundly influenced by social and political factors. Economic develop- ments forced traditional elites to resist or adjust to change. In East Prussia the large landowners had virtually insured against industrialization by mid-century, whereas the Saxon government was encouraging it as part of a drive for political centralization, but in southern and western Germany the rivalry between central and local bureaucracies retarded industrial development until mid-century. The role of non-economic factors is nowhere as clear as in the development of railroads which were "the major cause of the dichotomy between backward and advanced districts" since " 'self-feeding' growth at the favored centers was purchased at the expense of 'emptying' and progressive stagnation for what rapidly became the agricultural hinterland." Yet the location of railroads was always "a political decision" and "not a natural phenomenon at all, but a very human creation . . . being responsive to the push of political muscle first and the pull of marginal cost only second, if at all." Regional divergences reinforced other divisions within German society which together produced an increasingly tense and explosive mix by the eve of World War I. Thus the effects of industrialization were divergent, if not indeed contradictory: while integrative in encouraging national consciousness and culture, it also was disintegrative in producing divergent tendencies in different areas.

L. L. FARRAR, JR.
Boston University
Massachusetts

ALEXANDER VUCINICH. *Social Thought in Tsarist Russia: The Quest for a General Science of Society, 1861– 1917.* Pp. ix, 294. Chicago, Ill.: The University of Chicago Press, 1976. $15.50.

This erudite work is a very useful and instructive introduction to the role of representative members of the Russian intelligentsia in molding and shaping public opinion in Russia. It stresses the impact on their studies of western intellectuals from the abolition of serfdom in

Tsarist Russia (1861) to the October (Bolshevik) Revolution (1917). There is no reciprocal evidence of an impact by the Russian intelligentsia on the works of western intellectuals during the period in question. Strictly speaking, Vucinich provides for the first time, to my knowledge, a comprehensive and scientific definition of subjective and objective sociology in all its ramifications, through both a "Russian prism" and a western interpretation.

Although the terms *intelligentsia* and *intellectuals* are used synonymously here, in Tsarist Russia the intelligentsia did not embrace all intellectuals. The Russian intelligentsia, as such, a product of the nobility, clergy and military distinction, represented no party or profession, but rather the conscience of the people. Many twentieth-century intellectuals, who have claimed to speak for the masses (populism), actually represented political parties—in the case of the Bolsheviks, one party, the Communist Party. These intellectuals were materialists rather than idealists. Actually, it was the Bolshevik intellectuals who put an end to the leading role of the idealistic Russian intelligentsia.

This work helps to explain why F. M. Dostoyevskii, the giant of nineteenth-century Russian literature, elevated Jesus Christ above everything, even above *truth*. The impression is given that every leading contributor among the cultured intelligentsia dealt with in this book—including P. L. Lavrov, N. K. Mikhailovskii, B. A. Kistiakovskii, M. M. Kovalevskii and A. A. Bogdanov—sought to ameliorate the plight of the *narod*. Some advocated celestial (religious) means, others terrestrial (secular) to achieve their common goal. It became evident to V. S. Solovyov, whose lectures strongly influenced Dostoyevskii, that neither theology nor ideology alone could satisfactorily solve human and social problems. Thus Dostoyevskii arrived at the conclusion that we must have both religion and science, especially as regards the Russian people (p. 104). Since Christ personified both the deity (theology) and man (ideology), world problems could be solved, according to

him, only by applying the teaching of Russian Orthodox Christianity.

Professor Vucinich writes intelligently and clearly. His book is a solid, meaty contribution on a very important subject—interesting and valuable.

IVAR SPECTOR
University of Washington
Seattle

EUGEN WEBER. *Peasants into Frenchmen: The Modernization of Rural France, 1870–1914.* Pp. 615. Stanford, Calif.: Stanford University Press, 1976. $20.00.

France's delayed entry into the modern world and the persistence of local characteristics have both perplexed and intrigued historians. *Peasants into Frenchmen* by Eugen Weber tackles this controversial issue and concludes that the crucial transformation occurred between 1870 and 1914. He argues that the spread of roads and railroads gradually undermined the isolation of rural communes and exposed them to modernizing forces. The fragmentation and local idiosyncrasies of 1870 had yielded to national unity. Local dialects and illiteracy gradually gave way to a national tongue and a reading public. New industry and skills invaded formerly isolated regions to weaken traditional modes of life and labor. Weber thus views the early Third Republic as France's transition to modernity.

In the first of three sections, Weber analyzes France's characteristics before 1870. Much of rural France, and particularly the less developed southwestern portions, still lived at bare subsistence standards. Semi-barbarians occupied a rural wilderness in which local solidarity and regional autonomy reinforced a dislike of outsiders. Mistrust confronted all strangers; even governmental agents were viewed as alien intrusions. Old systems of coinage and measurement resisted standardization or replacement by the franc and metric system. Even the French language had to compete with a multiplicity of local dialects. A population whose habitats were miserable and food supplies limited felt little sense of national unity. On the eve of the Third Republic, France's sizable rural population still lived in an uncivilized state of poverty, superstition, and local fragmentation.

Into this self-contained world moved the agencies of change which would fundamentally alter peasant society. Weber's second part focuses on those forces, foremost among which were the new roads and railroads envisaged by the Freycinet Plan and laws of the early 1880s. Although the major roads and rail-beds had been laid earlier, strategic concerns had motivated their layout. Not until the 1880s were the rural roads and branch line railways built which would pull the isolated countryside out of its autarky and into a market economy. Second only to road building in transforming the peasantry was the contemporaneous introduction of compulsory, free schooling. France's expanding bureaucracy needed trained and educated civil servants. Peasants learned because education offered material rewards. Other subsidiary agents of change also contributed their part: migration advanced literacy; military service proved an agency for acculturation; a large artisanate transmitted national values to the rural world as did participation in the practice of politics; and the declining role of the church facilitated acceptance of modern ideas. Thus, numerous forces undermined rural isolation and exposed the French peasantry to national influences.

Weber's last section explores the effects of change on the rural situation. This part of the book is rather disappointing since Weber focuses on such minor phenomena as the declining role of rowdy festivals, charivari forms of justice, folk wisdom, music and dance rather than returning to the major issues raised in Part I. He might have spelled out the impact of change on problems of poverty, justice, language and civilization to reinforce his important conclusion that roads, schools and military service fundamentally altered the countryside and incorporated rural France into a modern, unified nation. Although Weber leaves certain issues insuffi-

ciently developed, his massive, well-documented study is a major contribution to the literature on French social history.

MARJORIE M. FARRAR
Boston College
Chestnut Hill
Massachusetts

UNITED STATES HISTORY AND POLITICS

PHILIP S. BENJAMIN. *The Philadelphia Quakers in the Industrial Age, 1865–1920.* Pp. ix, 301. Philadelphia, Pa.: Temple University Press, 1976. $12.50.

All Americans suffered extraordinary stresses in the fifty years following the Civil War as the nation responded to industrialism and mass urbanization. But few were so severely strained as the Philadelphia Quakers. Traditionally they had tried to remain apart from the larger society, members of an island community seeking to perserve its cultural uniqueness and sectarian spiritualism. By World War I, however, the Friends had lost much of their cultural exclusiveness. They found themselves in positions of business leadership and deeply involved in the political and moral issues of the time. Moreover, their own ranks had been fractured by splinter groups such as the Hicksites, Gurneyites, and Wilburites, contending units formed in reaction to the stresses of the new urban life.

The late Philip Benjamin, professor of history at Temple University, has captured the central dilemma of the Philadelphia Quakers as they emerged from the pre-industrial society. Using a sample of some 710 Quakers and the records of five Friends Meetings of Philadelphia, he applied sound social scientific methods to develop a profile which demonstrates the social condition of the Quakers, their influence in the community, and the shifting condition of their sect. Benjamin identifies essentially the same conflicts for the Quakers of Philadelphia in the Gilded Age and Progressive Era that Frederick Tolles and Gary B. Nash had already found for the Quakers of the colonial era. In both times the Friends' attempts to remain apart from the growing society were frustrated as they found themselves increasingly a part of the socioeconomic elite unable to preserve their "unworldliness." Benjamin's Quakers criticized the capitalist excesses of their age but often found themselves among the city's captains of industry and commerce. They were never entirely at ease participating in the political and social reforms of the time, but many became active in the temperance movement and in efforts to clean up corruption in Philadelphia politics. And like their colonial predecessors, some were thought to have an inordinate passion for education and the arts.

Benjamin builds a convincing case that the Philadelphia Quakers maintained their "quietism" fairly well until the turn of the century. Even social feminism and women's suffrage, contrary to the traditional view, were not championed by the Quakers until the 1910s. It was in that decade, also, that they marshalled their spiritual resources to promote militant organizations for the rights of blacks and struggled energetically for pacifism during the World War. The Philadelphia Quakers had emerged from an exclusive, conservative community into a progressive body of civil libertarians actively supporting programs of social change.

Historians of modern America have rarely taken an interest in the Quakers except as pacifist leaders. Benjamin's study has corrected that by placing the Philadelphia Quakers into the larger context of the total American scene. He has woven them skillfully into the history of their city, and he has proven in the process that good religious history can be combined with sound urban history.

ROBERT DETWEILER
San Diego State University
California

ALEXANDER DeCONDE. *This Affair of Louisiana.* Pp. x, 325. New York: Charles Scribner's Sons, 1976. $12.50.

The thesis of this book is that the Louisiana Purchase of 1803 was a logical consequence of an earlier Anglo-American and American expansionism and set the pattern for other expansionist activities by the United States in the nineteenth century. The thesis is neither new nor very important, and the chapters that bear heaviest on this interpretation are the weakest ones in the book. Large use of expressions such as "aggressive people," "the lust for lands," "imperial desires," "implicit coveting of Louisiana," "limitless territorial ambitions," "ruthless land hunger," and "despoiling of Indians" (pp. 34–37, 243), when applied to Americans only, suggests that Spaniards and Frenchmen, by contrast, were generous and altruistic in their New World ventures and that they came by their empires innocently. As such, the book is one of many works on different phases of American foreign policy that are tilted against the United States, almost as though this were a requirement for securing approving nods from publishers' readers of manuscripts.

As for abstract right in empire-building in America, whether by Spaniards, Frenchmen, Englishmen, or Americans, a strong case can be built against them all. But in the New World, no less than in the Old, abstract right did not govern; and so aborigines were dispossessed in one way or another and empire-builders used dubious arguments to justify their actions, not only against Indians but also against each other. As for Americans, it must be said that they conducted themselves in accordance with standards which, as Mr. DeConde correctly observes, they had inherited from England, and which were the standards obtaining in international diplomacy of their day. Had they not done so, the United States could not have been born, or having been born, could not have lived as a nation. Insofar as there could be any "right" to expansionism in America, perhaps it belonged more nearly in the United States, a strong and rising nation in North America, than to nations on the other side of the Atlantic whose destinies were not so vitally linked with this hemisphere.

The heart of Mr. DeConde's book consists of chapters dealing with the immediate background and the consummation of the Louisiana Purchase. These chapters are well done and one is carried along by the high drama they describe. But the interpretative chapters, as noted, are slanted and detract from what is otherwise a useful synthesis of literature on the Louisiana acquisition.

JENNINGS B. SANDERS

Kensington
Maryland

JEANNE GUILLEMIN. *Urban Renegades: The Cultural Strategy of American Indians*. Pp. viii, 336. New York: Columbia University Press, 1975. $10.95.

NIELS WINTHER BRAROE. *Indian and White: Self-Image and Interaction in a Canadian Plains Community*. Pp. viii, 205. Stanford, Calif.: Stanford University Press, 1975. $8.50.

These books describe how two bands of Indians faced alien and tacitly hostile cultures, and survived. They neither withdrew into isolation nor wholly assimilated, the first because they could not, the second because they would not. Rather, they *adapted*, and their culture with them. The process is a fascinating testimony to the resilience of culture, related to both cases by perceptive and sensitive social scientists. Both books should be included in the standard bibliographies of the subject, and read together.

There are problems. "*Urban Renegrades*," for instance, is a misleading title. Its subjects, the Micmacs, are not renegade in the city. Boston and their shuttle migrations between Boston and

Nova Scotia have become an integral part of Micmac culture. Indeed, author Guillemin emphasizes that the Micmacs are part of the fully one-third of United States and Canadian Indians who are effectively urban people. And she insists in Vine Deloria's phrasing that if we are to understand Indians, we must transcend the stereotype of a "food-gathering, berry-picking, semi-nomadic, fire-worshipping, high-plains-and-mountain-dwelling, horse-riding, canoe-toting, bread-using, pottery-making, ribbon-coveting, wickiup-sheltered people." The trouble is that for all the protestations, there is a sense in the text (and surely in the title) that Professor Guillemin feels that the Micmacs ought to be and would be happy, better-off, and better "down home," quite for the sake of the wickiups, fire-grilled salmon, and Manitou.

This may be unfair to what is on the whole an excellent and illuminating inquiry. Whatever her sentiments may be (and she devotes one chapter of six to scrutinizing them), Professor Guillemin deftly summarizes the history of the Micmacs, the nature of their tribal organization, their mores, values, mode of relationship with each other, and economy. While the temptations of jargon are sometimes too sweet ("An individual may theoretically interact with anyone and the frequency, purpose, and quality of interaction, and the number of people interacted with can vary by choice" [p. 70]), the author typically writes with a clarity and verve that her senior colleagues might well admire.

Niels Braroe does too. In *Indian and White*, he describes another Canadian community, a small band of Crees who live on a tiny western plains reserve. Unlike the Micmacs, who leave their ancestral home in order to earn their living, the Crees gain their sustenance in "Short Grass," working casually for white ranchers, cutting fence posts for sale, and collecting government stipends as reservation residents. Their travelling, also considerable, is for cultural purposes, to attend Sun Dances during the summer, for example, or to visit other Cree communities. This reverse image of the Micmac pattern takes on more meaning in light of Professor Braroe's theme—that the Short Grass Cree are constantly confronted by the problem of preserving spiritual self in the face of the local white society's definition of them as "profane persons" —and one method of thus accommodating is to conceal attributes defined as "Indian."

Like Guillemin, Braroe ably establishes historical context, clearly defines his problem and resolves it with thorough reference to the large and often contradictory anthropological literature. Also as in *Urban Renegades*, however, and less happily, a sort of primitivist sentimentalism creeps into the text and the effect, however distant from the author's intention, is downright patronizing. Thus, Professor Braroe describes the attempt of two Cree brothers to found a herd of cattle, and even instances of Indians swearing off alcohol almost sadly. They are described as attempts "to win a place with whites" (p. 122). Again, when "most indians . . . voice a desire to be self-supporting, to own land and cattle," it is "as their white neighbors do." Band members are judging "their own behavior by white standards" (p. 172). Surely there is nothing intrinsically Caucasian, Canadian, Bourgeois, or Anti-Indian about preferring a full stomach to privation. Surely there are other merits to abstaining from alcohol than confounding a social stereotype.

But it would not do to conclude on this note. The foible is hardly an ethnological monopoly. And within ethnology, there are few who will not profit from reading this book.

JOSEPH R. CONLIN
Centre for the Study of Social History
University of Warwick
Coventry
England

CORNELIUS J. JAENEN. *Friend and Foe: Aspects of French-Amerindian Cultural Contact in the Sixteenth and* *Seventeenth Centuries.* Pp. 207. New York: Columbia University Press, 1976. $12.50.

LOUISE K. BARNETT. *The Ignoble Savage: American Literary Racism, 1790– 1890.* Contributions in American Studies, No. 18. Pp. xii, 220. Westport, Conn.: Greenwood Press, 1976. $13.95.

These two studies, despite their differences in subject and period, attempt to expose the racism underlying white attitudes towards Native Americans. Jaenen feels these attitudes have distorted our histories while Barnett finds they have distorted our literature.

Jaenen, who is concerned with the French-Indian contact situation, begins with a chapter on French views of the Indian's humanity, descent from Adam, and ranking in the order of nature, before exploring various attempts by the French to integrate the Indian into French-Canadian culture. For the security of New France, the French implemented a policy of forced Indian acculturation pursued through missionization, education, and resettlement of the Indians. In all three areas, according to Jaenen, the French were frustrated in their goals by their misunderstanding of the complex Indian cultures which functioned as an integral part of their environment. In the end, Native American cultures changed, but this change was due more to disease and alcohol than to any French policy.

Although Jaenen blames French racism and cultural differences for the French failure to assimilate the Indians, he does not adequately discuss the economic goals of the colony that conflicted with the governmental goals. Seasonal nomads were essential to the fur trade and it was not in the traders' interest to make Indians sedentary. Although the government theoretically pushed for the settlement of the Indians, given the economic reality of New France, it did so only half-heartedly.

Jaenen's study goes far towards bringing together not only the French side of the story, but also the ethnohistorical material that has often been neglected. A basic weakness of the book, however, lies in Jaenen's generalizations about "Amerindian culture" when in reality he is dealing with many different Native American cultures.

In *The Ignoble Savage*, Barnett studies literary racism in a singularly American literary genre, the frontier romance of the first half of the nineteenth century. The "Indian as devil" stereotype which dominated the colonial captivity narrative from the seventeenth through the eighteenth centuries persisted in the frontier romance which flowered after 1820 under the influence of English romanticism in general and Scott's Waverley novels in particular. Largely limited to the psychological archetypes of heroes and villains, the frontier romance portrayed only the pre-Columbian Indian as a noble savage. Once in contact with white culture, Indians became aggressive "evil savages" who continued to degenerate as white culture triumphed.

According to Barnett, frontier romances were functional to the New Nation. They justified white expansion, since while the reader might feel sympathy for the Indian's loss of land, less guilt would be generated if the Indian could be portrayed as a "persecuter of whites." Romances also offered proof of racial superiority by demonstrating that in both physical and mental endowment Indians were inferior to whites. Finally, the frontier romance served the cause of nationalism by offering the Indian as a symbol of nature, to be sacrificed at the altar of civilization. Slaying the Indian, the "serpent in the New World garden," became for Americans a patriotic duty, "a rite of passage from which they emerged a new people."

Although Barnett presents a penetrating examination of racist views in a literary genre, she does not adequately account for the structural changes in the genre at the end of the eighteenth century and again in the mid-nineteenth century. Furthermore, she does not consider historical factors, other than nationalism, in her treatment of racist attitudes in literature.

ROBERT E. BIEDER

Center for the History of the
   American Indian
The Newberry Library
Chicago
Illinois

LAWRENCE J. KORB. *The Joint Chiefs of Staff: The First Twenty-five Years.* Pp. vii, 210. Bloomington: Indiana University Press, 1976. $10.95.

In the spate of writings about the American military system that has poured forth since 1945 little attention was paid to one of the most significant bodies in that system, the Joint Chiefs of Staff (JCS). Most of these studies were concerned with the whole range of the military establishment, and it is the complaint of Professor Lawrence Korb that they treated the JCS "only peripherally." Korb thinks that the agency deserves separate and special treatment. The JCS is one of the "most controversial" and one of the "least understood" institutions in the American political system, he writes. His book should help to redress the balance.

Korb begins his study with an "overview" of the JCS today, outlining the organizational structure of the agency and describing its functions. In discussing the latter role he properly emphasizes a fact that is probably not generally realized, that the Chiefs are "divorced from the operational realm," that they do not have "any command authority of their own." But he hastens to add that in every war or military crisis, because of their nearness to the seat of power in Washington, they have exercised a strong influence in the operational area.

Following his overview, Korb discusses the men who have served on the JCS since its creation by executive order in World War II and its legal incorporation in 1947, providing a sketch of each individual. In a critical vein he describes the selection process and concludes that it produces narrowly edu-

cated and "combat-oriented line officers" who usually have not been able
to rise above the "parochial interests"
of their particular service. This devotion
to their service controls what the Chiefs
do in what Korb calls "the battle of the
Potomac," the conflict to get the biggest
slice of the military budget. It is this
competition, not consideration of national policy, that determines military
policy, Korb claims.

The section of the book that will interest most readers is the one dealing with
the "operational role" of the JCS in the
Korean and Vietnam wars. In the former
conflict the Chiefs supported the decision to intervene although they believed that Korea was of slight strategic
importance to the United States; they
accepted the dictum of the civilian authorities that Communist aggression had
to be contained. They also supported
President Truman in removing General
MacArthur in what Korb calls their
"finest hour." Their hour in Vietnam he
characterizes in uniformly critical terms.
They helped to provoke the aggressive
American reaction to the North and they
insisted on ever escalating the conflict,
he charges. In their demands they went
beyond the thinking of most of the
civilian authorities. Korb pushes his con-
demnation to extreme lengths in suggesting, in a strange hindsight observation, that the Chiefs should have re-
signed en masse in 1965 and thus forced
a halt to the war.

Korb thinks that the JCS still contains areas of "continuing weakness."
The members allow themselves to be
"intimidated" by political leaders into
supporting policies they should oppose,
and they are not sufficiently innovative
in the policy process. But he sees hope
in the future. The present Chiefs, he
believes, are "possibly the most well-
rounded group" ever to sit on the agency,
and they should be able to provide the
leadership needed in today's world. Professor Korb has provided us with a
challenging book; it may not be always
right but it is well worth reading.

T. HARRY WILLIAMS
Louisiana State University
Baton Rouge

DAVID ALLAN LEVINE. *Internal Com-
bustion: The Races in Detroit, 1915–
1925.* Contributions in Afro-American
and African Studies, No. 24. Pp. xii,
222. Westport, Conn.: Greenwood
Press, 1976. $13.50.

This short book, full of valuable insights, is a contribution to understanding the history and interrelationships of
Progressives, urbanization, and white
ethnic groups, as well as black Americans. It focuses on the chain of developments in Detroit between 1915
and 1925 which culminated in the racial
violence of 1925 and the Ossian Sweet
case.

In the early years of this century Detroit was undergoing changes at a pace
so rapid that existing institutions failed
to cope with them. Population growth,
which made it the fastest growing city in
the United States, was made up largely
of European immigrants and blacks
from the South. By 1915, 74 percent of
the population was either foreign-born
or of foreign parentage. A black population of less than 7,000 in 1910 grew to
80,000 by 1925. The author says that his
study "is an example of this change
and a demonstration of how one city
tried to organize and direct its members in answering the call of progress"
(p. 9).

Much of Detroit's growth was due to
the phenomenal growth of the automobile industry. Levine includes a fascinating synopsis of how Henry Ford's
promise of wage of $5 a day lured would-
be workers and aggravated some urban
problems, while at the same time the
"Ford Sociological Department" engaged in a program of "Americanization"
and moral uplift among Ford employees.

Detroit was regarded as a model of
Progressive reform, a city with an unusually large number of civic-minded
business and industrial leaders. The
Employer's Association of Detroit, the
most powerful group in the city supported Americanization programs for
foreigners and supported the Urban
League, but its on-going mission was to
perpetuate the open shop. The Board of
Commerce had as its slogan "Every

industrial employee a home owner," but the desperate housing situation for blacks was the major reason for the explosions of the 1920s. There was an Urban League, which dissident blacks said was the only channel through which blacks could reach the white power structure. The League tried to find jobs for black newcomers, a disproportionate percentage of which were for female domestics. For black men there were "nigger" jobs which whites would not take. Yet in the face of these conditions the League used some of its resources to promote the Detroit Dress Well Club in an effort to improve the image of black migrants in the white mind.

The lesson of this book is the tragic inadequacy and superficiality of the efforts of the Progressives, business and industrial leadership, and social agencies. The author suggests a parallel between the situation in the 1920s and 1967.

EMMA LOU THORNBROUGH
Butler University
Indianapolis
Indiana

ROLAND J. LIEBERT. *Disintegration and Political Action: The Changing Functions of City Government in America.* Pp. ix, 223. New York: Academic Press, 1976. $12.00.

This study, based on the relevant data of 676 cities with a 1960 population of at least 25,000, is concerned with the scope, in a functional sense, of city government in the United States. A central finding of Professor Liebert is that the most important predictor of the functional scope of any one municipality is its age; that is, when it first realized a population of 25,000. On the whole, the author notes that older cities are more multifunctional and exhibit a politics of accessibility, while newer municipalities deliver a somewhat restricted scope of services and are characterized by a decision-making process dominated by experts.

Several interesting observations are set forth by Professor Liebert. He notes that the range of services provided by municipalities varies considerably. For instance, only about one-quarter of the total sample of cities are responsible for primary and secondary education (in most communities this is the province of the school board); while, almost ninety percent provide parks and recreation services. Further, he carefully analyzes the impact of historical factors on structuring local delivery systems.

Students of urban government identified with the "consolidationist approach" will not welcome the findings set forth for, as the author demonstrates, the relative limited functional scope of the newer city governments and the consequent importance of special purpose governmental units, most prominently special districts and authorities, mean increasing governmental fragmentation in the metropolis. At least implicitly, Professor Liebert negatively views this development as well; what he fails to note is that there is a good deal of horizontal cooperation in the metropolis engendered by local units and councils of governments.

This is a good study carried out with rigor; it provides a *meaningful* contribution to the study of local government and politics. However, I wish Professor Liebert had devoted more attention to the impact of federal and state policies in structuring the functional activity of local government.

NELSON WIKSTROM
Virginia Commonwealth University
Richmond

SPARK M. MATSUNAGA and PING CHEN. *Rulemakers of the House.* Pp. 208. Urbana: University of Illinois Press, 1976. $7.95.

U.S. Representative Spark M. Matsunaga and Professor Ping Chen present a critical study of the House Rules Committee. Matsunaga, as a participant and observer of the Rules Committee for the past ten years, provides the reader with first hand knowledge and experience of the formal and informal actions of the Rules Committee. The authors' purpose is to demonstrate ". . . that the historical role of the Rules Committee is one of searching for a balance between its own goals and those of House Leadership" (p. xi). The authors studied the Rules Committee for a twenty-year period (1957–1976), interviewed fifty-nine House Members over a four-year period (1970–1974), interviewed three former chairmen of the Rules Committee, and interviewed chairmen of other House committees and Rules staff members.

Their study begins by examining the role of the Rules Committee. The committee is viewed as an instrument or arm of House leadership by both House Republicans and Democrats. Furthermore, over two-thirds of the Democrats interviewed agreed that the Democratic committee members had to be loyal to the party platform. Less than one-third of the Republicans interviewed agreed that their party committee members had to be loyal. Both parties agreed that the Rules Committee must attempt to satisfy House expectations and leadership.

The authors examine and critically analyze the powers and functions of the Rules Committee (Chapter 2). Through the use of these powers and functions, the authors describe how the committee (1) exercises substantive control over legislation, (2) establishes regulations for debate, (3) determines when to yield to House leadership, (4) forces a bill to the floor, and (5) settles other committees' jurisdictional disputes.

Chapters Three, Four and Five discuss sanctions against the Rules Committee, recruitment, and goals of the Rules Committee members, respectively. Sanctions are imposed by House membership if their expectations are not fulfilled by the Rules Committee. The recruitment of members on the Rules Committee is determined by tangible and intangible qualifications, regional and state expectations, candidate expectations and candidate nonexpectations. Once a member of the committee, members have goals they wish to accomplish. These may be prestige and influence, constituency and re-election benefits, and the like.

Chapters Six and Seven focus on the role of the Rules Committee chairmen and the decision-making behavior of committee members, respectively. The tenure of three former chairmen is examined (1955–1974) and divided into five periods based on each chairman's reputation. The identification of each period was determined by the relationship that existed between the Rules Committee chairman and House leadership and other committee members. The authors performed special studies to analyze committee member behavior in decision-making. Consistency studies were used to analyze the 'divided vote' from the 85th–93rd Congresses. The Rice Index of Cohesion was utilized to determine the party voting patterns of the Rules Committee members. Federal District Outlay studies were used to analyze the relationship between constituency interests and the voting behavior of committee members.

The authors conclude that (1) the history of the committee has been one of accommodation between leadership and independence and (2) committee survival is dependent upon the majority of the House approving its decisions. The authors furnish several tables to support their analyses and claims throughout their work. Three appendices provide useful information to the reader.

In sum, the authors' work represents a significant contribution to the literature in the field. The book will appeal to those scholars, students, and observers who have either a special or general interest in the legislative process.

MITCHELL F. RICE
Prairie View A & M University
Texas

WILLIAM HOWARD MOORE. *The Kefauver Committee and the Politics of Crime, 1950–1952.* Pp. xii, 269. Columbia: The University of Missouri Press, 1974. $12.00.

HUMBERT S. NELLI. *The Business of Crime.* Pp. xiii, 314. New York: Oxford University Press, 1976. $12.95.

The great American success story has many variants, and some of the most impressive began in Europe with immigrant boys making their ways through Ellis Island to discover that there was, indeed, gold on the pavements of the New York streets and beyond. Fame and fortune was the lot of relatively few, and the many found that there were barriers of prejudice, language, and the solidarity of the older settlers in the way of achieving even a modest competence. These twice-told tales are cherished elements of the melting pot myth; they nourish our claim to a new and vital culture.

They also have a gothic parody. Among the huddled masses who made their way to our shores were thousands from the tormented southern provinces of Italy. The most exploited and poorly governed people of western Europe, they brought with them traditions of hard work and hostility to authority. Poverty, disorder and the sense of exploitation had driven many southern Italians into criminal activity. Whatever the truth may be about the Mafia in this country— and that is not settled in either of the books under review here—it was an authentic subculture in Sicily for generations before the first Sicilians arrived in our cities. It is not surprising that its vocabulary, at least, has been institutionalized here, even if substantial doubts persist about the links between criminal organizations in the old country and the new. What is certainly true is that a great many southern Italians found a criminal opportunity structure easily accessible. Preying at first on each other with the terrifying imagery and violence of *la mano nera* —The Black Hand—they eventually discovered that prostitution, gambling and, with the arrival of Prohibition, the traffic in liquor combined to offer opportunities in enterpreneurial crime which rivaled and outstripped those conventional opportunities that attracted their law-abiding contemporaries. Outside the controls which function for conventional commerce, they used violence of the most extreme variety in place of take-over bids and manipulation of the stock and commodity markets to advance their interests. Their con-

tribution to our cultural traditions is ineradicable. Our fascination with organized crime has already created a folk literature of fiction and non-fiction which rival the *Elder Edda* or the *Song of Roland.*

Maybe through such epics as Mario Puzo's *The Godfather* we will have achieved all the understanding we will ever have of the Italian contributions to organized crime. Certainly the passing parade which Dr. Nelli hustles through his pages does no more than numb the understanding. He has relied almost entirely on newspaper sources to pull his history together, and evidently has been unwilling to edit out any of the bloody engagements, the ugly triumphs, or the front page horrors which he has culled from the microfilms. Photographs of half-forgotten unworthies glower at the reader throughout the book, and the effect is like a wax museum. It is all very unfortunate. Nelli appears to have the equipment and the research for a book which will put the Italian share of organized crime in the larger context of Italian-American history. He has told us far more than we need to know or can absorb about the chronology and the dynasties of entrepreneurial crime, but enlightenment does not come with the abundant documentation.

For Dr. Moore the task was different. Obviously a conscientious historian with an awareness of the responsibilities of his discipline to assist the reader in an understanding of the past, he has relied on the mass of reports of the Kefauver Committee's hearings, the newspaper reports of the time, and the growing literature of organized crime. He found it impossible to assemble an oral history out of the Kefauver Committee members or its staff; these principals are all dead.

What he has been able to give us is a competent account of the Committee's origins, the conduct of its investigation and its findings. He concludes that the whole episode was a good show, an effective advancement for the career of its ambitious principal, Senator Kefauver, but a failure in either bringing out the truth about organized crime or in promoting effective legislation for its control. But like Dr. Nelli, Moore is unable to winnow the masses of detail which he accumulated, with the result that the reader has the same sense of a parade of half-forgotten names from the fifties, an era which is already slipping into the unreality of the archives. His conclusions are true enough but their significance is not demonstrated by their consequences. A specialist in the history of the fifties will find Dr. Moore's monograph a useful account of an important episode in the political history of the times. For an understanding of its significance he will have to think for himself.

JOHN P. CONRAD
The Academy for Contemporary
    Problems
Columbus
Ohio

REXFORD G. TUGWELL. *The Compromising of the Constitution: Early Departures.* Pp. iv, 188. Notre Dame, Ind.: University of Notre Dame Press, 1976. $8.95.

Rexford G. Tugwell has had a long, varied, and distinguished career in academic and public life—most notably perhaps as a member of Franklin Roosevelt's brain trust. Currently he is a Senior Fellow in Political Science at the Center for the Study of Democratic Institutions. The theme he reiterates in this essay is that the Federal Constitution, adequate for the time it was written and the result, in part, of compromises relevant to the politics of the framers, has become in many respects obsolete. Later Americans living under conditions markedly different from those of the late eighteenth century are governed under a document more mystical than real, whose provisions, if taken literally, are hopelessly outdated. The Constitution does not specifically say government may undertake to relieve the ills plaguing an industrial society or to promote health and education, or to control the nation's economic condition. Such actions can be justified only by implication and are subject to varieties of interpretations. Consequently we do

not know what we can or cannot do when action becomes imperative. In Tugwell's mind the fault lies in the failure of the framers of the Constitution to provide an efficient amending process. In lieu of this defect the original meaning of the Constitution has been altered by the executive, congress, and especially by the Supreme Court. Whatever the framers had in mind regarding the judicial power, Tugwell argues, they could not have expected that the justices would rewrite the Constitution. For this purpose they specifically provided for two methods of amendment. What they did not foresee was that one would be extremely difficult and the other practically impossible. Inasmuch as they did not include the word "interpretation" among the powers granted to the judiciary, they obviously expected that alterations would be made only by amendment. While the Supreme Court had, in fact, no discernible mandate it was to engage in an immense enlargement of the original meaning of the Constitution. But as a product of judicial interpretation the Constitution has become more and more ambiguous, a fundamental law Americans could not understand or rely upon, but only revere. Other branches of government were also to swell their own jurisdictions. Adapting Cardozo's locution he charges that administrative law "when it exceeds the limits of legislatively directed regulation, is implication run riot" (p. 159). Some persons who have recently been placed in an impossible predicament by the doublethink, *Catch-22* requirements laid down by HEW might agree with Tugwell, and deplore the failure of Congress to insist that its agencies adhere to, rather than violate the intention of the Civil Rights Act of 1964. Yet the political process for a nation as large as the United States and composed of so many diverse elements often produces a situation in which only bills vague enough and subject to varied interpretations will win the support of enough diverse interests groups to provide a majority for enactment.

Tugwell as a minimum seems to be

calling for a new procedure for amending the constitution. But in referring to the audacity of the men who in 1787 abandoned the Articles of Confederation and started anew, he remarks: "Such boldness, regarded as admirable in 1787, would be equally admirable at the Constitution's bicentennial" (p. 172). But is the problem one that can be solved by a new constitution? Does our predicament stem from a constitution unclear as to whether government may act? It has been a long time since the Court struck down NRA. Has the constitutionality of recent federal programs even been challenged? Our dilemma may be that there is no consensus as to what our problems are, and little agreement as to appropriate solutions. Can we presume that a new constitution, no matter how detailed or specific its text may be, will allow resolution of differences political in nature? Will not protagonists continue to differ and to subject even such a constitution to varieties of interpretation?

JACK M. SOSIN

University of Nebraska
Lincoln

SOCIOLOGY

MARGARET ADAMS. *Single Blessedness: Observations on the Single Status in Married Society.* Pp. v, 264. New York: Basic Books, 1976. $12.50.

"Capitalist imperialism (or neo-colonial capitalism)," according to the author, is the ultimate villain responsible for the deprecated, ambiguous lot of single persons, especially single women, in contemporary society. Proceeding from Marxist and feminist premises, the author has plenty of blame left for psychiatrists, who represent singleness "as psychopathic and indicative of narcissism, neurotic withdrawal from intimate relationships, and a schizoid personality."

The author is a social worker who has read widely, theorizes ably at both the psychological and sociological levels, and whose writing contains a pungency based on her resentment of the stereo-type of the single woman. The data of her study derive principally from depth interviews with twenty-seven people. She concentrated on women but does include material from interviews with men.

The author's sociological analysis leads her to speculate that "the single status begins to receive respect and support at the stage of social development when maintaining population growth is of less immediate importance than . . . expanding economic productivity. . . ." At another point her speculations include the possibility that "the dinosaurlike institution of marriage as understood today may subside into obsolescence as the need for population control turns the family into a redundant, if not actually antisocial, system."

After considering "psychology's persuasive assaults" on, and its "anathematizing proscription" of, singleness, the author develops the argument that singleness calls for "psychological autonomy," and that although the single state implies a "predictable loneliness," it does not preclude the possibility of emotional investment and commitment. Indeed, she asserts that the single life is laden with opportunities for varied social relationships and concludes that this freedom, in contrast to the rigidity of familial roles, fosters a capacity for abstract ideas and intellectual interests and a greater readiness for experimentation among the single.

This reviewer sympathizes with the author's complaints about the labeling of the single woman but is dubious about the Marxist supporting argument. Singleness has been a deviant status in pre-industrial as well as in "capitalist-imperialist" societies, and it seems probable that Engels was wrong in believing that women enjoyed a universally higher status before the onset of industrialization. It is reasonable to argue that the family's importance might be expected to dwindle with the growth of concern about overpopulation. What has been going on for decades is a decline in the birth rate and an increase in the emphasis on the family as a source of emotional support and gratification although the mounting divorce rate and the declining marriage rate can be construed as evidence that the family has numerous failures in fulfilling the affectional function. Finally, it seems possible that the decline in the birth rate may generate such alarm that the family will suddenly find new honor.

Whether one agrees or disagrees with most of the argument of this book, one comes away with the refreshing feeling of having encountered a stimulating thinker and a cogent writer.

ROBERT F. WINCH
Northwestern University
Evanston
Illinois

SHIMON AWERBUCH and WILLIAM A. WALLACE. *Policy Evaluation for Community Development: Decision Tools for Local Government.* Pp. v, 286. New York: Praeger, 1976. $22.50.

The appearance of this new monograph in the Praeger Special Studies Series should be noted by two intersecting audiences in the urban studies field. First, it will be of interest to those urban generalists who wish to follow from a certain distance research trends in the urban community planning profession and, second, it will be of interest to planning professionals with a specific interest in what is going on in the area of computer simulations and models. This reviewer, an urban sociologist, is reviewing the book taking the role of the former audience, which is probably greater among the readers of *The Annals.*

Three early chapters of the book in the course of about 50 pages are a descriptive history of urban planning trends from the Colonial period to the present or the "New Planning"—that is when the large computers entered the picture. There is really nothing new by way of fact or interpretation in these chapters. It is the familiar story of the dominance of economic considerations, the market mechanism, and the singularity of profit motive as the guiding hands in American urban development and land-use plan-

ning. These factors were to some degree modified of course with the advent of the planning profession in the middle of this century.

The early chapters are really a lead-in for the core of the book, which is the exposition of several rather technical and *ad hoc* computer models. In the author's own words, "The purpose of this research is not to prescribe the best community development plan for a municipality but, rather, to describe techniques that can help the local policy-maker evaluate the fiscal and socio-economic impact of community development alternatives on the municipality." It is a disjointed feature of the book that the historical chapters discuss planning trends for the largest cities of the country while the ensuing technical chapters, developing the evaluation and decision impact model, probably of necessity are addressed to planning problems in the *smaller* communities of the nation—in one application to a town of 1,500. The book has three appendices and 58 tables, figures and exhibits.

IRVING LEWIS ALLEN
The University of Connecticut
Storrs

SHERBURNE F. COOK. *The Conflict Between the California Indian and White Civilization.* Pp. xi, 522. Berkeley: University of California Press, 1976. $24.75.

Between 1940 and 1943, Sherburne F. Cook published six essays which appeared as Volumes 17, 18, and 21–24 of the *Ibero-Americana* series. In this labor of love, Cook, a distinguished animal biologist, turned to the field of history and studied the effects Spanish and American invaders had on the California Indians during the century after 1770. The essays that emerged from this research were truly major contributions to Native American historiography—a field receiving only scant attention before 1945. In 1976, the essays, long out of print, remain works of fundamental importance in California anthropology and history, and their reemergence is both welcomed and appreciated.

The essays are of unequal length and importance. The two that should be read, and studied, and contemplated are included here as Parts One and Three: "The Indian Versus the Spanish Mission" and "The American Invasion, 1848–1870."

In the former essay, Cook not only discusses carefully the intended goal of Franciscan missionaries but, more important, he shows the effect their efforts at assimilation had on Native Americans. Reviewing an enormous amount of historical data, he shows clearly the misery endured by Indians wrenched away from a life of freedom and forced to live in a foreign environment (missions) together with Spaniards dedicated to destroying their heritage and spirit. Cook leaves no stone unturned as he examines population declines, fugitivism, rebellion, and the destruction wrought by disease (especially syphilis), poor sanitation, change of climate, and much more. He also offers important data on twenty-seven Indian tribes—most of which have disappeared—that inhabited California and numbered 133,550 when the Spanish came.

However, despite the destructive effect of Spanish rule and the ultimate failure of their efforts, Cook rightly contends, in "The American Invasion, 1848–1870," that Spaniards were kind and thoughtful compared with the interlopers from the United States who followed them. Americans did not force natives to live in missions; they simply took the Indians' habitat and made it their own, forcing Indians to endure a new environment in their own homeland. California natives "were subjected not to invasion but to inundation" (p. 256), Cook maintains; and they suffered more—far more—as a result. Even though Spaniards considered Indians inferior, they at least believed natives could be saved and uplifted by conversion; Americans were interested only in material goods—land, gold, silver—and considered Indians temporary obstructions to be destroyed

along the bloody road to material success. Spaniards forced natives to be a part of their society; Americans rigidly excluded them from admission. Cook and subsequent researchers have concluded that the impact of American settlement was three times as destructive to natives as that of Spanish predecessors.

Unfortunately, although this volume honors Cook's essays and rescues them from contemporary obscurity, it does not honor Cook himself. The anonymous editor could have enhanced the work by including an introductory essay on the life of Sherburne Cook and emphasizing why and how he got interested in California Indians. It would also have been fitting to show clearly the importance of Cook's work today, and not leave to reviewers the task of paying proper tribute to this scientist who labored long and hard in a field which then attracted only a few scholars and their students to these topics whose importance is second to none in this nation's history.

ARTHUR H. DEROSIER, JR.
The University of Mississippi
University

SAMUEL C. HEILMAN. *Synagogue Life: A Study in Symbolic Interaction.* Pp. xii, 306. Chicago, Ill.: The University of Chicago Press, 1976. $12.95.

Professor Heilman has presented us with a most interesting and lively description of the purposes, the activities and the functions of the synagogue in terms of a sociological analysis from the perspective of interactional symbolism. He has very prudently admitted in his chapter "Final Words" that he has not presented a "full view" of the synagogue (p. 262) because such a view demands a variety of perspectives. On the other hand, this sociological view cannot be exclusive, as can be seen, for example, by his psychological analysis of the "joking" that goes on in the synagogue. Even the religious dimension inevitably creeps into his analysis. He wisely points out that for a person to be in the "shule" (a yiddish expression meaning synagogue) could be a combination of prayer, study and "sociability." He has attempted to portray the synagogue as a dynamic institution —a task in which he has eminently succeeded. Commendable are his well chosen quotations at the beginning of each chapter, his painstaking first chapter of "Backgrounds, Beginnings and Definitions" and his efficient summary called "Final Words." The Glossary, Footnotes and Bibliography are indeed quite useful.

While the term "symbolic interaction" is normally interpreted to apply to human beings that interact with each other through some contact and thus produce a behavior modification, Heilman maintains that the activities themselves as social forces interact with each other. An example of this phenomenon is what he calls the "interaction between liturgical and social in common prayer." To this extent, gossip becomes an activity which affects even the activity of prayer, and not always in the negative sense. His analysis of the types of gossip and joking as a form of "social obligation" makes for a lively and even amusing piece of reading. While these two activities are technically forbidden and looked down upon by the laws of synagogue decorum, as a social expression they have managed to play a significant role in the social dimension of the synagogue. Heilman has capably analyzed even the chanting, group singing and religious study that go on in the synagogue as interactional activities of great value. It also appears in his study that synagogue activity is not restricted to the four walls of the synagogue structure.

A review must present some constructive criticism. In this light I would have liked to see the author analyze how the interaction involved in synagogue activity is different from other institutional systems of interaction. There surely must be something unique about each social system. Also, some of his statements seem questionable. For example, saying that the prayer book is enhanced in its sanctity by contact with the Torah Scroll or that Tzizith

(fringes) gain their sanctity by contact with the Torah Scroll is indeed not accurate. It is also not completely accurate to state that inspiration is diluted when using "other's words" or praying in public. If anything, these characteristics often add inspiration to prayer. Also, his analysis of the role of women in prayer is slightly misleading. Private prayer for a woman is not a privilege which she may assume. It is an obligation, the same as it is for a man. Women's expression of "Jewishness" at home and with family does not entirely preclude time for public gathering and prayer. Women are obligated to hear the Megillah reading for example, to take part in the Seder as well as other religious obligations.

All in all, we are indebted to Professor Heilman for presenting us with this dynamic and well written study which will interest both scholar and layman.

SAMUEL J. FOX

Merrimack College
North Andover
Massachusetts

MARTIN E. MARTY. *A Nation of Behavers.* Pp. 239. Chicago, Ill.: University of Chicago Press, 1976. $8.95.

Religion has already served as a means of social demarkation for Americans. This is to say that through their religious identities, Americans tend to differentiate among themselves. Though early settlers were limited to few denominations, demographic changes, migrations and dissent caused a multiplication of faiths and factions. Nevertheless, scholars attempting to understand American religious life (as well as theologians and laymen hoping to make sense of it) have tended to use the same restrictive categories that have epitomized older, more established churches.

It is to "map" the terrain of religious life in contemporary America that Martin Marty, Professor of Christian History at the University of Chicago, presents us with *A Nation of Behavers.* More an essay than a book, it is the author's opinion that the most effective way to understand American Religion is through the behavior it engenders. Actions, rather than creeds, allow denominations to be differentiated from each other.

Marty examines the two most common approaches to the same issue, theological comparison and institutional analysis, and finds them wanting. Theology, he claims, is often apologetic and beside the point. It may serve to cover more salient differences between sects, such as geography and social status. To be a Congregationalist, wealthy and from Connecticut is largely one and the same.

Equally, institutional forms assumed by religious groups have become too similar to allow satisfying differentiation for their members. Organizational lines have steadily blurred. Even splinter fractions copy many of the very structures they found so repugnant in their parent body. In Marty's words: ". . . the suggestions that spirit-people could transcend institutionalism are denied by discussions of ministerial pensions . . . in Pentacostal newspapers" (p. 112).

The inadequacies of these forms of social boundary-setting came to the fore in the wake of the "identity incident" of the sixties and early seventies. Now, belonging and identifying in experiential and emotional terms outflank theological discussions or organizational forms. Congregants seek religious practices that put cognitive distance between them and others. It is thereby that they establish a positive and visible anchor to set themselves in society. This identity may be all the more important to the extent that it offers to its adherent a distinctive social location.

It is within this context that Marty analyzes the successes and failures of several religious manifestations. These include: Mainline Religion, Evangelicalism, Pentacostalism, the occult, ethnic religion and civil religion. In each case he rather pessimistically decides that new and creative religious identities will either fade in time or join the mainstream. He implies that deviations from the mainstream are often responses to outside, secular forces. Thus: "Main-

line churches suffer in times of cultural crisis and disintegration, when they receive blame for what goes wrong in society but are by-passed when people look for new ways to achieve social identity" (p. 71).

Marty's work is intelligently, almost pleasantly written. He is obviously at home with his material which is well-organized and direct. Yet there are some problems of a conceptual nature.

It may be, for example, that his work is time-bound. If, as he implies, the pendulum is swinging back toward the mainstream—and most deviating sects are so condemned—then his "identity incident" may be little more than a passing phase. Adherents, either on their own or through their churches, will ultimately return to the theological or institutional base that Marty dismisses. No doubt the base to which they return will have been changed, as well, in the process—but it will be the "mainline" nonetheless.

In addition, Marty is unclear as to cause and effect. At times it seems that religious groups engender certain social behaviors while at times it seems that those of similar social behavior seek out given religious sects. It may also be that the two are mutually reinforcing, and/or caused by some third, unknown, factor. The author never clarifies his thoughts in this area but simply employs these approaches indiscriminately as they suit his purpose.

Nevertheless, these weaknesses should not divert one from the value of the book. Professor Marty has argued convincingly for a non-theological, non-institutional understanding of American religion. What he says is literate and well-worth reading.

DAVID SCHNALL
The College of Staten Island
City University of New York

NOEL PARRY and JOSE PARRY. *The Rise of the Medical Profession.* Pp. 282. New York: International Publications, 1976. $17.50.

Sorokin's classic study of American social mobility (1927) suggests that individual hereditary transmission occurs within the professions of higher social honor and privilege which require intensive intellectual work and provide long term stability. The Parrys do not restrict explanation of all social mobility to the habits and background of the individual. They explore historically the maneuvers and consequences of a professional group's impact on the social standing of all its members. They regard the sociologists' lack of interest in group mobility as a blindness extending from the lack of concern with the middle class which, according to Marxist theory is to be absorbed by the proletariat, and the middle class's own preoccupation with individual striving and success. As a core element of the middle class, the authors view the professions as the vehicles of collective social mobility.

After providing the theoretical structure for a discussion of professions and social class in the first half of the book, a case study of the development of the medical profession in Britain is offered. The choice of both profession and country demonstrates the authors' wisdom in selecting a genuine and very provocative test of their thesis. Charles Newman's study of medical education in the nineteenth century is heavily relied on for historical data and assessment which ensures a reliable basis for the discussion. The views of medical leaders, economic changes, the growth of hospitals and state supported medical care systems have offered difficult challenges to the maintenance of the medical profession's monopoly up to the present. By keeping its membership limited and precise, with the roles of those with differing educations and duties separated by rank, fees and respect, the medical profession has retained its prestige as a group in which all its members share.

The Poor Law and successive legislated reforms which provided funds to support medical treatment for more citizens offered the greatest challenge to the profession which had exercised control over its members by restricting the number of highly qualified and

salaried physicians. Medical graduates found more opportunities to advance through service in the state supported medical systems, hospitals and private health insurance programs. Nevertheless, the almost inherent mechanism of a profession to ensure its members status within the middle class has continued to adjust to these unexpected and unwanted opportunities for growth and enlargement of its membership.

Since the authors do not accept the usual constraints of the historian not to comment on future possibilities, and after all this is the criterion of a good sociological analysis, several alternative forecasts for the next stage of development of the medical profession are discussed. The radical view of Illich (1973) in which medicine is simplified or as he phrases it: "The time has come to take the syringe out of the hand of the doctor, as the pen was taken out of the hand of the scribe during the reformation in Europe," (p. 252) is rejected for the moderate view that all members of society will actively participate in health preservation.

                              AUDREY B. DAVIS
Smithsonian Institution
Washington, D.C.

PAUL E. PETERSON. *School Politics Chicago Style.* Pp. xi, 304. Chicago, Ill.: University of Chicago Press, 1976. $15.00.

Some social science research appears to be facts in search of explanatory theory, some theory in search of facts. This study of school politics in Chicago appears to be factually overwhelming but theoretically still in quest of a theory to manage the facts. Professor Peterson has dedicated a large portion of his academic career to a thorough collection of data surrounding school board politics in Mayor Daley's Chicago. He has sought to impose upon the data what he calls "pluralist and ideological bargaining models" as well as "unitary" and "rational" models. The facts are pressed through the models and, unsurprisingly, every model has a meaning all its own.

The array of facts on teacher union politics, the meticulous detail concerning board members, internal factions on the school board—all these are provided in rich supply. There is a judicious use of interviews and spicy quotations to enliven the material and sharpen the issues. Statistical data and charts are used modestly to illustrate and supplement the presentation.

A few surprises are produced: Mayor Daley did not control the school board, even though he made all the appointments; elites do not dominate key decisions; interest groups seem relatively weak. Yet these points are not emphasized or developed by the author who is much more inclined to test out his models. Unfortunately, the model testing leads to inconclusive results, depending upon the model employed, as Professor Peterson admits.

The subject of school politics has attracted a number of social scientists who seem to find it in a miniature version of the political system. Professor Peterson does not find that close a connection between general municipal politics and school board politics. Instead, school board politics, even in America's most bossed city, are regarded as relatively autonomous. The separation of schools from ordinary politics seems to be fairly complete, on the evidence provided. Yet we have no comparative frame of reference. In most big cities school board politics are related to partisan and machine politics, at least indirectly. If those linkages are few in Chicago and if Mayor Daley was merely a pluralist bargainer in an autonomous universe which contained strong reform influence we should know more about how this happened in Chicago as compared to other big cities. The concentration of the research upon Chicago is intense, but this limits the value of the book for the understanding of school politics in general.

Bridging the gap between the educationists and the political scientists is a worthy enterprise. The attempt to introduce a more sophisticated methodology into school politics research is commendable. The balanced approach to sensitive issues such as school desegregation, collective bargaining and decentralization is refreshing, but the final and concluding chapter is simply not justified by the facts and models marshalled in this book. We cannot draw conclusions about educational policy-making in central cities based solely on the Chicago example.

JAY A. SIGLER
Rutgers University
Camden, N.J.

INO ROSSI, ed. *The Unconscious in Culture: The Structuralism of Claude Lévi-Strauss in Perspective.* Pp. ix, 487. New York: E. P. Dutton & Co., 1974. $6.95.

This lengthy volume of essays is an attempt to analyze and assess the theoretical and substantive contributions of Claude Lévi-Strauss and his structuralist method to contemporary social scientific thought. It is not a comprehensive or systematic discussion of Lévi-Strauss' work as a whole, but rather an attempt to deal in depth and from a variety of theoretical points of view with certain of the more crucial analytical and methodological issues arising out of his work. The essays, for the most part, have been contributed by scholars within the anthropological profession, and much of the emphasis is on the usefulness of Lévi-Strauss' approach for the analysis of the kinds of data anthropologists typically engage themselves with.

The book is divided into three main sections, each of which is introduced by a brief essay by the editor outlining the major issues to be discussed and anticipating the central points to be raised by each author. The first section is devoted to the theoretical foundations of Levi-Strauss' structuralism and to some of its historical antecedents, particularly within the field of linguistics. The major essays in this section are by the editor himself, with additional commentaries by George Mounin and

Marshall Durbin (on linguistic theory and structuralism) and Jacques Maquet (on structuralism and the analysis of myth).

The second section, entitled "Structuralism in Ethnography," has as its purpose "to offer a variety of ethnographic reactions to Lévi-Strauss' method to illustrate its peculiarities and strengthen its procedures." The section is balanced between criticism from those whom Rossi terms the "empirical anthropologists" (represented by Alice Kasakoff and John Adams dealing with Lévi-Strauss' analysis of kinship and myth, respectively, among an American Indian tribe with whom both have done field research), and support from anthropologists who find his methodology useful and stimulating as it is applied to their field data. In this latter group are Ross Crumrine and Barbara Macklin (with a joint paper) and Shin-pyo Kang. Finally in this section essays by Eric Schwimmer and Jan Pouwer suggest ways in which the structuralist method can be strengthened, illustrating their views with discussions of ethonographic materials with which they are personally familiar.

The third and final segment of this volume is the longest. It is a collection of essays in which structuralism is viewed critically from a variety of other epistemological and methodological perspectives within the social sciences. The contributions of Anthony Wilden, Stanley Diamond and Lawrence Krader may be characterized as predominantly critical in tone, while Yvan Simonis and Lawrence Rosen provide more favorable assessments in their comparisons of Lévi-Strauss' approach with those of other major contemporary theoreticians.

It is not possible in a brief review to discuss in any detail the various arguments put forward in this volume, nor is it appropriate to single out any one from among a large group of high-quality contributions. From the point of view of the general reader, it should perhaps be pointed out that this book is in no way an introduction to the work of Lévi-Strauss. Its major contribution is to the large and ever-increasing body of specialized literature on and within the structuralist school, and can best be appreciated by those already familiar with Lévi-Strauss' work and thought.

For the reader with an interest in further examination of some of the issues raised in these essays, and for those as well who would like some guidance into the literature on and by Lévi-Strauss and into the structuralist literature in general, Rossi's useful bibliographical resource note will be appreciated. It includes not only a basic bibliography of the writings of Lévi-Strauss himself, but, more important, an annotated description of the available literature on him and on structuralism, divided according to topic.

SYLVIA VATUK

University of Illinois
Chicago Circle

GERALD STUDDERT-KENNEDY. *Evidence and Explanation in Social Science.* Pp. 246. Boston, Mass.: Routledge & Kegan Paul, 1975. $20.25.

"An interdisciplinary approach" has as its focus a study of abstract theory building and the implementation of those theoretical frames to particular cases, and simultaneously, the building of theoretical abstractions which might emerge from the implementation of abstract theory. It is a circular process. The author selected several theoretical and methodological frames and sought to analyze those through particular cases. The cases are described in some detail, and are interspersed with comments, analyses and evaluations. They range from A. R. Radcliff-Brown's approach, E. E. Evans-Pritchard work, V. W. Turner's process to T. Kuhn's "Paradigms," H. Simon's "Decision Making," Mary Douglas' comments (to mention a few). There are evaluations from some theorists themselves about each other and the author's on evaluations about all.

Gerald Studdert-Kennedy (the author) locates the cases, theories and the participants under the several headings of: Equilibrium and Historical Change,

Versions of Structure, Scientific Inquiry, Statistical Models and Social Structures, Causes and Structure . . . Levels of Theory . . . ; and, the Disciplines of Economics, Psychology, Social Anthropology, Administration, Political Science, Sociology, Politics and History are used to illustrate the interdisciplinary nature of his own work.

Professor Studdert-Kennedy does not seek to build for himself a theoretical underpinning. However, he does share his epistemological orientation and implicit assumptions about the world of theory building. His epistemological abstract frame is a constant theme threading throughout as he talks about generalities and specifics. Consequently, one does not have to guess about his process, but may have questions about how that process is utilized.

This is a complex book, but the complexity is made understandable by its orderly arrangement. It contains so much, promises a great deal, attempts to integrate many kinds of theories, simultaneously makes fine distinctions between one method and another, and the author goes from one level of abstraction to another in order to demonstrate the relationship between general and specific interdisciplinary approaches. In regard to the latter, he said, "There may be other less acceptable reasons for increasing compartmentalization in the social sciences. It may have undesirable consequences which need to be offset by promoting interdisciplinary research and encouraging students to study for joint degrees." The suggestion does not deal with the epistemology necessary to bring about change. At best, interdisciplinary degrees at the macroscopic level are an expedient. Where they study is not as important as what. We need to know merely the things which connect at a basic level. It is virtually impossible to get into a theory of theories unless this is done.

While his chapter on "Causes and Structure" did not quite live up to its prior billing, some very powerful and impressive statements were made which are right on target. He advises the social

scientists, that no matter what level one is abstracting, he must focus on the central epistemological problem of causation in order to set in motion transformative relations. He, however, reduces the power of the statement by later stating that it is not necessary to relapse into the assumption of an impenetrable global functionalism, for data can be analyzed statistically and comparatively. This approach, in my judgment, does not lead us to an understanding of causation. And, to my amazement he chose economic theory as a prototype to illustrate this point, and the advancement of social science theory, as if economic theory and epistemology were not at two different levels of abstraction unless, of course, he has reference to G. L. S. Shackle's book entitled *Epistemics and Economics* (a fellow Englishman). But, even Shackle was hard put to blend the two levels in a mutative and transformative sense. Although, he began with the proposition that it was necessary to have knowledge about the theory of the origin of political economy, nature and the human predicament.

This book was a massive attempt, achieving a modicum of success. His attempt at moving from abstract theory to specific cases within a large framework is to be commended. And, this book has traces of genius and brilliance especially in the areas of substantive knowledge and expression. But it lacks consistent depth. This is from the point of view of a person in Public Affairs. The social anthropologists may have different feelings. Overall, Studdert-Kennedy's effort is the same as many in the social sciences: to make the social scientist a better theoretician and practitioner by moving beyond the scientific method and establishing the basis for a separate and unique theoretical process. On the basis of that effort I commend this book to the reading public, plus the cases are interesting and engaging.

WILLIAM J. WILLIAMS

University of Southern California
Los Angeles

ECONOMICS

MARION CLAWSON. *Forests For Whom and For What?* Pp. v, 175. Baltimore, Md.: The Johns Hopkins University Press, 1975. $11.95.

The most elemental statement one can make about the human race is that it confronts a natural environment in order to fashion that natural endowment so that it may derive an economic sustenance which enables it to subsist and, if possible, produce a surplus so that it may live in the grandest style compatible with existing technical knowledge. From the most primitive existence known to man to our most modern technical marvels, this is the human condition. One may be awed by nature but never cowed by it. Always man has successfully conquered his environment by dint of the application of his wit. This, in fact, is the unique endowment of man that separates him from other animals—his intelligence which enables him to create tools (technology) so that the natural environment can more effectively be harnessed to meet his unsatiable desires.

This is the answer to the query posed in the title of a most interesting book by Marion Clawson, *Forests For Whom and For What?* Moral philosophizing aside, my answer is that they are for man to fashion a technological system which enables him to produce at a minimum his means of subsistence and once that problem is resolved, then a surplus. This is not to say that is the way I would like it to be. But my ethical desires and esthetic preferences are not the turf on which this ballgame is played.

Clawson adroitly takes us through the thicket of public policy as it relates to forests so we are able to see the forest as well as the trees. His initial point of departure is one of economic efficiency, but he does not neglect the esthetic or ethical criteria in the course of his analysis. For this we should be grateful. Nor should we ignore our gratitude for having the issues of forest policy succinctly stated in a comprehensive discourse on the problem.

The one glaring weakness in the book is the absence of an historical context— and I mean an historical context as long as the life of some of the trees in the forest that Clawson is talking about. Failing this, the reader is left rootless in trying to assess both the desirability of the programs Clawson offers as well as the probability for their success.

HOWARD M. WACHTEL
American University
Washington, D.C.

ELCHANAN COHN and STEPHEN D. MILLMAN. *Input-Output Analysis in Public Education.* Pp. vii, 135. Cambridge, Mass.: Ballinger, 1975. No price.

Input-Output Analysis in Public Education concerns the flow of resources through public school systems and explanations of student performance partly based on variables manipulable in decision making. American educational institutions continue to find themselves in a financial crunch, leading to a search for efficiency models with an emphasis upon "value added" (p. 7). The underlying assumption of this study is that possibilities exist to reduce input costs without reducing the quality of educational output.

The first four chapters provide an overview of the concept of input-output analysis as related to educational institutions and a survey of literature concerning the educational production function. This production process is explored in chapters five and six for a sample of Pennsylvania secondary schools; the Pennsylvania Plan is detailed; and a simultaneous equations analysis is presented for dealing with a broad range of educational outcomes. In chapter seven, the well-known canonical correlation technique is used to construct a single index combining diverse outputs. The final chapter contains a brief discussion of mathematical programming as an alternative tool for educational input-output analysis.

The style is too detailed and technical for a survey and too concise and unsystematic for a text. However, in a readable way the authors adeptly weave the common thread of optimal input and output through many different areas of mathematical programming and statistics.

The reader will recognize the importance of rigorous management techniques to assist decision makers in allocating scarce resources. Perhaps the greatest value of the book lies in the authors' shared insight. Particularly in discussions of regression analysis, the authors emphasize using mathematical manipulation and statistical inferences to approximate input and output parameters. Clearly, this insight is useful; unfortunately, it is less clear whether the author's finesse is transferable to the educational field in real practice.

This important book has a potentially significant influence, particularly for doctoral students interested in educational planning, research, and simulation techniques. The authors accomplished their stated purpose. While the reviewers might quibble with choices of data and variables, we feel that the authors have made intelligent selections. We heartily recommend this book for its intended audience of students and statisticians, especially since competitive books comparable in coverage and level of presentation do not seem to exist. Specialists will find this book worthwhile for its 131 references.

BARBARA W. VAN DER VEUR and
ABDUL W. HAMOOD
Ohio University
Athens

ALAN DAWLEY. *Class and Community: The Industrial Revolution in Lynn.* Pp. viii, 301. Cambridge, Mass.: Harvard University Press, 1976. $17.50.

The emergence recently of a "new social history" reflects a distinct dissatisfaction with traditional historical research methodology—relying primarily on the papers of prominent individuals, public documents, newspapers. Focusing principally on the local level, relying on local manuscript collections and census tracts, these pre-

dominantly younger historians have sought to analyze more scientifically important historical questions. Alan Dawley's study of Lynn (Massachusetts) shoemakers falls within this school. In this monograph, Professor Dawley attempts to assess (1) the impact of industrialization on community and economic relations within one locale, (2) the process by which a village artisan was transformed into a capitalist urban industrial economy, and (3) why increasing social and economic divisions did not result in a radicalized, class conscious politics.

Intensively researched, *Class and Community* provides insights into the social, economic, and political life of an industrializing society. Professor Dawley details the role of capital in effecting industrialization and how an artisan household economy became an industrial economy based first on central shops and then on factories. He further describes the impact of these economic changes on communal and individual relations—the rise of the city, increasing class and social divisions, the professionalization of politics and services.

The study's narrative is disjointed; the reader is often confronted by a mass of information not wholly mastered by the author. Nor is there a clear sense of chronology—as to when these changes occurred and how they affected individuals and community over time. Professor Dawley also fails to develop clearly the relationship between economic and political/community change. When he does, his interpretations are distinctly impressionistic. Impressively challenging the conclusions of the Commons school and the traditional interpretations that geographic and occupational mobility and the opportunities for property accumulation precluded the development of class consciousness, for example, Dawley concludes that political democracy constituted the controlling "safety valve"—that is, it defused radical protest and contributed to a pluralist, interest group politics. Ironically, Dawley's study indirectly highlights the "new social" history's limited contribution as a more scientific approach to the study of history. The reader acquires no definite sense as to how values were formed or transformed, the changing or static basis for power and influence, and the author's major conclusions about the "safety valve" role of political democracy and the Equal Rights tradition are not based on evidence derived from census, newspaper, or manuscript sources.

If unevenly written and developed, this is nonetheless an important addition to the growing literature on 19th century urban, labor, and social history.

ATHAN THEOHARIS
Marquette University
Milwaukee
Wisconsin

ROBERT G. KEITH. *Conquest and Agrarian Change: The Emergence of the Hacienda System on the Peruvian Coast.* Pp. vii, 176. Cambridge, Mass.: Harvard University Press, 1976. $17.50.

In recent years there has been a burgeoning of interest in a set of topics relating particularly to the Third World, but also in part to Europe and Japan: peasantry, modernization, economic development, and colonialism. All the social sciences and several branches of history are now very much engaged. New journals have recently been started to accommodate this growing interest, such as *The Journal of Peasant Studies* and *African Economic History*. A remarkable number of excellent books have appeared which treat several of these topics simultaneously, books such as T. C. Smith, *The Agrarian Origins of Modern Japan*, C. Geertz, *Agricultural Involution*, G. Wright, *Rural Revolution in France*, B. Moore, *Social Origins of Dictatorship and Democracy*, L. B. Simpson, *The Encomienda in New Spain*, F. Chevalier, *Land and Society in Colonial Mexico*, T. S. Epstein, *Economic Development and Social Change in South India*, and I. Adelman and C. T. Morris, *Society, Politics, and Economic Development*.

Robert Keith's *Conquest and Agrarian*

Change: The Emergence of the Hacienda System on the Peruvian Coast is another of these good books, clearly written, intelligently organized, very informative, and based largely on primary sources; it also makes virtuous use of anthropological writing (Leach, Geertz, Rowe, Murra, and others). The book is solid historical description and analysis, free from the archaeologist's vice of compulsive guessing, free from the Marxian's vice of making strong analytical assertions without giving factual evidence to support the interpretation, and free from the "formalist's" vice of regarding early, pre-industrial economies as being merely minor variants of twentieth-century industrial capitalism, to be described in the supply and demand language of elementary economics (for examples, see H. K. Schneider, *Economic Man, The Anthropology of Economics*, A. G. Hopkins, *An Economic History of West Africa*, and D. North and R. Thomas, *The Rise of the Western World*).

After giving a sketch of some of what is known about (1) Indian "Coastal Society before the Spanish Conquest," in successive chapters Keith describes (2) "The Encomienda System," (3) "The Beginnings of Commercial Agriculture," (4) "The Age of the Gentleman-Farmer," and (5) "The Consolidation of the Hacienda System." The book ends with a seven page "Conclusion" comparing early colonial coastal Peru with other parts of Spanish America and summarizing the main reasons (explained throughout the book) for the emergence of haciendas:

The hacienda system [of relatively large plantations and agricultural estates] developed on the Peruvian coast in response to social and economic changes which took place during the century after the conquest. Of these changes, three were of primary importance: (1) the growth of the Spanish population . . . ; (2) the rapid decline of the Indian population in the disastrous epidemics of the sixteenth century, and later as a result of pressures generated by economic development; (3) the rise of agrarian markets to supply the needs of a sizeable Spanish urban population (p. 130).

Some minor quibbles: I would have preferred Keith to write a much longer book (his text is only 136 pages) so as to give us additional chapters on interesting matters only touched lightly in passing: the organization and employment of black slaves; an account of how much of what kinds of exports there were early on and an explanation of why there was so little foreign trade (an important reason, surely, why commercial agriculture developed so slowly); organizational and economic details on what is known about how the pre-conquest political systems controlled irrigation, and on the first haciendas established, particularly the manorial haciendas. Finally, although the book is very clearly written and agreeably free from highfalutin terminology, throughout Keith calls what the Spaniards extracted from the Indians "tribute," "surplus," and "exploitation," very treacherous terms, the latter two especially being condemnations of what one does not like rather than descriptions of what exactly was paid out and received back by the Indians. (Are the obligatory payments made today by Soviet collective farmers to their Government also "surplus" and "exploitation"? If not, why not?) It is better to describe these payments and receipts in detail than to label them (see, for example, pp. 28, 39, 65, 130–136, where the terms "surplus" and "exploitation" are used uncritically, that is, without explaining what they mean and without explaining why the use of these terms is justified).

GEORGE DALTON
Northwestern University
Evanston
Illinois

PETER H. ROSSI and KATHARINE C. LYALL. *Reforming Public Welfare: A Critique of the Negative Income Tax Experiment.* Pp. 208. New York: Russell Sage Foundation, 1976. $10.00.

The idea of trying out particular social programs on an experimental basis

before they are enacted into law has a compelling logic. Indeed, this has long been advocated by academicians believing in the "policy relevance" of social science, by politicians clamoring for scientific backing for their actions as well as by the taxpayer who sees the folkwisdom in such a common sense approach. But until the publication of Rossi and Lyall's *Reforming Public Welfare,* which evaluates the final project reports of the New Jersey–Pennsylvania Income Maintenance Experiment, there has been little knowledge of what happens when the experimental approach is actually attempted.

The idea of a negative income tax (NIT) as a replacement for the existing welfare system has attracted enormous interest since the federal government became poverty conscious in the 1960s. The Office of Economic Opportunity (OEO) turned to two groups, Mathematica, Inc. and the Institute For Research on Poverty at the University of Wisconsin, to conduct a 7.6 million trial of a variety of NIT plans over a three year period in four communities and to determine whether income maintenance would lead to reduced work effort on the part of recipient groups. As perhaps one of the "firsts" in policy related empirical social research, the NIT experience suggests many of the hazards and the potential payoffs for approaches of this kind.

Rossi and Lyall present a detailed critique of the experiment—its scope and design, the conduct of the field investigation, the findings and an analysis of some of the politics in carrying out the research. Although these authors laud the boldness of the experiment, on balance they see the project as seriously flawed. NIT was so narrowly conceived and designed that it produced only frustratingly inconclusive findings about labor supply questions; moreover, the measurement techniques and the data base were so defective that it is impossible to extrapolate these findings to the universe of the poor who would be the likely object of welfare reform.

Although these authors are critical of

the experimenters for being so limited, particularly for ignoring many social dimensions of the welfare problem and becoming obsessed with economic variables, I would say that this critique is also quite limited. Political constraints probably had as much if not more to do with the results of this experiment than anything else. Swift answers about only work response patterns were demanded by politicians in need of ammunition for the welfare reform issue in the late 60s; willing economists, prepared to ignore many of the social aspects of work patterns, dominated the experiment. They gave shaky and premature testimonial support to pro-reform forces in OEO and in Congress, eventually casting doubt on the scientific integrity of the whole project.

Although Rossi and Lyall see these events and report them casually, they never consider them systematically or suggest any conclusions about why and how key political forces were so determinative in shaping the results. This book is valuable for those concerned with the techniques for carrying out an experimental design, but the larger questions which experimental policy research raises remain to be answered elsewhere.

PAUL KANTOR
Fordham University
Bronx, N.Y.

ARNOLD R. WEBER. *In Pursuit of Price Stability: The Wage-Price Freeze of 1971.* Pp. xiv, 137. Washington, D.C.: The Brookings Institution, 1973. $5.95.

By introducing the wage-price freeze of 1971, the Nixon administration took the step of improving direct, enforceable controls on wages, prices, and rents under economic conditions not significantly distorted by war. Phase I— a ninety-day freeze on wages and prices —constituted the first step in a series of controls that moved through Phases II and III and into Phase IV. These policy steps, especially Phase I, enjoyed considerable public support. For some commentators it represented a proper

exercise of power by the government to check inflation. For others, it was a dangerous intervention that threatened market efficiency of free institutions.

This book, written by one of the advisors who served as the first Executive Director of the Cost of Living Council, recounts the development of the policies and strategies. It also tells the story of the improvised administrative organization, manned entirely by members from other governmental agencies. Especially illuminating is the discussion about the formulation of national economic policies in general and income policies in particular. And because the wage-price freeze of 1971 represented American loss of innocence in the use of peacetime controls, it is useful to review the lessons of the experience. Reaction to future temptation will be determined by whether the episode is remembered with pain or pleasure.

The strategy was to "talk tough but walk softly." To be sure, the freeze was carried out without attempting to "manage" the economy in any systematic way. Yet one must remember that the success of the freeze was facilitated by the fact that it was imposed on a cool economy marked by considerable slack in the labor force and industrial capacity. The record shows that by the end of 1971, the upward march of consumer prices at an annual rate of 4 percent suddenly slowed down to a rate of 1.6 percent. Wholesale prices, which had been rising at a rate of 4.9 percent, declined slightly. The U.S. balance of payments improved. The employment picture brightened. The experience reinforced a contention that governmental interventions can restrain wage and price increases temporarily, although the moderation tends to be greater on wages than on prices.

Notwithstanding the valuable contributions of the book, this reviewer remains skeptical about the whole undertaking. The author concludes that "the primary objectives of a freeze are to buy time to permit the development of more substantial economic policies [and the experiment] of 1971 fulfilled these objectives for the Nixon administration" (pp. 129–130). But, I submit, they did so only in the short run and at the cost of substantial damage in the long run. The policies of 1971 did nothing to remove the institutionalized constraints eroding the micro and macro supply functions but only further reinforced them. Consequently, the unprecedented coexistence of inflation and unemployment during the subsequent years had some of their stimulus in the shock of 1971.

JANOS HORVATH
Holcomb Research Institute
Butler University
Indianapolis
Indiana

OTHER BOOKS

ACHEBE, CHINUA. *Morning Yet on Creation Day.* Pp. 160. New York: Anchor Press, 1976. $2.50. Paperbound.

ACQUAVIVA, SABINO and MARIO SANTUCCIO. *Social Structure in Italy.* Pp. v, 236. Boulder, Colo.: Westview Press, 1976. $24.75.

ADAMS, J. MACK and DOUGLAS H. HADEN. *Social Effects of Computer Use and Misuse.* Pp. vii, 326. New York: John Wiley & Sons, 1976. $11.50.

ALLEN, FREDERICK S. et al. *The University of Colorado, 1876–1976.* Pp. vii, 319. New York: Harcourt Brace Jovanovich, 1976. $12.95.

ANDERSON, VERNON F. and ROGER A. VAN WINKLE. *In the Arena: The Care and Feeding of American Politics.* Pp. xi, 425. New York: Harper & Row, 1976. $6.95. Paperbound.

ANDRADE, VICTOR. *My Missions for Revolutionary Bolivia, 1944–1962.* Edited by Cole Blasier. Pp. xi, 200. Pittsburgh, Pa.: University of Pittsburgh Press, 1976. No price.

ASHCRAFT, NORMAN and ALBERT E. SCHEFLEN. *People Space: The Making and Breaking of Human Boundaries.* Pp. 200. New York: Doubleday, 1976. $2.50. Paperbound.

ASHLINE, NELSON F. et al., eds. *Education, Inequality, and National Policy.* Pp. vii, 199. Lexington, Mass.: Lexington Books, 1976. No price.

AUSTIN, LEWIS, ed. *Japan: The Paradox of Progress.* Pp. v, 338. New Haven, Conn.: Yale University Press, 1976. $20.00.

BANKS, OLIVE. *The Sociology of Education.*

Revised Edition. Pp. 294. New York: Schocken Books, 1976. $13.75. Paperbound, $4.95.

BARD, MORTON and ROBERT SHELLOW. *Issues in Law Enforcement: Essays and Case Studies.* Pp. v, 213. Reston, Va.: Reston Company, 1975. $9.95.

BEAGLEHOLE, J. H. *The District: A Study in Decentralization in West Malaysia.* Pp. 122. New York: Oxford University Press, 1976. $6.95. Paperbound.

BEATTY, JOHN LOUIS and OLIVER A. JOHNSON, eds. *Heritage of Western Civilization.* Vol. I. 4th ed. Pp. v, 433. Englewood Cliffs, N.J.: Prentice-Hall, 1977. $6.95. Paperbound.

BEATTY, JOHN LOUIS and OLIVER A. JOHNSON, eds. *Heritage of Western Civilization.* Vol. II. 4th ed. Pp. v, 414. Englewood Cliffs, N.J.: Prentice-Hall, 1977. $6.95. Paperbound.

BECKER, ERNEST. *Escape from Evil.* Pp. xiii, 188. New York: The Free Press, 1975. $2.95. Paperbound.

BELL, QUENTIN. *On Human Finery.* Pp. 239. New York: Schocken Books, 1976. $14.95.

BERTSCH, GARY K. *Values and Community in Multinational Yugoslavia.* Pp. vi, 160. New York: Columbia University Press, 1976. $11.00.

BINDER, VIRGINIA, ARNOLD BINDER and BERNARD RIMLAND, eds. *Modern Therapies.* Pp. v, 230. Englewood Cliffs, N.J.: Prentice-Hall, 1976. $8.95. Paperbound, $3.95.

BLAKER, MICHAEL K., ed. *Japan at the Polls: The House of Councillors Election of 1974.* Pp. 157. Washington, D.C.: American Enterprise Institute for Public Policy Research, 1976. $3.00. Paperbound.

BLANKEN, MAURICE. *Force of Order and Methods: An American View into the Dutch Directed Society.* Pp. vii, 174. The Hague: Martinus Nijhoff, 1976. No price.

BLONDEL, JEAN. *Thinking Politically.* Pp. 165. Boulder, Colo.: Westview Press, 1976. $15.75.

BODDEWYN, J. J., ed. *European Industrial Managers: West and East.* Pp. 560. White Plains, N.Y.: IASP, 1976. $17.95.

BONJEAN, CHARLES M., LOUIS SCHNEIDER and ROBERT L. LINEBERRY, eds. *Social Science in America.* Pp. 221. Austin: University of Texas Press, 1976. $10.00. Paperbound, $3.95.

BRAINERD, J. GRIEST, ed. *The Ultimate Consumer: A Study in Economic Illiteracy.* Pp. v, 230. New York: Arno Press, 1976. $15.00.

BROWNELL, BLAINE A. and DAVID R. GOLDFIELD, eds. *The City in Southern History:*

The Growth of Urban Civilization in the South. Pp. 228. Port Washington, N.Y.: Kennikat Press, 1976. $13.50. Paperbound, $6.95.

BUTLER, EDGAR W. *Urban Sociology: A Systematic Approach.* Pp. viii, 526. New York: Harper & Row, 1976. $13.95.

BUTTERWORTH, ROBERT LYLE and MARGARET E. SCRANTON. *Managing Interstate Conflict, 1945–1974: Data with Synopses.* Pp. v, 535, Pittsburgh, Pa.: University of Pittsburgh Press, 1976. $16.95. Paperbound, $6.95.

CAMPBELL, R. H. and A. S. SKINNER, eds. *Adam Smith: An Inquiry into the Nature and Causes of the Wealth of Nations.* Vol. I & II. Pp. 1623. New York: Oxford University Press, 1976. $62.50.

CHANDLER, DAVID. *Capital Punishment in Canada.* Pp. xi, 224. Toronto, Ca.: McClelland & Stewart, 1976. $5.95. Paperbound.

CHASE, HAROLD W. and CRAIG R. DUCAT. *Supplement to Edward S. Corwin's The Constitution and What it Means Today.* Pp. v, 284. Princeton, N.J.: Princeton University Press, 1976. $3.95. Paperbound.

CHEEK, N. H., JR. and WILLIAM R. BURCH, JR. *The Social Organization of Leisure in Human Society.* Pp. v, 283. New York: Harper & Row, 1976. $10.95.

CHIODI, PIETRO. *Sartre and Marxism.* Pp. vi, 162. Atlantic Highlands, N.J.: Humanities Press, 1976. $13.50.

CLAWSON, MARION. *The Economics of National Forest Management.* Pp. 117. Baltimore, Md.: Johns Hopkins University Press, 1976. $4.50. Paperbound.

CLIFF, TONY. *Lenin: All Power to the Soviets.* Vol. II. Pp. 412. New York: Urizen Books, 1976. $17.50. Paperbound, $7.95.

CLIFF, TONY. *Lenin: Building the Party.* Vol. I. Pp. 398. New York: Urizen Books, 1975. $15.00. Paperbound, $6.95.

COLLINS, DOREEN. *The European Communities.* Vol. I. Pp. vi, 128. Totowa, N.J.: Martin Robertson, 1976. $11.50.

COSER, LEWIS A. and OTTO N. LARSEN, eds. *The Uses of Controversy in Sociology.* Pp. v, 398. New York: The Free Press, 1976. $14.95.

CRAWFORD, ELISABETH and NORMAN PERRY, eds. *Demands for Social Knowledge: The Role of Research Organisations.* Pp. 276. Beverly Hills, Calif.: Sage, 1976. $15.00.

CZUDNOWSKI, MOSHE M. *Comparing Political Behavior.* Pp. 224. Beverly Hills, Calif.: Sage, 1976. $11.00. Paperbound, $6.00.

DAVIS, BERNARD D. and PATRICIA FLAHERTY, eds. *Human Diversity: Its Causes and Social Significance.* Pp. v, 248. Cambridge, Mass.: Ballinger, 1976. $13.50.

DAVIS HORACE B., ed. *The National Question: Selected Writings by Rosa Luxemberg,* Pp. 320. New York: Monthly Review Press, 1976. $16.50.

DE COPPENS, PETER ROCHE. *Ideal Man in Classical Sociology: The Views of Comte, Durkheim, Pareto, and Weber.* Pp. 174. University Park: Pennsylvania State University Press, 1976. $12.75.

DEDRING, JUERGEN. *Recent Advances in Peace and Conflict Research: A Critical Survey.* Pp. 249. Beverly Hills, Calif.: Sage, 1976. $12.00. Paperbound, $6.00.

DiCAPRIO, NICHOLAS S. *The Good Life: Models for a Healthy Personality.* Pp. v, 210. Englewood Cliffs, N.J.: Prentice-Hall, 1976. $8.95. Paperbound, $2.95.

DIKSHIT, R. D. *The Political Geography of Federalism.* Pp. x, 273. New York: Halsted Press, 1976. $22.50.

DION, LEON. *Quebec: The Unfinished Revolution.* Pp. ix, 218. Quebec, Ca.: McGill-Queen's University Press, 1976. $15.00. Paperbound, $7.50.

DOBYNS, HENRY E. and PAUL L. DOUGHTY. *Peru: A Cultural History.* Pp. 336. New York: Oxford University Press, 1976. $12.50. Paperbound, $3.95.

Documents on Disarmament, 1974. Pp. v, 918. Washington, D.C.: U.S. Government Printing Office, 1976. $8.60. Paperbound.

DOETSCH, RAYMOND N. *Journey to the Green and Golden Lands: The Epic of Survival on the Wagon Trail.* Pp. 112. Port Washington, N.Y.: Kennikat Press, 1976. $9.95.

DOLCE, PHILIP C., ed. *Suburbia: The American Dream.* Pp. 240. New York: Doubleday, 1976. $2.95. Paperbound.

DOLCE, PHILIP C. and GEORGE H. SKAU, eds. *Power and the Presidency.* Pp. xi, 339. New York: Charles Scribner's Sons, 1976. $12.50. Paperbound, $5.95.

EAGLETON, TERRY. *Marxism and Literary Criticism.* Pp. 96. Berkeley: University of California Press, 1976. $6.95. Paperbound, $2.65.

Ecological Consequences of the Second Indochina War. Pp. v, 118. Stockholm, Sweden: SIPRI, 1976. No price.

ELKINS, DOV PERETZ, ed. *Glad to be Me: Building Self-Esteem in Yourself and Others.* Pp. 138. Englewood Cliffs, N.J.: Prentice-Hall, 1976. $8.95. Paperbound, $3.95.

Executive Sessions of the Senate Foreign Relations Committee. Vol. III, Part I. Eighty-Second Congress, First Session 1951. Pp. 639. Washington, D.C.: U.S.

Government Printing Office, 1976. $5.25. Paperbound.

Executive Sessions of the Senate Foreign Relations Committee. Vol. III, Part 2. Eighty-Second Congress, First Session 1951. Pp. 700. Washington, D.C.: U.S. Government Printing Office, 1976. $5.65. Paperbound.

FAIR, RAY C. *A Model of Macroeconomic Activity: The Empirical Model.* Vol. II. Pp. vii, 234. Cambridge, Mass.: Ballinger, 1976. $17.50.

FARRELL, MICHAEL. *Northern Ireland: The Orange State.* Pp. v, 406. New York: Urizen Books, 1976. $10.00. Paperbound.

FINER, S. E. *Vilfredo Pareto: Sociological Writings.* Translated by Derick Mirfin. Pp. v, 329. Totowa, N.J.: Rowman & Littlefield, 1976. $15.00.

FINKLER, EARL, WILLIAM J. TONER and FRANK J. POPPER. *Urban Nongrowth: City Planning for People.* Pp. vi, 227. New York: Praeger, 1976. $16.50.

FISCHER, JOEL. *The Effectiveness of Social Casework.* Pp. vii, 342. Springfield, Ill.: Charles C Thomas, 1976. $19.75.

FOLEY, VERNARD. *The Social Physics of Adam Smith.* Pp. ix, 265. West Lafayette, Ind.: Purdue University Press, 1976. $11.95.

Foreign Relations of the United States, 1948: General, The United Nations. Part 2. Pp. ix, 508. Washington, D.C.: U.S. Government Printing Office, 1976. $8.50.

FOX-GENOVESE, ELIZABETH. *The Origins of Physiocracy: Economic Revolution and Social Order in Eighteenth-Century France.* Pp. 325. Ithaca, N.Y.: Cornell University Press, 1976. $15.00.

FRANK, ANDRE GUNDER. *On Capitalist Underdevelopment.* Pp. 113. New York: Oxford University Press, 1976. $1.90. Paperbound.

FRIEDENBERG, EDGAR Z. *The Disposal of Liberty and Other Industrial Wastes.* Pp. 280. New York: Doubleday, 1976. $2.95. Paperbound.

GELLA, ALEKSANDER, ed. *The Intelligentsia and the Intellectuals: Theory, Method and Case Study.* Pp. 224. Beverly Hills, Calif.: Sage, 1976. $12.00. Paperbound, $6.00.

GIVENS, R. DALE and MARTIN A. NETTLESHIP, eds. *Discussions on War and Human Aggression.* Pp. vi, 231. Chicago, Ill.: Aldine, 1976. $12.50.

GLASS, GENE V., ed. *Evaluation Studies Review Annual.* Vol. I. Pp. 672. Beverly Hills, Calif.: Sage, 1976. $29.95.

GLEJSER, HERBERT, ed. *Quantitative Studies of International Economic Relations.* Pp.

vi, 281. Washington, D.C.: Potomac Associates, 1976. No price.

GOLANY, GIDEON. *New-Town Planning: Principles and Practice.* Pp. vii, 389. New York: John Wiley & Sons, 1976. $25.00.

GOLDMAN, RALPH M. *Contemporary Perspectives on Politics.* Pp. v, 454. New Brunswick, N.J.: Transaction Books, 1976. $14.95.

GREENBLATT, SIDNEY L., ed. *The People of Taihang: An Anthology of Family Histories.* Pp. xiii, 305. White Plains, N.Y.: IASP, 1976. $15.00.

GREENSTONE, J. DAVID and PAUL E. PETERSON. *Race and Authority in Urban Politics: Community Participation and the War on Poverty.* Pp. ix, 364. Chicago, Ill.: University of Chicago Press, 1976. $5.95. Paperbound.

GRENE, MARJORIE. *Philosophy In and Out of Europe.* Pp. 180. Berkeley: University of California Press, 1976. $7.95.

GRIFFITH, WILLIAM E., ed. *The Soviet Empire: Expansion & Détente.* Pp. v, 417. Lexington, Mass.: Lexington Books, 1976. No price.

GUINTHER, JOHN. *Moralists and Managers: Public Interest Movements in America.* Pp. 280. New York: Anchor Press, 1976. $2.95. Paperbound.

HAIM, SYLVIA G., ed. *Arab Nationalism: An Anthology.* Pp. 271. Berkeley: University of California Press, 1976. $3.85. Paperbound.

HAMBERGER, JOSEPH. *Macaulay and the Whig Tradition.* Pp. vii, 274. Chicago, Ill.: University of Chicago Press, 1976. $17.50.

HANSEN, NILES M. *Improving Access to Economic Opportunity: Nonmetropolitan Labor Markets in an Urban Society.* Pp. 208. Cambridge, Mass.: Ballinger, 1976. $15.00.

HARE, A. PAUL. *Handbook of Small Group Research.* 2nd ed. Pp. v, 779. New York: The Free Press, 1976. $19.95.

HARTZLER, H. RICHARD. *Justice, Legal Systems and Social Structure.* Pp. viii, 134. Post Washington, N.Y.: Kennikat Press, 1976. $12.50.

HAYDEN, DOLORES. *Seven American Utopias: The Architecture of Communitarian Socialism, 1790–1975.* Pp. ix, 401. Cambridge, Mass.: MIT Press, 1976. $16.95.

HEATH, ANTHONY. *Rational Choice and Social Exchange.* Pp. vii, 194. New York: Cambridge University Press, 1976. $16.95. Paperbound, $5.95.

HELLINGER, STEPHEN H. and DOUGLAS A. HELLINGER. *Unemployment and the Multinationals: A Strategy for Technological*

Change in Latin America. Pp. vii, 158. Port Washington, N.Y.: Kennikat Press, 1976. $12.50.

HELLMAN, ARTHUR D. *Laws against Marijuana: The Price We Pay.* Pp. 210. Urbana: University of Illinois Press, 1975. $10.00.

HENRY, FRANCES, ed. *Ethnicity in the Americas.* Pp. vi, 456. Chicago, Ill.: Aldine, 1976. $22.50.

HOFMANN, ADELE D., R. D. BECKER and H. PAUL GABRIEL. *The Hospitalized Adolescent: A Guide to Managing the Ill and Injured Youth.* Pp. ix, 249. New York: The Free Press, 1976. $14.95.

HOWELL, DAVID. *British Social Democracy.* Pp. 320. New York: St. Martin's Press, 1976. $16.95.

HUTCHINS, ROBERT M. et al., eds. *The Great Ideas Today, 1976.* Pp. 473. New York: Praeger, 1976. No price.

Improving Urban America: A Challenge to Federalism. Pp. 283. Washington, D.C.: ACIR, 1976. $3.00. Paperbound.

KAMENKA, EUGENE, ed. *Nationalism: The Nature and Evolution of an Idea.* Pp. 135. New York: St. Martin's Press, 1976. $12.95.

KASULAITIS, ALGIRDAS. *Lithuanian Christian Democracy.* Pp. v, 244. Chicago, Ill.: Draugas, 1976. No price.

KATZNELSON, IRA. *Black Men, White Cities: Race, Politics, and Migration in the United States, 1900–30, and Britain, 1948–68.* Pp. ix, 219. Chicago, Ill.: University of Chicago Press, 1976. $3.95. Paperbound.

KELLEHER, CATHERINE MCARDLE. *Germany and the Politics of Nuclear Weapons.* Pp. vii, 372. New York: Columbia University Press, 1975. $15.00.

KEMP, JACK and LES ASPIN. *How Much Defense Spending is Enough?* Pp. 64. Washington, D.C.: American Enterprise Institute for Public Policy Research, 1976. $2.00. Paperbound.

KENDRICK, JOHN W. *The Formation and Stocks of Total Capital.* Pp. vii, 256. New York: Columbia University Press, 1976. No price.

KENNET. WAYLAND, ed. *The Futures of Europe.* Pp. 242. New York: Cambridge University Press, 1976. $14.95.

KESSLER, LAWRENCE D. *K'ang-hsi and the Consolidation of Ch'ing Rule, 1661–1684.* Pp. vii, 251. Chicago, Ill.: University of Chicago Press, 1976. $22.00.

KINTON, JACK, ed. *American Ethnic Revival.* Pp. 203. Aurora, Ill.: SSSR, 1977. $9.95. Paperbound, $6.95.

KNIGHT, C. GREGORY and JAMES L. NEWMAN, eds. *Contemporary Africa: Geography and Change.* Pp. v, 546. Englewood Cliffs, N.J.: Prentice-Hall, 1976. $14.95.

KONING, HANS. *A New Yorker in Egypt.* Pp. 265. New York: Harcourt Brace Jovanovich, 1976. $10.95.

KORB, LAWRENCE J., ed. *The system for Educating Military Officers in the U.S.* International Studies, no. 9. Pp. 172. Pittsburgh, Pa.: University of Pittsburgh Press, 1976. No price.

LASKY, MELVIN J. *Utopia and Revolution.* Pp. ix, 726. Chicago, Ill.: University of Chicago Press, 1976. $29.95.

LAUER, ROBERT H., ed. *Social Movements and Social Change.* Pp. v, 292. Carbondale: Southern Illinois University Press, 1976. $10.00.

LEE, J. M. et al. *The Scope of Local Initiative: A Study of Cheshire County Council, 1961–1974.* Pp. viii, 208. Totowa, N.J.: Martin Robertson, 1976. $12.50.

LEVIN, GILBERT, EDWARD B. ROBERTS and GARY B. HIRSCH. *The Persistent Poppy: A Computer-Aided Search for Heroin Policy.* Pp. vii, 229. Cambridge, Mass.: Ballinger, 1975. No price.

LEVITAN, SAR A. *Programs in Aid of the Poor.* 3rd ed. Pp. v, 146. Baltimore, Md.: Johns Hopkins University Press, 1976. $9.00. Paperbound, $2.95.

LYELL, WILLIAM A., JR. *Lu Hsün's Vision of Reality.* Pp. 365. Berkeley: University of California Press, 1976. $14.50.

MACBRIDE, ROGER L. *A New Dawn for America: The Libertarian Challenge.* Pp. 111. Ottawa, Ill.: Green Hill, 1976. $5.95.

MACMULLEN, RAMSAY. *Roman Government's Response to Crisis: A.D. 235–337.* Pp. v, 308. New Haven, Conn.: Yale University Press, 1976. $17.50.

MAESTRO, MARCELLO, *Gaetano Filangieri and His Science of Legislation.* Pp. 76. Philadelphia, Pa.: American Philosophical Society, 1976. $6.00. Paperbound.

MANCKE, RICHARD B. *Squeaking By: U.S. Energy Policy Since the Embargo.* Pp. 181. New York: Columbia University Press, 1976. $8.95.

MARTINEZ, TOMAS. *The Human Marketplace: An Examination of Private Employment Agencies.* Pp. 159. New Brunswick, N.J.: Transaction Books, 1976. $8.95.

MCDONALD, FORREST. *The Presidency of Thomas Jefferson.* Pp. v, 201. Lawrence: University Press of Kansas, 1976. $12.00.

MCDONALD, WILLIAM F., ed. *Criminal Justice and the Victim.* Pp. 288. Beverly Hills, Calif.: Sage, 1976. $17.50. Paperbound, $7.50.

MERTON, ROBERT K. *Sociological Ambivalence and Other Essays.* Pp. vii, 287. New York: The Free Press, 1976. $12.95.

MILLER, KENT S. *Managing Madness: The*

Case against Civil Commitment. Pp. ix, 185. New York: The Free Press, 1976. $9.95.

MILLER, WARREN E. and TERESA E. LEVITIN. *Leadership and Change: The New Politics and the American Electorate.* Pp. vii, 267. Cambridge, Mass.: Winthrop, 1976. $10.00. Paperbound, $6.95.

MILNES, BARRY BRACEWELL. *Eastern and Western European Economic Integration.* Pp. 218. New York: St. Martin's Press, 1976. $18.95.

MITCHELL, DANIEL J. B. and ROSS E. AZEVEDO. *Wage Price Controls and Labor Market Distortions.* Monograph Series, No. 16. Pp. 174. Los Angeles: University of California Press, 1976. $5.50. Paperbound.

MOORE, ROBERT and TINA WALLACE. *Slamming the Door: The Administration of Immigration Control.* Pp. vii, 126. Totowa, N.J.: Martin Robertson, 1976. $5.00. Paperbound.

MOSHER, FREDERICK C., ed. *Basic Documents of American Public Administration, 1776–1950.* Pp. v, 225. New York: Holmes & Meier, 1976. $14.00. Paperbound, $6.95.

MOSTOFSKY, DAVID I. *Behavior Control and Modification of Physiological Activity.* Pp. iv, 504. Englewood Cliffs, N.J.: Prentice-Hall, 1976. $17.95.

MULLEN, WILLIAM F. *Presidential Power and Politics.* Pp. 294. New York: St. Martin's Press, 1976. $12.95. Paperbound, $4.95.

MUNRO, J. FORBES. *Africa and the International Economy, 1800–1960.* Pp. 230. Totowa, N.J.: Rowman & Littlefield, 1976. $12.00. Paperbound, $5.75.

MURPHY, ARTHUR W., ed. *The Nuclear Power Controversy.* Pp. iii, 184. Englewood Cliffs, N.J.: Prentice-Hall, 1976. $9.95. Paperbound, $3.95.

NAUSEKM, LOUIS, ed. *Changing Campaign Techniques: Elections and Values in Contemporary Democracies.* Pp. 274. Beverly Hills, Calif.: Sage, 1976. $17.50. Paperbound, $7.50.

NEAL, ARTHUR G., ed. *Violence in Animal and Human Societies.* Pp. viii, 229. Chicago, Ill.: Nelson-Hall, 1976. $11.00.

NEWMAN, SIMON. *March 1939: The British Guarantee to Poland.* Pp. vii, 253. New York: Oxford University Press, 1976. $14.25.

OWEN, A. L. RIESCH. *Selig Perlman's Lectures on Capitalism and Socialism.* Pp. vii, 183. Madison: University of Wisconsin Press, 1976. $12.50.

OWEN, HENRY and CHARLES L. SCHULTZE, eds. *Setting National Priorities: The Next Ten Years.* Pp. ix, 618. Washington, D.C.: The Brookings Institution, 1976. $14.95. Paperbound, $6.95.

PERS, JESSICA S. *Government as Parent: Administering Foster Care in California.* Pp. v, 124. Berkeley: University of California Press, 1976. No price.

POLSBY, NELSON W. *Congress and the Presidency.* 3rd ed. Pp. v, 206. Englewood Cliffs, N.J.: Prentice-Hall, 1976. $7.95. Paperbound, $3.95.

POST, JAMES E. *Risk and Response.* Pp. vii, 206. Lexington, Mass.: Lexington Books, 1976. $17.00.

Powers of Congress. Pp. vii, 357. Washington, D.C.: Congressional Quarterly, 1976. No price. Paperbound.

RADA, EDWARD L. and KAN WU, eds. *Self-Help in Pacific-Asian Development.* Pp. vii, 172. Los Angeles: University of California Press, 1975. $7.95.

RIDLEY, CHARLES P. *China's Scientific Policies: Implications for International Cooperation.* Pp. 92. Washington, D.C.: American Enterprise Institute for Public Policy Research, 1976. $3.00. Paperbound.

RODES, ROBERT E., JR. *The Legal Enterprise.* Pp. ix, 181. Port Washington, N.Y.: Kennikat Press, 1976. $13.50.

ROSENTHAL, DONALD B., ed. *The City in Indian Politics.* Pp. 256. Faridabad, Haryana: Thomson Press Ltd., 1976. No price.

ROSSITER, CLINTON. *The Supreme Court and the Commander in Chief.* Pp. v, 231. Ithaca, N.Y.: Cornell University Press, 1976. $15.00. Paperbound, $3.95.

SAID, ABDUL A. and LUIS R. SIMMONS, eds. *Ethnicity in an International Context.* Pp. 241. New Brunswick, N.J.: Transaction Books, 1976. $12.95.

SARTORI, GIOVANNI. *Parties and Party Systems: A Framework for Analysis.* Vol. I. Pp. vii, 370. New York: Cambridge University Press, 1976. $10.95. Paperbound.

SCHEIBER, HARRY N., HAROLD G. VATTER and HAROLD UNDERWOOD FAULKNER. *American Economic History.* Pp. 514. New York: Harper & Row, 1976. $18.95.

SCHILLER, HERBERT I. *Communication and Cultural Domination.* Pp. 127. White Plains, N.Y.: IASP, 1976. $7.95.

SCHWARTZ, THEODORE, ed. *Socialization as Cultural Communication: Development of a Theme in the Work of Margaret Mead.* Pp. 269. Berkeley: University of California Press, 1976. $15.00.

SCOTT, DAVID L. *Financing the Growth of Electric Utilities.* Pp. vi, 120. New York: Praeger, 1976. $15.00.

SEIFER, NANCY. *Nobody Speaks for Me:*

Self-Portraits of American Working Class Women. Pp. 447. New York: Simon & Schuster, 1976. $10.95.

SHAPIRO, STEPHEN and HILARY RYGLEWICZ. *Feeling Safe: Making Space for the Self.* Pp. v, 148. Englewood Cliffs, N.J.: Prentice-Hall, 1976. $8.95. Paperbound, $2.95.

SHLAIM, AVI, ed. *International Organisations in World Politics: Yearbook, 1975.* Pp. 228. Boulder, Colo.: Westview Press, 1976. $27.50.

SKINNER, ANDREW S. and THOMAS WILSON, eds. *Essays on Adam Smith.* Pp. xiv, 647. New York: Oxford University Press, 1976. $37.50.

SMITH, BRIAN C. and JEFFREY STANYER. *Administering Britain.* Pp. 288. Totowa, N.J.: Martin Robertson, 1976. $11.50.

SOMBART, WERNER. *Why is There No Socialism in the United States?* Pp. x, 187. White Plains, N.Y.: IASP, 1976. $17.50.

SPIERS, M. *Techniques and Public Administration.* Pp. 250. Totowa, N.J.: Martin Robertson, 1976. $10.00.

SPULBER, NICHOLAS and IRA HOROWITZ. *Quantitative Economic Policy and Planning: Theory and Models of Economic Control.* Pp. xi, 413. New York: W. W. Norton, 1976. $16.95.

STEIN, PETER. *Single.* Pp. vii, 134. Englewood Cliffs, N.J.: Prentice-Hall, 1976. $7.95. Paperbound, $2.95.

STEINBERG, JONATHAN. *Why Switzerland?* Pp. vii, 214. New York: Cambridge University Press, 1976. $12.95.

STEINER, GILBERT Y. *The Children's Cause.* Pp. viii, 265. Washington, D.C.: The Brookings Institution, 1976. $9.95. Paperbound, $3.95.

STEWART, PATRICIA R. *Children in Distress: American and English Perspectives.* Pp. 285. Beverly Hills, Calif.: Sage, 1976. $12.00. Paperbound, $7.00.

SULLIVAN, MICHAEL P. *International Relations: Theories and Evidence.* Pp. v, 385. Englewood Cliffs, N.J.: Prentice-Hall, 1976. $12.50.

SYRETT, HAROLD C., ed. *The Papers of Alexander Hamilton, April 1799–October 1799.* Vol. XXIII. Pp. vi, 728. New York: Columbia University Press, 1976. $20.00.

TEITELBAUM, MICHAEL S., ed. *Sex Differences: Social and Biological Perspectives.* Pp. 232. Garden City, N.Y.: Anchor Press, 1976. $2.95. Paperbound.

TURNER, JONATHAN H. *American Society: Problems of Structure.* 2nd ed. Pp. vi, 306. New York: Harper & Row, 1976. $8.95. Paperbound.

VAN ONSELEN, CHARLES. *Chibaro: African Mine Labour in Southern Rhodesia, 1900–1933.* Pp. 326. New York: Urizen Books, 1976. $17.50.

WATSON, ALAN. *Rome of the XII Tables: Persons and Property.* Pp. ix, 195. Princeton, N.J.: Princeton University Press, 1976. $15.00.

WATT, DONALD CAMERON. *Too Serious a Business: European Armed Forces and the Approach to the Second World War.* Pp. 202. Berkeley: University of California Press, 1975. $8.50.

WENDZEL, ROBERT L. *International Relations: A Policymaker Focus.* Pp. 286. New York: John Wiley & Sons, 1977. $7.95. Paperbound.

WESSEL, ANDREW E. *The Social Use of Information: Ownership and Access.* Pp. vii, 244. New York: John Wiley & Sons, 1976. $15.95.

WHITE, KERR L. and MAUREEN M. HENDERSON, eds. *Epidemiology as a Fundamental Science: Its Uses in Health Services Planning, Administration, and Evaluation.* Pp. vii, 235. New York: Oxford University Press, 1976. $6.95. Paperbound.

WILKIE, JAMES W., MICHAEL C. MEYER and EDNA MONZON DE WILKIE, eds. *Contemporary Mexico: Papers of the IV International Congress of Mexican History.* Pp. 875. Berkeley: University of California Press, 1976. $27.50. Paperbound, $12.00.

WOOD, W. D., ed. *The Current Industrial Relations Scene in Canada 1976.* Ontario, Ca.: Queen's University Press, 1976. $35.00.

ZABEL, JAMES A. *Nazism and the Pastors.* Dissertation Series 14. Pp. vii, 243. Missoula: University of Montana Press, 1976. $4.50. Paperbound.

INDEX

The American Academy of Political and Social Science

3937 Chestnut Street   Philadelphia, Pennsylvania 19104

Origin and Purpose. The Academy was organized December 14, 1889, to promote the progress of political and social science, especially through publications and meetings. The Academy does not take sides in controverted questions, but seeks to gather and present reliable information to assist the public in forming an intelligent and accurate judgment.

Meetings. The Academy holds an annual meeting in the spring extending over two days.

Publications. THE ANNALS is the bimonthly publication of The Academy. Each issue contains articles on some prominent social or political problem, written at the invitation of the editors. Also, monographs are published from time to time, numbers of which are distributed to pertinent professional organizations. These volumes constitute important reference works on the topics with which they deal, and they are extensively cited by authorities throughout the United States and abroad. The papers presented at the meetings of The Academy are included in THE ANNALS.

Membership. Each member of The Academy receives THE ANNALS and may attend the meetings of The Academy. Annual dues for individuals are $15.00 (for clothbound copies $20.00 per year). A life membership is $500. All payments are to be made in United States dollars.

Libraries and other institutions may receive THE ANNALS paperbound at a cost of $15.00 per year, or clothbound at $20.00 per year. Add $1.50 to above rates for membership outside U.S.A.

Single copies of THE ANNALS may be obtained by nonmembers of The Academy for $4.00 ($5.00 clothbound) and by members for $3.50 ($4.50 clothbound). A discount of 5 percent is allowed on orders for 10 to 24 copies of any one issue, and of 10 percent on orders for 25 or more copies. These discounts apply only when orders are placed directly with The Academy and not through agencies. The price to all bookstores and to all dealers is $4.00 per copy less 20 percent, with no quantity discount. Monographs may be purchased for $4.00, with proportionate discounts. Orders for 5 books or less must be prepaid (add $1.00 for postage and handling). Orders for 6 books or more must be invoiced.

All correspondence concerning The Academy or THE ANNALS should be addressed to the Academy offices, 3937 Chestnut Street. Philadelphia, Pa. 19104.